Illuminati Hunter

Copyright Ethan Harrison 2015
All rights reserved.
ISBN 978-1-914195-70-9
Illuminati Hunter.com

'Without doubt one of the most gripping and important books I've ever read. Don't bother reading other books. Cut to the chase. Read this one.'

Claire Palmer, Editor International Times, 2015.

Original book photographed 2012.

© Ethan Harrison 2015

The rights of Ethan Harrison to be identified as the author of this work have been asserted by him in accordance with the Copyright, Designs and Patents Act of 1988.

All rights reserved; no part of this publication may be reproduced, stored in a retrieval system, or transmitted in any form or by any means, electronic, mechanical, photocopying, recording or otherwise without the prior written consent of the publisher or a licence permitting copying in the UK issued by the Copyright Licensing Agency Ltd. www.cla.co.uk

ISBN 978-1-914195-70-9

Book design and layout by Ethan Harrison. Production management by UKBookPublishing.Com.

Foreword

After this brief introduction the following text, apart from the addition of the footnotes and the appendix, is an exact reprint of a book that I found in the secondhand book market under Black Friars Bridge in London in 2012. Originally published in 1913 by Necromancer, a small English publishing house that has since vanished, it seems to have enjoyed only a limited release as, after much extensive searching, I have not been able to find another copy anywhere in the world.

There are several reasons that inspired me to republish this book. Mainly, because it is a fantastic adventure written in a surprisingly modern way which I feel the contemporary reader will relish. But also, when I checked the story's details on the internet, to my astonishment, many of them, however unbelievable, were backed up by existing records, or so close that it was impossible to thnk that they could all be coincidence, hence the addition of the footnotes so that you can see for yourself.

If this extraordinary tale is true, then it would throw a completely new light on to what is already a remarkable period of history. I'm sure that you'll find it fascinating, especially if you have a laptop at your disposal and use the website addresses listed in the appendix, or you have the E Book version with the embedded hypertext links.

I hope that you enjoy researching the background of this incredible adventure as much as I did and that, of course, you are as thrilled by this truly amazing story.

E.T. Harrison 2015.

ILLUMINATI HUNTER

Adam Weishaupt & The Eye of Horus

By Sebastian P. Drechsler

Published in Great Britain by Necromancer Press 1913.

Introduction

This volume is formed from a collection of memoirs discovered in 1898 at the University of Munich in Bavaria. Sebastian Pierre Drechsler was a student and eventually lecturer at Ingolstadt University between 1783 – 1800, before the faculty was closed down. He later went on to become Professor and then Director of History at Munich University until he retired in 1835. It is understood that the original memoirs were dictated by the scholar on his deathbed (circa 1852) and that he had not wanted them to come to the public's attention for 'some time' after he died so as not to besmirch his fine reputation achieved after many years working within academe. He was on record to have made claim that they would be valuable 'To those in the future who are already illuminated, or are ready to come into the light.' It should be noted that the transcript was dictated to an Englishman, a court stenographer by trade, who was not fluent in the Bavarian tongue but the far-sighted Professor had understood that his scribe's natural dialect was fast becoming the international language of the world and so, by means of this translation, would secure the text's widest readership when it eventually saw the light of day. This detail and the fact that it is a vocal record would explain the sound effects, British measurements, occasional vernacular and the constant personal observations of a humorous nature.

A. Jones Editor Necromancer Press 1913.

To My Darling Francesca.
I Will Never Forget You.

Order from Chaos
'Ordo ab Chao'

I, Sebastian Drechsler, finding myself of sound mind but failing body, at the grand old age of eighty-seven, in the year of our Lord 1852, do finally commit these words to paper and solemnly swear that, though much of the following text may at times sound unbelievable, it is, in fact, a true and accurate account of the extraordinary adventures in which I played my part as a young man in my homeland of Bavaria many, many years ago. Also, I truly hope that, if the text has survived as long as I have intended before coming to the public's attention, then the incredible tale you are about to read no longer contains a very necessary warning for the world. But, if that is the case, then may God Almighty have mercy on your pathetic souls.

It was a ghastly night. The wind whined in the chimney and the rain lashed about in the dark trees creaking outside my window. In my bed, I thrashed around anxiously listening to the storm pass over until, at last, I fell into a deep, deep sleep.

I awoke in a terrible dream. In this hellish vision, I was climbing a monstrous mountain of writhing, naked bodies and, far below me, lay an eternal blackness which I knew was the abyss. Way above me, radiating from the summit of this enormous pyramid of flesh, shone the brightest light that I had ever seen. So bright, that I knew it was also the abyss. As I climbed, I could feel the faces of those beneath me, their ears, their lips, their teeth, all of them imagined through my fingertips, for I dared not look in case I caught one of their desperate stares. Under my feet, I could feel their shoulders, their knees, and their cold hands grasping at my skin, but I fought hard to break their grip and, even though I knew that it would be the end of everything, I clambered on towards the terrifying light over the wall of people as they called out their awful cries.

I woke with a gasp, covered in a cold sweat and filled with a dreadful sense of foreboding. It was at that moment, sitting up in my bed shivering with fear, that I first decided I would visit Professor Van Halestrom. I was sure that I had overheard some of my fellow students saying that the eccentric scholar had the skill to read dreams and I had to know what this vision meant. That was how it all began for me. It was all because of my dream. As I pulled my nightshirt about me and tried to go back to sleep, it would have been impossible for me to imagine the incredible adventures that fate now held in store. Indeed, had I known the extraordinary series of events that my first real meeting with the Professor was to set in motion, and the effect it was to have on my future, and indeed the future of the whole world, then I might never have decided to go to see Van Halestrom at all.

For back then, I was merely a freshman student at the University of Ingolstadt, immersed in the study of history, philosophy, canon law, and the pursuit of women. A simple lad from a small village, recently arrived in a big city and trying to make the same acclimatisation to his thoughts as with his new location in life. No mean task for a man who had received as strict an upbringing as mine and had inherited his father's stifling self-consciousness. A trait that I was more than ready to shake off, so that I could find out what was out there in this brave new world and discover, within me, a brave new self.

Ah, but I digress. This tale is of such great importance that it must be told properly. So I shall begin…

Chapter 1

Innocence and Reason

Though my nightmare had put me in a frightful state of mind, I was in a much better mood as soon as I had begun my walk to Ingolstadt University on that fresh spring morning in May 1784. The city streets were bustling with townsfolk and traders and artizans all going about their daily business and the smells of early summer mixed pleasantly with those wafting from the river Danube which filled the air with a sweet scent that thrilled the senses. Another thing that thrilled the senses about this new and exciting place to which I had moved but nine months ago from the distant village of Tuffengarten, was that *here* there seemed to be pretty girls around every corner and, back in Tuffengarten, there were no pretty girls at all. Believe me, I had looked.

I smiled hopefully, but with little effect, at another lovely young maiden as I crossed the street outside the university and strode through the grand old gates. Back then, of course, I had no idea why my lack of success persisted with members of the fairer sex. I knew that I wasn't a bad looking chap, although, sadly, it was still only my mother who would say so.

I was almost six foot tall, well-built with thick brown hair and even had a charming face sporting a proud chin and a noble set of features. Too proud and noble for all the girls, or so I thought. In reality, of course, I was a spoilt brat and a total idiot especially when it came to women and, as such, spent most of my lonely days with my head stuck soundly up my Bavarian arse. Though the inexperience of youth kept me blissfully unaware of these crucial facts, so, in my innocence, and bad dreams aside, I had every reason to have a spring in my step that day, because I knew one thing for certain. For a young man with a thirst for learning - this was the time to be alive.

For the Great Enlightenment was everywhere. The thoughts of men like Rousseau, Newton, Voltaire, Copernicus and Galileo were sweeping away the old ideas of the past and resigning their hocus pocus to the rubbish bin of history. Oh yes, this was the time to be young and open-minded, and the best place to be both these things was Ingolstadt University. With one of the finest reputations in all of Europe, which meant the known world, I was indeed very lucky and very proud to be attending this esteemed institution, though perhaps not trying as hard at my studies as I could, as any '*truly enlightened*' student never should.

I strolled through the university's open front door and into the shadows of the hallway then, after establishing with the campus clerk that Professor Van Halestrom was finishing his morning lecture and that I may watch from the gallery, I made my way to the appropriate hall and quietly let myself in. The auditorium was packed with students as his lectures were always very popular and I squeezed myself amongst the crowd at the back.

I had first met the scholar at the university chess club when he had congratulated me on my victory over one of the other professors and we had talked of chess and military campaigns and great battles of the past. I had found him both very learned and very personable at the same time, which was in complete contrast to all the other teachers that I had met. Looking around, I saw undergraduates from other courses who obviously felt that they could learn something though their particular subjects were unrelated. They were probably right. At a stalworth fifty-five, the grey-bearded but eagle-eyed Van Halestrom was at his peak, and famous for delivering thoroughly illuminating lectures encompassing many themes. That morning was no exception.

"And that is why, gentlemen, the inherent problems of a debt-ridden monetary system make it anathema to civilised society. This system will always produce aggregated capital over too wide a range which, in turn, produces an undesirably large gap between the haves and have-nots. As we have already learnt, this will lead to a problematic rise in crime, illness, child mortality, spread of disease, general suffering, and all the associated revolutionary political upheaval that they bring in their wake. This particular form of capitalism can be shown as a pyramid; the majority living on the bottom while only a few occupy the pinnacle at the very top. In my opinion, the shape that *should* be aspired to when creating a system of trade and equity, is, in fact, the sphere. For it has no spike - No high - No low, and is the most harmonious of shapes within Greek geometry."

He energetically sketched on the blackboard as he theorised, "It is the shape that matter, or energy, most readily assumes, suggesting that there is equilibrium within the system. It is also, and I believe this no coincidence, the most common of all natural forms in the universe and, of course, a perfect mirror of our own naturally balanced world."

He finished a cleverly detailed drawing of the earth before turning to the audience and taking a small bow with his fingertips together. A short silence was followed by an exuberant wave of applause which swept the hall and which he graciously accepted by raising his palms and calling out, "Thank you! Thank you! Although I am flattered, your praise will not stop me from being extremely cross with you if you do not read Herr Adam Smith's *'Wealth of Nations'* and write a five thousand-word essay on it by next week. I would also urge anyone who is not a student of this class to read this volume as it is very instructive and outlines the rather ominous global economic realities of our future."

With this, he collected his things and walked out of the hall. I left with the other students who gossiped excitedly about what they had heard before I made my way to the Professor's study where he was enjoying a cup of tea and a smoke of his pipe.

He welcomed me with typical aplomb, "Ah, Herr Drechsler, good to see you. Would you like some tea? It's Darjeeling, a particularly pleasant flavour I think you'll agree."

After briefly discussing how my studies were going, he asked me the purpose of my visit and I told him about my odd dream. Upon hearing my description, to my astonishment, he calmly said, "I have recently had the same one."

Flabbergasted, I begged him, "But what could it mean, sir?"

Speaking with casual authority he stated, "It is the hidden secret of capitalism, my friend: The greatest conspiracy of them all. A vile trap in which you will be condemned to climb over the rest of humanity to reach your own pitiful end, and the powerful light that you saw at the top was 'The Eye of Horus': The Illuminated One. Lucifer himself."

Well, quite understandably, all I could do was sit there in his leather chair completely dumbfounded and, so much so, that I thought I might be back in my horrendous nightmare.

Whilst I tried to make sense of these bizarre statements, he surprised me once more and, taking some tobacco from his pouch, he asked, "Would you consider yourself a good horseman, my lad?"

I was still too busy thinking about 'The Illuminated One' to answer properly and let out a protracted, "Err ..."

Regardless of my confusion, he carried on, "Only I heard some of my students mentioning that you were very accomplished in the saddle." He looked me over as though evaluating my capacities for something of which I was uncomfortably unaware, before puckering on his pipe and adding, "I may have a small task for you. A matter of little consequence. Can you use a gun?"

This was another jump in the proceedings and I finally found my tongue. "If the matter is of such little consequence, sir, why should I need to use a gun?"

"I understand that your father is a gunsmith, so I presumed that you'd be familiar, to a certain degree, with using... *guns*?"

He flicked his eyebrows and lit his pipe with an ingenious set of flints all contained within one hand-held miniature box. Feeling a little off guard already, these remarks of a more personal nature unsettled me further. It was true that I was a dab hand with a horse and known for doing tricks in the stables on my beautiful white mare Petrova. Also, as a member of the university shooting club, it was common knowledge that I was a good shot, and that my father was a gunsmith, but that the Professor knew of it was a surprise to me.

I felt a little trapped and replied politely but firmly, "I am a simple freshman, Herr Professor, as you know from our brief meetings at the chess club. I am but nineteen years old and know nothing about the indecencies of city life, so how I could be of any use to you in this matter, however small, is something that I cannot even begin to imagine."

This was not entirely true. I had enjoyed a number of secretive adventures back in Tuffengarten, mostly running away from angry farmers and tavern landlords.

The Professor seemed to sense this. "Oh, don't do yourself down, Sebastian. You've an excellent mind for one thing. Remember, I've seen you beat Professor Kandinsky at chess, and he was a champion back in his day. You're here at the university for another, which means you're willing to learn. You've a ready wit, which always comes in handy, and you've got a horse which I'd bet a month's wages on to win against a thoroughbred." He puffed on his pipe and concluded with a wink, "And a month's wages here at the university is quite a lot."

With this, he looked unnervingly right into my eyes and came away with a broad smile. "You also look as though you fancy a bit of an adventure. It's a good look. I've seen it before.

Sometimes in the mirror, sometimes in my students, but always in the face of a man with a desire to live a life that's his own. So what d'you say? Will you run a small errand for me and collect a letter from a messenger out on the road to Stuttgart?"

I didn't know what to make of the man as he sat there looking me up and down and engulfed me in another ring of pipesmoke. My parents had warned me of the dangers of accepting offers from strange men in the city and, with all this staring into my eyes, I was feeling as uneasy as I had since arriving in Ingolstadt the previous September. I had thought him an eccentric intellectual up until this moment, but a tiny shudder ran up my spine when I remembered him casually mentioning '*Lucifer himself.*'

This made up my mind for me. "I'm afraid I must refuse, sir. I hope you don't mind, but I promised my parents..."

"I fully understand, my lad, but if you change your mind there's fifty thalers in it for you, which I'm sure you'll find useful. Now, if you'll excuse me, I have another lecture to prepare."

"...Of course, Herr Professor..."

His abrupt dismissal brought on another wave of anxiety in me and I quickly stood to attention then performed a very low and overly earnest bow and clicked my heels together as my father would have when taking leave of someone socially superior. I immediately regretted it and caught his eye, but he chuckled, "Good luck, my friend. See you at chess club."

I wandered back up the gloomy corridor going through everything that he had said. If I was so interested in discovering my *new self*, why had I not jumped at his exciting offer faster than a rat scurrying up a drainpipe? I cursed my self-consciousness and blamed it on my father's influence. After all, whatever the eccentric professor had said about my dream, it was only a dream and he was merely an unconventional old gentleman. As a man of reason, I should not be scared of either.

So lost in my thoughts was I, that I nearly walked into another student coming the other way before leaving the darkness of the building and returning back into the bright spring sunshine. Maybe it was the beaming rays of sunlight that snapped me from my ruminations, but I suddenly remembered: Jan Kolher, my best friend from Tuffengarten was coming to stay. I was meant to meet him at ten o'clock at the coaching inn, but I had been so consumed by my dream, and everything else, that I had completely forgotten.

At that moment, the bells of St Maria's church rang out through the streets and I counted the chimes fearing the worst, nine, ten, oh dear, eleven times. I was late. Very late indeed. [1]

---

1. Professor Van Halestrom & Ingolstadt University. Unfortunately, there is no record of a Professor Van Halestrom working at Ingolstadt's university at this time, but staff records are rare, at best, so this is quite unsurprising. By 1784, Ingolstadt University was regarded as one of the most influential institutes of higher learning in europe and the free-thinking spirit that flourished through The Enlightment's Age of Reason, widely regarded responsible for the French and American revolutions, was reflected in the culture of the campus. The university was finally closed down in 1800 by the then Elector of Bavaria, Maximilian IV and, though it is claimed that this was due to a lack of funds, it is suspected that it was because the institution was considered so revolutionarily secular, by the broadly Christian authorities, that it posed a direct threat to the government'.

Chapter 2

Old Friends

The second that I arrived at the coaching inn I spotted my old friend waiting outside amongst the throng of travellers and horses and townspeople. There were a couple of reasons that I saw him so easily. Firstly, his unruly crop of bright orange hair clashed so violently with his vulgar green clothes that he could have been seen by a blind man. Secondly, unlike myself, Jan Kohler was found most attractive by members of the opposite sex and, though the scoundrel had barely got there himself, he was already accompanied by two pretty young ladies.

It was not his looks that attracted the women to him. He would be the first to admit that he was no oil painting - and perhaps no watercolour either. Neither was his figure so alluring for, though he was nearly as tall as me, well, to put it bluntly, he was fat. No, the secret of his attraction lay not in his physique, nor his features. It was immediately obvious to anyone who met him that he was very, very funny and that's why the ladies liked him. And that's why I liked him too.

"Jan Kohler!" I halooed, "How the devil are you?"

Fast as lightning he cried, "As happy as a hungry Chinaman who's just found a huge dog in his kitchen and twice as good for seeing you. You're late!" We hugged, before he held me at arm's length and chortled, "You, Sebastian Drechsler, will never change, so I am unsurprised to see that, as usual, you have not."

"You too are as I remember and your face is pulling exactly the same stupid expression that it was when I saw it last Christmas."

"And yours, Seb, is as simple as it ever was. Not ugly mind, but simple. And tell me, my old friend, *since that time*, has it felt the fair hand of a woman in the throes of a passionate embrace, or has it just remained simple?"

I squirmed with embarrassment in front of his new coquettish friends who were both giggling at me. He butted in, enjoying his enduring advantage with the ladies, "Well then, old boy, simply help yourself to one of mine. This is Amelia, and this is Eva." He bowed at the tittering girls and jollied, "Now take me where I can eat. I was on that stagecoach for twelve hours and at least twice as long at this miserable coaching inn waiting for you and, in that eon, I have found that neither serves a good breakfast."

Jan was certainly my best childhood friend, though, to be honest, there were no others who qualified as candidates. We had only fought once when we were boys, a fight which he had won using his superior weight to hold me down. After that, the pair of us had become best friends, riding, fishing, shooting with guns borrowed from my father's workshop, and talking about girls at great length, though enjoying their pleasures to a lesser extent and always he more successfully than me.

This was something of which I had always been a little jealous and he knew it. Jan had not been able to afford to come to university and had admitted that he was not of the right temperament. In truth, his Latin was worse than a donkey's and no way near the required standard for higher education. Though he had claimed that he thought *the pursuit of academia pretentious*, I secretly suspected that he was envious of my academic pretentions. So, in a way, our jealousies balanced out. Anyway, his uncle had found him a job at the local moneychangers in Ingolstadt so, having found myself a little lonely after moving there, I had promised to look after him until his room was vacated, as he always cheered me up. Funny old beggar that he was.

I took him and our lady friends to the nearest place where we could get something proper to eat and, at Herr Fassbender's on Milchstrasse, we did precisely that. Jan had certainly lost none of his great humour and we laughed so much that the whole afternoon passed without me thinking once about the Professor or my troubling dream. Later on, we moved to a bierkeller popular with the student fraternities and the jokes and drinks flowed as we reminisced into the night.

It must have been eleven o'clock when, returning from the privy and not finding the girls or Jan at our table, I noticed them gathered round a shy young couple sitting in the corner. Jan was holding out his handkerchief in one hand and an empty beer mug in the other and blathering, "Ladies and gentlemen." He pointed a swaying finger at the seated man and slurred, "That's you, sir," before belching and carrying on, "For your hearty entertainment, I shall now turn these two objects into a piece of meat." The blaggard wrapped his handkerchief around the mug, gripped it between his thighs, then placed the lady's hand underneath and proudly boasted, "Behold, have you ever seen such magic? What a frankfurter eh?"

There was a pause while everyone looked at Jan's groin then at the triumphant grin of his face before the girls' tittering burst into a mighty howl. Surprisingly, the young woman resolutely holding the phallus aloft joined in with the laughter but, for her poor companion, this was the last straw. He stood up and slapped Jan round the face with his glove - of all things - which only made the girls laugh even harder and this final humiliation was too much for him. He grabbed Jan by the ear and dragged him through the tavern and into the street where honour could be satisfied, and, seeing that the fool was carrying a sword, I ran after them to try to prevent any unnecessary bloodshed.

I hurried outside to find Jan wobbling around in front of the eager duelist who was thankfully having trouble freeing his rusty blade from its scabbard. Oblivious of any impending danger, Jan kept repeating, "It's a frankfurter! A frankfurter! Do you see? And when I say frankfurter of course, I mean cock!"

The girls came out along with a few of the other young bucks and, flustered by the crowd, the man lost his patience and raised the scabbard anyway, presumably to bludgeon some manners into Jan. My old friend finally took exception to this and they briefly wrestled for it, until Jan suddenly let go and pitched the would-be knight backwards through the window of a china shop.

Though the fight would have embarrassed the class of a kindergarten, the crash was loud enough to be heard at the city gates and even drew a few fearful screams from the ladies. Sure enough, as Jan and I helped the clumsy idiot from the wreckage, we could already hear the shouts of the night watchmen approaching fast. Suffice to say, within a minute we were arrested and, another thirty after that, locked in jail.

Our fortunes continued to wane when we discovered that '*d'Artagnan*' was the son of a local magistrate and so, unsurprisingly, he was set free while we were charged with affray. The jailer told us that the authorities held a dim view of the antics of drunken students and, though Jan relentlessly argued that he was not a student, we were told the fine would be more than ten thalers each and that we would be locked up till the morning. Languishing in our cold, damp cell that night, listening to Jan's snoring and the rats scurrying around in the darkness, I had already decided what I would do come the morning and freedom.

Chapter 3

The Doctor

"It wasn't my fault I keep telling you," complained Jan for the umpteenth time as we trudged away from the jail in the first cold light of day.

"But then, in a much truer sense, yes it was." I could not lie.

"How can I be blamed for another man's lack of humour?"

"Maybe you could have guessed he was not going to find your joke amusing in the first place."

"Perhaps, but then I couldn't have guessed he was going to fall through the window. Anyway, it was an excellent joke. A frankfurter. Get it? A frankfurter!"

"Yes, yes, I get it. Now could you please stop repeating it at the top of your voice, it's making my head pound even harder."

"You've changed since you've become a student, Seb. Back in Tuffengarten you'd still be laughing about this in a week's time."

Maybe he was right. Maybe I did feel as though I had more responsibility on my shoulders here in Ingolstadt. I knew that I felt a burden of duty to my parents not to let them down and to flourish in my studies before, hopefully, graduating. Since my enrolment the previous September, I had not committed a single transgression and, although I was a little behind in my work, maybe more, I had not come to the attention of my superiors.

This indiscretion would change all that. I knew that the city council was in constant contact with the university's administration, so this incident would definitely be reported. We reached my lodgings and entered as quietly as possible, then sneaked up to my room as it was still very early in the morning and I did not want to wake my nosy landlady Fraulein Warburg.

Sadly, my guffawing friend made too much noise going up the creaking stairs and she came into the hallway, calling up from below, "Is that you, Herr Drechsler? I know it is as you did not come back last night. You shouldn't come in at this hour because you will wake my other guests, *and* you still owe me two month's rent!"

Jan sniggered under his breath, "She'll wake the whole street up if she doesn't shut up, never mind this house."

I told him to shush and we reached my room on the top floor. I let Jan have my bed, ate a tiny breakfast of bread crusts and cold coffee, filled my satchel with books, then quietly sneaked back downstairs and made my way to the university.

The weather had changed and a grey drizzling mist hung over the city. Whilst threading my way through the lanes, I reviewed my accounts, although no lengthy calculations were necessary. I had been swindled a little in the first few months after arriving in Ingolstadt, as all freshmen were, or so I had been told, though mainly by those who did the swindling. Also, the books that I had bought for my studies had been more expensive than I had planned. Combined with my habit of a little drink, purely for social reasons you understand, the feeding and stabling of Petrova, and indeed myself, I had already been feeling the pinch.

This last complication of one broken window, nine smashed chamber pots, two counts of affray and the subsequent eleven-thaler fine, had pushed me over the edge. Now I was broke. I had been reluctant to inform my parents of my money troubles, not wanting to worry them, especially my mother. Though I was sure that my father would have simply said that he could have purchased the same necessities for a fraction of their actual price, as he would no doubt have been able, '*back in his day.*'

I had already decided to accept Professor Van Halestrom's interesting offer. Not only would it give me a good opportunity to explore my new self, but the money would be essential if I was to keep up with my deluge of debts. So keen was I to resolve my financial woes, that I had planned to see him before my first lecture which was three hours of canon law, but I realised that I would now not have the time. I cursed Jan's pranks and also my selection of subjects.

Canon law was my least favourite of these. Being no genius, or wealthy young man, I had only been able to attend university under the patronage of our local lord, Count Von Friedrich. Fortunately, this philanthropic minor aristocrat, having no offspring of his own, occasionally took it upon himself to sponsor the education of Tuffengarten's more promising young men, and the latest of these was me. Although this arrangement meant there was an added sense of responsibility, knowing that my parents would be greatly humiliated back in the village were I to let them down, it also meant that I had to study a mixture of topics which were pre-selected for me, to make it easier to; '*obtain proper employment on entering the modern environment of work,*' - apparently. After I had graduated and found suitable employment, I was expected to reimburse the Count's estate over the following years.

This was fair enough, but canon law? I didn't enjoy it for several reasons. Mainly because it was immeasurably complicated and incalculably dull, but also, to me, lawyers, whether they worked for the church or not, seemed like professional liars, clever charlatans who would literally say anything, although very correctly and persuasively, to get what they wanted, and this was simply immoral. Another reason was my teacher, Herr Adam Weishaupt. Although incredibly intelligent and, amazingly for a head of faculty, still only in his early thirties, he was also cold, aloof and was possessed of a strangely menacing air. Indeed, such was his icy character, that it had earned him the nickname,

'The Doctor,' amongst the fraternity, as he always made his students feel like they were about to go under the surgeon's knife. Late students were also his pet hate, so, on hearing the bells of St Maria's ring quarter to eight, I pulled up my collar, put my head down and marched a little faster through the drizzle that was turning into rain.

I made it in the nick of time and, not wishing to draw attention to myself, found a seat at the top of the auditorium. Exactly as the hallway bell rang eight o'clock, Weishaupt imperiously strode out onto the stage with his black gown wafting behind him. He took his place behind the lectern and watched the rain-soaked stragglers come in with a disapproving frown until, after the last had taken his place, he began, "Good morning, *finally*, gentle..." only to be interrupted by one more latecomer, Herr Grubber, a portly chap with a look of constant surprise on his face.

The youth bowed in the doorway and panted, "Sorry, sir…"

Weishaupt coolly intoned, "Tell me, Herr Grubber, do you think the ancient civilisations of the past could have ever achieved their glorious triumphs, which still resonate throughout our modern world today, if their citizens had perpetually turned up late for everything?"

Grubber looked even more surprised than usual and spluttered, "I was run into by a horse in the town square, sir, I…"

"It was not a question, Herr Grubber!" snapped Weishaupt, "It was a rhetorical statement of empiric fact. Now sit down! You will report to me afterwards. Let this be a lesson to you all. Bad timekeeping will not be tolerated in this class. Now open your books at page seventy-seven and, *hopefully*, we can begin."

It was a good job lippy Jan was not there, or we would have been expelled before the good Doctor could have shouted 'Habeas Corpus!' I put my head down, along with everyone else, and the lesson began.

Perhaps it was the previous night's drinking and incarcerations, or simply plain boredom, but I drifted off then woke with a start and tried to compose myself. Luckily, Weishaupt had not noticed and, as I glanced around, I saw that a couple of my fellow students were also dozing. It was dark up at the back of the hall and I guessed that his eyesight was not good enough to see those of us in the shadows. I forced myself to concentrate, thinking that I should at least try to take something in, if only for the sake of my parents and perhaps, more importantly, to simply stay awake.

The Doctor droned on, "In this classic case of canon law the orders in the constitution clearly define our legally binding claimant to the rendering and inscription of new legislature, be that disposed to a country of colonies, rightful heir, or royal sovereign. i.e. King, or Queen."

He paused as if pondering his notes, before peering over his spectacles and meditatively continuing, "This may be a moot point as one can envisage a time in the future where society organises itself properly and we shall see the abolishment of the aristocracy, property, social authority, nationality, and the return of the human race to a happy state. A single family without artificial needs or useless sciences, with every father being a priest and a magistrate. These priests would not teach a type of religion which most of you would be familiar with, but more a God of Nature."

His concentration was broken by the hallway bell marking the end of morning classes, but he re-focused with irritation upon seeing the haste that we all showed in leaving. He shouted out above the din of his departing students, "Herr Grubber! I trust you have not forgotten our meeting?" and gestured to the foot of the lectern. The dejected student slowly made his way to the bottom of the stairs and Weishaupt escorted him out.

I followed behind them, keeping at a safe distance and watched Weishaupt show Grubber inside his private chambers. The Doctor briefly caught my eye, before slamming the door and growling at Grubber while I hurried off. [2.]

I knocked on the Professor's door and he bade me to enter, greeting me with his usual affable smile. Before I could speak, he started, "I'm so pleased you have decided to accept my offer. I was actually expecting you a little earlier so, perhaps, an incident befell you last night that prevented you from coming sooner?"

I froze in his doorway like an old man crossing the street who has realised that he is about to be run over by a stagecoach.

"But… how did you know I would come?"

"It was in your eyes, lad. And the eyes have it."

---

2. Johann Adam Weishaupt. This immensely intriguing historical figure was certainly lecturing at the University of Ingolstadt in 1784. Although S. Drechsler refers to him as 'The Doctor,' Adam Weishaupt was Dean of Canon Law at the faculty and the first non-Jesuit to hold this position in over ninety years. It is one view that the young academic's education at the hands of the Jesuit priesthood, which would have been extremely harsh, was the reason that he adopted his revolutionary anti-Christian philosophies. By this time, he is known to have denounced his Roman Catholicism and adopted the doctrines of the Hermetics, Manicheans, and those that revolved around astrology, alchemy, magic, and the mysteries of ancient Egypt, taking special interest in the pyramids at Giza.

Chapter 4

Mystery under the Serpen's Caput

I left the university with fifty thalers in my pocket, a gun under my belt, and, in my satchel, an ingenious star clock, along with a map and a list specifying times, directions, distances, et cetera, et cetra, all down to the last detail. The Professor had told me that there would be no need to take the gun on this occasion, but that I should keep it because it might be useful in the future. I guessed that the older man was overreacting to the possibility of highwaymen out on the country roads. No matter. I was pretty confident of my riding skills. In fact, I had never been beaten on my beautiful Petrova, a superb gift from my generous parents.

I had history classes through the afternoon, so it was close to six o'clock when I finally returned home to report my excellent news to the, no-doubt, still sleeping Jan Kohler.

I was right. The lazy oaf was still in my bed but sufficiently awake to moan, "Where have you been? I need some coffee and some idiot has left the pot on the wrong side of the room."

"If you get up now, I'll buy you a whole pot of coffee and the largest meal on the menu from the finest café in town."

"Have you sold your head? No, wait, you wouldn't get two thalers for that piece of mutton."

"Be quiet, fool. I have found employment from within the university which could lead to more work in the future. Very well paid work too."

"That's the student crowd for you. Always sticking together and keeping the good jobs for themselves, like cats licking each other's arses."

"That's ridiculous you idiot. Professor Van Halestrom's a friend of mine, and he would still be a friend had I met him outside the confines of the university. Anyway, this work has nothing to do with anything academic. It's more like the sort of thing that we used to get up to back in Tuffengarten. You know? Horses, and riding, and being secret."

"So what is it then? What do you have to do?"

"All I have to do is pick up a letter and deliver it to my master without it being opened."

"Sounds simple enough. What's the pay like?"

"Fifty thalers a letter."

"I'll be ready in less than a minute!" he clamoured excitedly, "Then you can keep your promise and buy me the most expensive dish on the menu." He scrambled from the bed in a flurry of sheets and began throwing on his clothes and jabbering, "I don't know why but, for some reason, expensive has always been my favourite type of everything."

We went for a slap up binge at Café Teure Küche on Friedrichshofen, the best spot in town and enjoyed every extravagance on the menu. Jan had me in hysterics and wooed the waitresses with his larks and excellent humour. After this indulgence, I paid off our fine and the rent, vowed to keep my expenditure down and waited to start my first job, which was not to be completed until the weekend. So I concentrated on my studies and even the erratic Jan calmed down as he prepared for work himself at the moneychangers.

Presently, the Sunday night of my task came around and I remember it like it was yesterday. Leading Petrova from the stables onto the lane behind my lodgings with her shoes lazily echoing along the cobbles and the warm evening breeze carrying rich aromas of honeysuckle from the banks of the Danube which brought back pleasant memories of summer nights spent as a boy. Gazing up into the heavens, I thanked my good fortune. It was a perfectly clear night and the glittering constellations shone so bright that I could have easily found my way by the stars alone. Not only was the Serpent's Head striking down to the western horizon like a signpost, but a huge waxing moon lit up the firmament like one almighty chandelier. After checking the contents of my satchel one last time, I mounted Petrova and set off for the road to Stuttgart and my intriguing rendezvous.

The first part of my journey was as uneventful as any that I have ever made, and I only saw a handful of people on the road as I travelled to the meeting point, which lay half a league south of the village of Kosigen at the turning for Katzenstein Castle. There I was to meet a mysterious rider to whom I was to say nothing other than the code word, 'Minerva,' and hear from them only the reply, 'Goddess of war,' whereupon, I was to be handed the envelope which I would bring back to Ingolstadt and deliver to Professor Van Halestrom the next day.

'Easy money,' I reckoned and galloped on through the countryside, which was so magically bathed in moonlight that night as to convince a man that he was in a dream. While my thoughts drifted to the beauty of the landscape, I recalled Weishaupt's words 'God of Nature' and they resonated within me as I swept along. Some three hours later, I spotted Katzenstein Castle on a small hillock a mile or so away and was so impressed by its sturdy but graceful architecture that I spent a wistful moment admiring its silhouette set against the night sky.

I could afford to rest for a while. I was ahead of time. I knew this because of the star clock that the Professor had lent me from which I took a reading every half hour. He had told me that he would *'perform minor but painful surgery'* on me if I lost it because it had once belonged to Kepler, the famous German astronomer. Having only known the eccentric Professor for a few weeks, I was a tad sceptical about this, but it was unimportant who had owned it before, it was very useful on that starry night.

After setting the outer dial of the device to the correct date, the time was indicated by a chronological marker on the central yoke when a spy hole in the mechanism's edge was aligned with the planet Venus and, two pins on its base, with the horizon. I took another reading: Half past eleven. Half an hour to go and only a couple of miles left to travel. I spurred Petrova off and kept my eyes open for the meeting place.

It had always been my plan to turn up early, believing it better to be safe than sorry. Also, the Professor had told me that the same messengers were used as often as possible to ensure the safety of the letters so, naturally, I presumed that the other rider would arrive on time having had made the journey before. After finding the fork in the road, I waited under the canopy of a large maple tree, where I could see the junction and the stars but remain hidden from the moonshine. [3]

At exactly twelve o'clock, the rider galloped up the road and brought his powerful chesnut mare to a halt at the junction in a cloud of dust. I watched him wheel about while I put the star clock away before trotting out from my hiding place. This seemed to unsettle the horseman, who had perhaps expected his regular ally to be on the road. He calmed his mare as I approached and I pulled Petrova up a length away from her nose. I felt a whiff of unease when I realised that, along with his black cloak and tri-corn hat, my accomplice was wearing a neckerchief round his face and I had not thought of concealing my own identity.

---

3. <u>Katzenstein Castle.</u> This impressive fort, originally built in the Middle Ages, is situated thirty miles west of Ingolstadt on the road to Stuttgart and is featured on the map at the beginning of the book. It will look exactly the same as when S. Drechsler saw it and can be viewed on the internet for those wishing to verify the authenticity of the author's account. Bavaria is home to hundreds of similar castles. The Serpen's Caput constellation, also reffered to as 'The Serpent's Head,' points down to the western horizon in the summer months and can be viewed by E book readers on the <u>Star Gazer</u> app.

Was this a mistake? Had the Professor forgotten to mention that I should disguise myself? 'Stupid old bird,' I cursed, though somehow this didn't ring true. It was then that the secretive rider spoke.

"You're new."

I was startled. Not only had this idiot broken our solemn rule; to say nothing apart from the code word, but it was a woman idiot. Also, I could detect a French accent. Never a good sign. 'Well that's no surprise,' I thought, 'she's probably never done this sort of thing before.' But then how could she have known that I was new? I argued with myself briefly before whispering, "Minerva," in case it was a test of my fallibility.

"Oh, *that*," she impudently sighed, "Very well, if it pleases you, *Goddess of war*."

Damn this wench's insolence. Someone should take her over their knee and give her a good spanking. I would report her disobedience to Professor Van Halestrom and recommend that her services be terminated forthwith and that a substitute, preferably male, be found to replace her. Also I was annoyed that, whilst she could see my disapproval, I could not see her reaction because -Damn it!- I was sure that she was laughing at me behind her neckerchief. I stuck out a glove, expecting the handover to occur as pre-arranged, that was to say promptly and without fuss but, to my further annoyance, she simpered, "Aren't you going to say *please* first?"

This was too much and I lost my temper. To hell with the rules and I hissed under my breath, "You have spoken to me three times now, which I know you know is forbidden."

"You don't have to whisper, sweetheart," she scoffed, "We're in a forest, on a lonely track, in the middle of the countryside, at twelve o'clock at night, which narrows down the chances of meeting a stranger and makes using a password a bit stupid.

Password for this - Password for that, they all think they're so important, well I've got a lot more important things to remember than a hundred different passwords thank you very much." Her horse stirred and she settled it with a tug on the reins before carrying on - after a fashion, "*Very well then.* Here you are."

She reached under her cloak and pulled out an envelope sealed with a large blob of wax and passed it over. I eased Petrova forward half a length and took the letter then stuffed it in my satchel. Closer now to the impertinent woman, I could see that she had the most beautiful eyes and, much to my surprise, one of them winked at me before she called out, "Take care, Herr *Junge-Kinda*. There are a lot of people out there who don't obey the rules."

With this, she reared her horse and made off in another shower of dust. I watched her gallop away back up the road and, for some reason, stayed there for a moment staring into the dark after she had disappeared, until collecting myself and checking that the satchel was fastened tight before making off as well. Riding all the way home at a steady canter, I stopped only twice, once for water and once again to rest my beauty at the top of a hill. I arrived home around four o'clock, stabled and fed her, then returned to my lodgings where I slept only a few hours before rising once more to prepare myself for classes. When I awoke, the spare bed was empty as Jan had already gone to his first Monday of work.

Two minutes after my first lecture was over, I was proudly standing before the Professor's door with my trusty satchel by my side. After checking the letter's position amongst my other papers, I composed myself, knocked smartly and, expecting my eagerness to come as a surprise, was most deflated to hear, "Come in, Sebastian!"

Chapter 5

Fine Work if You Can Get It

I found Van Halestrom sitting at his desk stirring a pot of tea. He beamed through the cloud of steam and said, "That went well. Did it not? Although you had a problem with our comrade? Yes? The girl with the beautiful eyes who doesn't obey the rules."

I was starting to wonder if sending this man a letter had any purpose whatsoever, as he would obviously know what was written in it before reading a word.

I joked, "Wouldn't it be easier for messages to be sent to you on the wind?"

"Yes, and cheaper too, but I have not yet developed the skill to the extent that it renders written correspondence obsolete."

He chuckled to himself and, such was his off-handedness, I could not tell whether he was joking or not. I sat down and passed him the envelope which he exchanged for a cup of tea. "You'll like this one. East Indian," he remarked and inspected the letter for a moment, then faced it back to me and asked, "Recognise the seal?"

I shook my head, having never seen the unusual crest before. It depicted a spear crossed with an axe and, pointing downwards in the middle, an arrow. Looking closer, I noticed that on the end of the spear was the Phrygian cap of liberty and, around the axe, a bundle of birch rods, or the 'fasces' of the state.

The Professor explained, "These symbols have existed for thousands of years, but are merely opposite sides of the same coin. The arrow represents the power behind them both and, in the end, it means only one thing. Revolution. In this particular case," he flipped over the envelope. "It's a revolution planned by the Bavarian Illuminati."

"The Illuminati?" I choaked. Of course, I had heard rumours of such an order, but thought tales of its secret control of heads of government and the aristocracy hypothetical, at best, and downright fanciful at worst. The type of ludicrous thinking typical of the students who drop out of university and end up in the opium dens round the docks in Frankfurt. But before I could say so, the Professor's incredible gift for mind-reading beat me to it and he sagely pointed out, "Before you try and tell me it's the type of ludicrous thinking typical of the students who drop out of university and end up in the opium dens round the docks in Frankfurt, I can prove without a shadow of a doubt, that there is indeed a sinister organisation which seeks to gain secret control of the heads of government and the aristocracy." He smiled sphinx-like before finishing, "Hardly hypothetical theories and downright fanciful tales now, eh, Herr Drechsler?"

It was not the last time that he would respond in such an extraordinary manner and, although he did it many times, I never did quite get used to it. I tried to bring myself around. Though I understood the outlandish claim, my young mind was having a problem accommodating a conspiracy of such huge proportions.

"Surely, sir, these are simply imaginary forces dreamt up by fearful delusionists to explain anything strange that occurs in the corridors of power but, after the proper officials have been set to work getting to the truth of it, an explanation soon comes to light."

"And everybody lived happily ever after? It sounds as though *you* are the one with the fanciful notions, sir. Could it be rationally expected that dark forces would *not* try to control those in places of power, and those corrupted not discovered if their actions remained unscrutinised and in the shadows? It is a good thing that you don't see the evil that can lurk in the hearts of men. It means that you project your own moral principles onto those around you and especially those above. It is part of the way we are conditioned to think. It does you proud, young Drechsler. Never forget that. It also means you are at the first level and ready to enter the next."

I pondered this for a moment, wondering what he might mean, until I felt obligued to ask, "And what is the next level, sir?"

"To understand that the first level is simply not the case."

This thought halted my mental faculties. I had not been expecting it at all, as it seemed to contradict the initial understanding. Sensing my confusion, he went on, "There are many things that you might know about the true ways of the world, my lad, but for me to tell them all to you now would leave us both with beards long enough to reach the floor. Although tell them you I will, as time passes. This information will bring you great understanding, but also great moral problems. It will be up to you to solve these as well as you can. Perhaps it would be best to remember that nothing is *ever* truly what it seems, as this will make it easier for you to understand precisely what you need to know." *4.

---

4. The Bavarian Illuminati. This society, the most infamous of all secret societies, was founded on May 1st 1776 in Bavaria. From a very modest beginning of five members, after much administrative, financial and organisational help from other 'free-thinking' collaborators, by 1784 its ranks had swollen to as many as three thousand. Membership included many well-connected and influential figures, such as; Johann Wolfgang von Goethe, Johann Gottfried Herdér, and the Dukes of Gotha and Weimar. So much has been written about the order by hundreds of notable historians, and their less reliable counterparts, that it is hard to deny any other quasi-political organisation, apart from perhaps the Freemasons, has been responsible for such speculative hysteria, intriguing legend and conspiratorial myths which still continue to this day.

This was such an esoteric speech that it asked ten times as many questions as it answered. I felt my forehead crease and my mind want to start reading from the top of a very long list of questions.

He spotted this and raised a finger. "As I said, there is not enough time right now. So we must make that for another day. You have excelled, Sebastian. I will be in touch. Good day, my friend."

I finished my tea and stood to shake his hand, permitting myself a slightly less exaggerated bow which he seemed to appreciate, and I left his rooms. Over the following weeks, I performed many similar errands, meeting the same cocky, masked lady at the fork in the road near Katzenstein Castle and then delivering the messages to the Professor the following day. Sometimes he asked me to take the letters to a farmhouse twenty miles to the east of Ingolstadt, where I would hand them over to a kindly, old lady called Frau Hoffmeister. "One of our agents," he informed me.

It seemed strange that this nice old lady could be an agent of ours, but what did I know? Anyway, she was not the female ally who most intrigued me, because I quickly found myself developing a deep fascination for the masked rider in black.

Her unladylike demeanour only worsened as our meetings continued and I was soon smitten with her irreverence and mystique. I had to check myself on a few occasions when I realised that I was falling for a woman whose face I had never seen, and of whom my parents would definitely not approve. Still, what did I care? No one would ever know of her, or my failure to win her heart, which I was convinced was bound to happen as soon as she discovered my true feelings for her. For she was aloof, confident, and worldly-wise, while I was naïve, nervous, and immature, and she probably thought me a boy.

But, although it was the strangest of relationships, it was still a relationship, and, however fleeting and absurd, I knew that I would miss it painfully were it to end.

At our next encounter, I sensed that our task might be more dangerous than I had first imagined. She arrived ten minutes late, looking uncharacteristically shaken and glancing over her shoulder, but still found time to breathlessly mock me from behind her neckerchief.

"Better looking *and* more punctual than your predecessor, Herr Junge-Kinda. Still, no man can have everything, or so it would seem." She passed me the envelope and I asked a question that had been playing on my mind.

"What happened to the one who worked before me?"

"Ah. His face was not as simple as yours. I think he is doing something less profitable now."

She kicked her horse's flanks and flew off with even more haste than usual, calling back, "Take care, Herr Junge-Kinda! I would miss seeing your pretty face, however simple it was!"

Her uneasiness seemed to imply danger, so I left as fast as her and completed the journey home in record time. However, on the way back, I had the strangest notion that I was being followed, but put this down to my paranoia caused by the lady's skittishness. Nevertheless, I decided to take the Professor's gun on my next errand, even though I sensed that somehow this decision may tempt fate. Returning to my lodgings, I successfully scaled the stairs without stirring the ever-vigilant Fraulein Warburg but, on entering my room, forlornly cast an eye over the empty bed where Jan would have usually been asleep. He had recently moved out to his own lodgings and, having not seen him for a couple of weeks, I was beginning to miss him and his jokes, jokes that would have started the very moment I came in and told him of my latest adventures.

I had been in the habit of making them seem less interesting than they were, as I thought that I had detected a hint of envy after he had started work proper and realised the drudgery of his days compared with mine. I resolved to go and see him as soon as I had the time. Whenever that would be? Work was piling up for my upcoming exams in July and I had much revision to complete, but I was determined to make time for the sake of my friendship.

More urgently, I knew that I must rest before my busy day began and soon fell into a deep sleep then started to dream. In my dream, I met the mysterious lady-in-black at the usual fork in the road, but this time, when she handed me the letter, I grabbed her and pulled her towards me. She swooned in my arms and I tore off her black neckerchief to finally reveal her beautiful face but, to my horror, I found a hideous skull with maggots spewing from the eye sockets and falling down over the grey teeth.

I jumped back into my skin from the world of Morpheus with the bells of Saint Maria's chiming in the distance and panicked, "Was that seven or eight? Please God, don't let me be late today." For it was Wednesday. Canon law day.

Fearing the worst, I sprinted along my usual route determined not to be late for The Doctor's lecture. This grim prospect was not helped by the haunting vision of the maggot-filled skull still fresh in my mind as I raced through the university gates.

From the emptiness of the corridors, I calculated that I was late by at least a quarter of an hour, so well within the zone that would result in a major dressing-down. When I reached the door of the lecture hall, I grimaced as I entered but, to my surprise, Weishaupt calmly continued talking and, without taking his eyes from his lectern, nodded to a seat near the front. I gently closed the door and made my way over as quietly as I could, then sat down, certain that he was waiting till his notes allowed it to unleash a barrage of scathing taunts. So I was further mystified when, after a few minutes, still none were forthcoming. My classmates also noticed this inexplicable suspension of authority, and I was aware of some sneering from those around me because of this apparent preferential treatment. My surprise, along with their distrust, carried on until the end of the lecture and I gradually shrunk lower and lower in my seat.

When the hallway bell sounded, I took care to leave as surreptitiously as possible, hiding amongst some of my more bookish fellow students, and was halfway through the door when I heard from behind, "Herr Drechsler?"

I turned round to find Weishaupt approaching and was greatly unnerved to witness something which I had never seen before - a smile upon his face. He spoke disingenuously, "Don't worry, young man, you've done nothing wrong. I'd like a private word with you in my chambers, that's all." Then the darnedest of things. He put his arm around my shoulder in front of everyone directly contravening the strict rules of behaviour between a student and his professor. I instantly became aware of the antipathy of my colleagues for this inexplicable breach of etiquette. He kept his hand there for five more awkward seconds and pointed me in the direction of his chambers. Somehow I had the feeling that he'd done this on purpose, but struggled to understand why? 'He really knows how to put you off balance,' I thought. 'First one way, then the other.'

Of course, I dared not protest and let him show me to his door and open it for me. My mind raced through the unpleasantries that I was about to receive; a private dressing-down, a fine, or, worst of all, to be ridiculed in front of the rest of the class for the remainder of term. How on earth could I have known what fate actually held in store as I nervously edged into Adam Weishaupt's chambers that morning in June?

Chapter 6

A Fly in the Spider's Web

Weishaupt closed the door behind me and I was surprised to find a treasure trove of antiques and ornaments filling the room. The walls were covered by an extensive library along with many portraits, certificates and maps in gilded frames and, at the back behind a mahogany desk flanked by two leather chairs, a large globe stood in between a couple of fine marble busts on plinths. Also, I noted, spread across the entire floor, an exotic Asian rug.

"Take a seat. Make yourself comfortable," offered my host, pulling up a chair and sitting down behind his desk. He seemed calm so, in turn, I tried to relax and lowered myself into the other as he carried on, "We enjoy all privileges here. I shall ring for some refreshments." He picked up a tiny bell from the table and gave it a shake.

I doubted whether this pathetic tinkle would disturb anyone as I hardly heard it myself, but low and behold, a pretty young maid immediately appeared at the service door bearing a tray carrying two *ample* cups and a fresh smelling pot of coffee.

Weishaupt grinned like a crocodile that had found a bucket of fish. "It's always best to have a plan for every little detail, don't you think? The little pleasures in life are so agreeable."

I did not know whether he was referring to the coffee or the maid and found it hard diverting my attention from her buxom figure as she wiggled back out of the room.

He watched my eyes as she closed the door and commented, "She's very attractive. Is she not?"

Whatever he was up to, it seemed pointless to lie, and anyway I thought she might be listening at the door as she must have been to hear him ring his miniscule bell.

I spoke a little louder than I needed, disguising my general unease with a confident air. Remember, this was the Sebastian of the future, not the self-conscious soul of the past living in his father's shadow. "Very attractive indeed," I answered with awkward bravado, "One would be blind or a liar to say otherwise."

He regarded me with a calculating smile before setting out the coffee. Placing a cup down in front of me he asked, "So, tell me, Herr Drechsler, what do you think of my chambers?"

"Very impressive, sir. A little something from everywhere." I gazed round at the collection of artifacts and, spotting a framed chart similar to one that I had noted in a book in Count Frederick's library in Tuffengarten, I attempted to air what little knowledge I had, "That is a Persian calendar if I'm not mistaken?"

"Well spotted, Herr Drechsler. You are correct. Though, it is actually known as a Zoroastrian calendar. According to that it is the month of Chardad and the year is 1154 AD."

It occurred to me that having two calendars might be an unnecessary complication in a life where keeping up with one already posed enough problems and I asked, "Is it not difficult holding two contradictory ideas in one's mind at the same time, sir?"

"On the *contrary*," he flicked his eyebrows, " It is the secret of a life where all things have a paradoxical nature: To have two opposing sides apparent at all times."

This man was even more oblique than Professor Van Halestrom and I wondered if all university lecturers had the same disregard for saying what they meant when in private. His eyes ranged around the room, obviously inviting me to point out something else. Whatever was going on, it was not the dressing-down that I had expected so I continued to play along. My attention was drawn to the two gleaming busts behind him and I mentioned,

"One is Vivaldi, I recognise the nose, but the other is less familiar and the inscription is too small to read from here."

"Ah, it is my great friend, the philosopher, Immanuel Kant. I believe you'll be studying him next year. He suggests that the answer to life lies in three questions; What can I know? What ought I do? What may I hope for? And he considers that the answer to the second and third depends on the answer to the first, and that our duty and our destiny can only be determined after a thorough study of our experiences."

I was more than aware of Kant's philosophy but now, oddly, found myself feigning ignorance and it struck me that this was not something that I would usually do. Sensing that it was the Doctor's demeanour that was having this effect on me, I hid my real thoughts and hoped that he would not notice. He gave the globe next to him a lazy spin then stopped it with a tap of his finger.

He eyed me over while I sipped my coffee and said, somewhat unpredictably, "You're a very interesting student, Herr Drechsler. Your marks are excellent and you obviously have a keen intellect."

I was pretty sure that he knew at least one of these statements was untrue, but again said nothing and let him carry on none the wiser - if, indeed, he ever was.

"It is in my power to grant students who possess a thirst for knowledge entry to an elite society of young scholars known as The Owl of Minerva. Within its ranks are many promising individuals like yourself from a wide variety of backgrounds. This group comes together once a month on the full moon at the Chapel of Liebfrauenmünster in the centre of town. The next meeting takes place this Saturday night and I would like to extend an invitation to you."

I was intrigued to hear the Roman Goddesses's name again as

it had been the password for my first meeting with the mysterious lady-in-black. Though, a little apprehensive about accepting, I was going to go anyway out of plain curiosity when he added, "It is a great honour to be invited to the Minerval gathering. Maybe it would appear rude to turn down such an invitation."

This seemed like a veiled threat but, once more, I tried to conceal my real feelings and replied innocently, "I would be most honoured to attend, sir."

I smiled and gulped down the rest of my coffee, placed my cup back on the tray and politely observed, "I have to be at Professor Lipstad's history lecture in a moment."

He accepted my excuses and stood up to offer me his hand which I took, noticing it to be a little cold. I bowed and turned to go, certain that there was no chance he was going to ring his bell once more and summon back his little beauty.

Upon leaving, I made my way directly to find the Professor to tell him what had happened. Although Van Halestrom had never mentioned it, something told me that a certain rivalry existed between the two gentlemen and therefore I guessed that our brief discussion would be of interest to him. But, when I knocked, there was no answer and, after trying once more, I despondently walked away to my next lecture.

Over the next few days, I tried several more times to find the Professor, but to no avail, and eventually his clerk told me that he was not due back at the faculty until the start of next week. This would be after the meeting at the Owl of Minerva and, by Friday, I was growing increasingly nervous about attending and suspected that this would not have been the case had I been able to speak to Van Halestrom beforehand. It was also the night that I had planned to visit Jan and I rued the unfortunate timing, but promised myself that I would see my friend in the following days.

Before I knew it, Saturday had arrived and, after a hard day spent studying my books and deliberating my decision, as I had given my word to a university lecturer, I finally got changed and went to find the Chapel of Liebfrauenmünster.

Had I known exactly what was going to happen on that sticky summer's evening back in 1784, then instead of bounding up the steps and innocently strolling down the chapel's colonnade, I would have been on my knees on the pavement outside, humbly praying to God to protect me. I distinctly remember passing between the pillars and glancing around the shadows, thinking to myself, 'This might be good, and it might be bad.' Silly me. I should have known that it was pretty much all going to be bad. But that's the naïve optimism of youth for you. And that's what might have saved my life. In the end. *5.

---

5. The Owl of Minerva (Athena). These meetings facilitated an academy in which young initiates of the Illuminati could be selected and groomed for higher positions within the organisation. The class of Minerva was a relatively low rank in the scheme of things. However, it was the soul of the Order and functioned as a sort of assembly line for recruits. Candidates advanced from *Novice* to the *Minerval degree* where they were properly vetted, scrutinised and indoctrinated. Another revealing aspect of owl symbolism was to remind its initiates that the Illuminati does its bidding at night.

Chapter 7

The Owl of Minerva

At the chapel's entrance I was most pleased to find a pair of enchanting young maidens in classical vestal gowns standing either side of the double doors. Owing to the money that I had earned working for Van Halestrom, I was now quite wealthy by my usual standards, so, after paying off my debts, settling my rent and buying Petrova a brand new saddle and bridle, I had splashed out on a dashing new outfit befitting a man of my growing financial status. I could tell that the nymphs appreciated it and hoped that they might find their way inside later to inspect its tailoring more closely. The fairer sex had been increasingly on my mind and, having not seen the sultry lady-in-black for nearly a week, I was seriously craving some female attention. There seemed to be beautiful women everywhere in my life, but I never had the time or the excuse to become better acquainted. The maidens smiled rather more knowingly than their vestal garb should have allowed, before one of them passed me a decorative mask which I briefly inspected then put on and, before I could think of anything to say which was as dashing as my outfit, the other girl opened the doors and I stepped into a dim passageway.

Two rows of candles flickered along the walls as the doors closed behind me and, as the reverberations faded, I began to hear the sound of many voices coming from the far end. I sidled up to a pair of red velvet curtains and tentatively pulled them apart.

"This must be the place," I said to myself, upon seeing forty or so other guests wearing similar masks mingling about in a dark cavernous chamber. At the far end of the hall stood an enormous statue of an owl lit by four blazing candelabra around its feet, each the size of a man. 'The Owl of Minerva,' I presumed.

The flames threw eerie flickering shapes over the bottom of the statue, leaving the bird's austere features shrouded in shadow.

I slipped between the curtains and, as I noticed that everyone in the place was drinking from a silver goblet, I felt a tap on my shoulder and turned to find a man and a woman adorned in the same mock classical garb as the girls outside. The woman handed me a silver cup which the man skillfully filled from a barrel under his arm, before they both silently nodded and tiptoed away into the crowd. I made my way between the guests, sniffing at the drink and trying to ascertain its contents. As well as a goodly amount of alcohol, I could also detect another ingredient, something sickly sweet which I had smelt before, but could not quite place where.

My concentration evaporated on hearing a familiar voice ring out, "Of course it's alright to drink it *now*. I've had my cup filled three times already. These chaps are my favourite type of innkeep, as they need no pay nor any other encouragement to go about their business. Which, as any man worth his weight in wine will tell you, is a damn fine thing indeed."

It could not be anyone else but Jan Kohler, appropriately disguised in a mask of the nature spirit Pan. Taken aback to say the least, to find him here on this night for 'promising individuals,' I approached the small group surrounding him. But, before I got there, I recognised another voice which stopped me in my tracks like no other could have.

"Go on, darling, have another. You're so funny when you're drunk and I want to laugh."

I could not believe it. Draped over Jan, and wearing an alluring nymph's mask, was the lady-in-black. A surge of envy swept over me as the woman, whose breath-taking figure was now fully revealed by a tantalising fawn's outfit, began to kiss my oldest friend.

I stared with incredulity as Jan tongued for Bavaria whilst idly holding out his silver goblet to have it refilled by another attentive servant. The embrace lasted long enough to embarrass the landlord of the busiest brothels in Babylon but still I held my breath. Twisting my jealousy further, the group around them cheered encouragement with some copying their performance and entwining themselves around each other. Unable to accept what I was seeing, at last, I gasped and turned away.

Any other woman with any other man would not have had the same profound effect on me and I took an impulsive draw from my goblet then skulked behind a column. After a moment, I could not help but peek again and was further mortified to see them in an even more lustful pose. Heartbroken, I turned my back once more and gulped down several more slugs of the brew.

A drum roll sounded, drawing everyone's attention to the burning candelabra at the feet of the owl where Weishaupt appeared dressed in a white hooded gown and raised his hands to welcome the crowd. "Good evening, brothers and sisters! I am so glad to greet those who will carry the light of progress and knowledge into the future. Everyone here tonight has earned the privilege of admission into this renowned sect, dedicated to personal empowerment and public freedom. I want you all to share your youth and beauty on this full moon of Gemini. To enjoy each other's desires and throw away your cares from the past. To allow yourself to move seamlessly into your bright new futures."

He bowed, casting his head in shadow like the ominous bird looming above him and chanted, "O thou great symbol of all mortal wisdom, Owl of Bohemia, we do beseech thee, grant us thy counsel." He rose, catching his face in the light of the flames then called out, "Now let the rite begin!"

A band struck up and two lines of frolicking vestal maidens

escorted by musicians, filed out from behind the statue. They mixed with the guests and, as dancing and debauchery quickly broke out, Weishaupt enjoyed an arrogant grin before bowing deeply and disappearing back into the darkness.

The mood in the chamber was rapidly mounting into an orgy. I tried to spot Jan and my lady but their places had now been taken by another pair of lewd revellers. It seemed as though the nymphs in the vestal gowns were leading events in the room and enticing everyone to join in with their wanton behaviour. While I watched from behind the safety of my column, I heard splashing from my side and found another servant refilling my goblet. He had hardly finished when one of the maidens took my hand and, lowering her eyes in the most seductive of ways, dragged me into the cavorting throng. Despite myself, I meekly let her lead me on, until I could take no more and pulled her towards me.

She swooned in my arms and I took my advantage but, as I tasted my lips upon hers, I suddenly remembered where I had smelt the potion before. The docks in Frankfurt. It was opium! Realising this, and that I did not want my-lady-in-black to see me with this other woman, even though I had seen her with my best friend, I fought to control my carnal instincts. My head may have been swimming in primordial desire, but I could still feel the prickle of pride and my orthodox upbringing chiming at the back of my faltering consciousness.

I pushed the maiden away and made for what I thought must be the entrance. Luckily, none of the servants tried to force me back inside to fornicate with the revellers but, as I recovered from this frightening prospect, I found myself in a different candle-lit hallway to the one through which I had entered. Rather than return to the pulsating romp that lay behind me, I carried on and stumbled between another set of velvet curtains into a darkened chamber containing some statues and large potted plants.

I slumped down on a stone bench and spilled the goblet as the powerful drugs took hold. Trying to steady myself, I held my face in my hands but the room began to spin around and around. I felt that I was going to vomit and promptly did so - once - then immediately felt my head begining to clear as I took some steadying breaths. The ringing in my ears slowly subsided to be replaced by a muffled slurping sound coming from somewhere behind me. I could not quite fathom what it was and so, rather unsteadily, I got up to have a look.

In the shadows at the side of the room, I saw them. One was clearly Jan Kohler groaning from behind his Pan mask with his green trousers round his ankles, and the other, still wearing her nymph's mask and kneeling in front of him, I was sure was the lady-in-black. I began to feel sick again and lurched back through the curtains, knowing that I simply must get away.

I fell back into the main hall where the huge owl was now overseeing what had descended into a full-blown orgy. This wasn't what I had expected at all. I had thought that everyone would have been gently ambling about deliberating *The Age of Reason*, which would have made me seem like a romantic maverick. I had been looking forward to regaling my fellow sectists of how I 'almost' used a gun in anger, and how I 'almost' wooed a woman, whose face I could 'almost' see, who was now in the back room with my best friend 'fully' in her mouth. What a fool I'd been. In reality, I was a scared college boy out of his depth, put in a position that he had always thought he wanted, but now could only gawp around like a prig and not join in at all.

Another drum roll sounded and Weishaupt reappeared at the base of the owl. He raised his hands to halt the musicians and called out to us, "Now, my Minerval brethren, it is time to perform the Cremation of Care. Come now, those who seek the real truth of light. Join me in praise for our glorious Molech!"

I struggled to see what this frightening Canaanite god had to do with the 'truth of light.' But, still in a state of shock after the scenes that I had already witnessed, my jaded curiosity once again got the better of me and I took a couple of steps closer.

Despite the darkness, I could make out a tiny recess in the floor around the base of the owl and noticed that it was filled with a transparent fluid. One of the male servants appeared with a reed basket and set it on the liquid then gave it a push towards Weishaupt's feet. As the basket floated across the pool, I could have sworn that I heard a baby cry and that I saw a tiny hand appear from the canopy but, before I knew it, to my horror and bewilderment, the pool turned into a blazing fire which engulfed the basket in a flash. The powerful flames illuminated the owl, Weishaupt raised his arms, the musicians played ever faster and the party went into an accelerated stage of debauchery.

I started to feel sick again and clasped my mouth with one hand whilst using the other to push my way through the romping mob which writhed about me in every direction. To my relief, I found the original set of curtains, blundered through them and staggered up the passageway then burst out the front doors. Fortunately, the guardian maidens were no longer there to see me floundering through the colonnade wiping the vomit from my chin and I assumed that they were back inside giving their all for Molech.

Taking one last look behind me, I threw away my mask and stumbled down the steps leading back to the road. I had only got fifty yards when I was alarmed to see a large shaven-headed man with a heavy black moustache appear from behind a tree and approach me in the most unsettling of ways. He rudely blocked my path and demanded, "Are you Sebastian Drechsler?"

Somehow the question was so simple that it threw me for a second before I answered, "Well… yes. I suppose so…"

The sturdy swine produced a gleaming knife from behind his back which turned my innards to gravy. I only had time to see the blade glinting in the moonlight, and consider that the night had been bad enough already without this bastard murdering me in the street, when there was a sudden swishing noise from over my shoulder and an arrow appeared in his chest with a blood-curdling 'Crunch!'

The man was as shocked as I was but, from his open mouth, coughed a gut full of blood which splashed right across my face. I involuntarily wiped myself - again - as he reeled backwards and ended up slumped against the tree. I stood staring at the macabre sight for a moment not knowing what to do, before glancing behind me towards the chapel in the direction from which the arrow had come. There was no one there to suggest who might have fired the shot that had, almost certainly, saved my life. Unless, that was, they had been aiming for me? My heart began to pound even faster.

What in God's name was going on? One thing was certain - I wanted it to end right away. I saw that my hand was covered in blood and asked myself what I was still doing there? That was an easy question to answer. Nothing that would lead to any good. So, without further ado, I fled. It was an excellent piece of fleeing of which I am still proud to this day. I especially recall sprinting past a couple going the other way who wished me, "Goodnight." As you may imagine, this was hard to reciprocate knowing that they were going to find something up the street which was going to ruin their evening stroll. I ran all the way home in a blind funk and stayed up till three o'clock in the morning washing the blood from my clothes. Though I scrubbed long and hard, I could not remove the stains, nor the visions from my mind, which still persist to this day and will always serve as a bloody reminder of the worst time that I ever spent on a student's night.

*6.

---

6. The Cremation of Care Ceremony. S. Drechsler's recollections strangely bear much in common with ceremonies known to take place at a yearly party held for the world's elite at <u>Bohemian Grove</u> in California. Though, judging by the available video footage it appears that no one is actually hurt during the ritual. <u>The owl</u>, in this case, is sometimes referred to as <u>Molech</u>. In antiquity Moloch, the Canaanite deity, is represented as a legless bull with arms. This pagan god would be worshipped by the Israelites during times of apostasy (<u>without religion</u>) and is associated with the <u>sacrifice of children</u>. Lev.18:21, *'Neither shall you give any of your offspring to offer them to Molech.'*

Chapter 8

No Rest for the Wicked

I awoke with a start in my bed. By now I was getting used to waking up soaked in sweat after being plagued by horrific dreams. In my latest vision, I was being chased by a huge owl for stealing its opium. Even sleep was not allowing me a safe haven and I certainly could find none in my waking life. The moment I lifted my head from the pillow the look of horror on the bald man's face shot back into my mind and, all at once, the previous night's harrowing events came back in a flood of dark recollections. I shuddered and half-swooned with emotion then buckled with fear and remorse as the entirety of the ordeals returned to haunt me. "Jan," I sighed, "How could it possibly be?" I shook my head trying to cast out the odious memories, but it didn't work and I got out of the bed which now seemed somehow dirty.

I fumbled across the room and doused my head with water from the bowl by the window then gazed out across the rooftops. It was a pleasing view. Blossoming trees and pretty houses nestling up to the city wall all basked in pleasant morning sunshine and, here and there, the spires of Ingolstadt's churches pointing up to the sky with their chiming bells filling the air.

'That's what I need,' I thought. 'A church.' Not being the most pious of Christians, unlike my devout parents, I had not been to church since I had moved to this place almost a year ago. Now I noted how much had changed in that time, and how my soul yearned for something everyday and normal. Something that reminded me of home. As I came to a happier state of equilibrium, I remembered that, it was Sunday after all.

While I collected these thoughts, there was a commotion downstairs. My irritable landlady was scolding some poor soul who had made the mistake of arriving too early in the morning. The hubbub steadily came closer until I realised that, whoever it was, must be coming to see me, as they had come too far up the stairs for there to be any other alternative. My stomach churned as the voices approached and I imagined a town watchman, or another bald man with a knife, or even Jan come to boast - that might be even worse. My God! What if it was my lady?

"Control yourself Sebastian," I murmured, hearing a man's voice mingling with Fraulein Warburg's as a cane knocked smartly on my door. I timidly made my way over but, considering that I had nowhere to run and, indeed, nothing to hide, I flung the door open only to find - Professor Van Halestrom.

Well, it was my door this time so I spoke first and asked, rather indignantly, "Forgive me, sir, but what in Heaven's name are you doing here?"

He smiled inscrutably and said, "I was going to church and had the feeling that you'd like to come along."

I frowned deeply as it seemed that whenever I saw his face it was always calm and wise, while mine was awash with stupefaction. His smile turned to a grin as the ringing church bells wafted in through the window.

Five minutes later, we were picking our way through the crowds of townsfolk all dressed smartly in their Sunday clothes while I pestered him for all I was worth. "One day, sir, you have to explain to me how you perform the miracle where you tell me what I'm going to do before I know I'm going to do it myself."

"Ah, but then, Herr Drechsler, you would never have the chance to surprise yourself and, believe me, that would be permanently disappointing."

I frowned at his unsatisfactory answer, but carried on undeterred, "I'm sorry, sir, but as I understand it, nearly everything that comes from your lips seems to be a riddle."

"Is not life a riddle, my friend, and our purpose to understand it?"

He had been prevaricating in the same infuriating manner whilst I had got dressed and we left the house. Now, as we walked through the crowds in the clear light of day, I felt that I simply must find out what was going on in my new chaotic life and that, somehow, his timely appearance was not entirely a coincidence. I pressed on, "But, Herr Van Halestrom, I feel there are several extremely pressing matters of the gravest concern to which I must find explanations."

Finally, he stopped, looked me in the eye and said. "I think you're right.. I believe it is time for you to attain the next level of understanding. You've had time to grasp what you have already learnt and now you realise that all is not what it seems. I believe you truly know this, because you have seen it for yourself. Also, I believe that you have changed your behaviour to adapt to this new uncertain reality. And that, at times, you have pretended to be something that you are not, in order to gain some sort of control. This is the way we learn - through our experiences."

This was true enough. I had certainly seen some unbelievable things, and had also pretended to be something that I was not. Though, how the Professor knew of it was a mystery to me. Never mind. For once there seemed to be a fairly logical progression of ideas. Maybe things were finally starting to make sense.

The two of us set off again and I relaxed at the prospect of discovering something that I needed to know. We came to a pleasing avenue, the trees of which created a canopy of shimmering green above us. One hundred yards up ahead, neatly framed by the leafy branches, rose the spire of St Bartholomew's Church and, regarding the building's uncomplicated symmetry, a calm fell over me as we strolled along. "So you think you can tell me what I want to know, Professor?"

"I will try, Sebastian."

I took a deep breath and tried to pick the first and most pertinent question from the hundreds rampaging through my mind, but realised that I could not think of one which I could fairly ask and reasonably expect him to answer. I became frustrated. All this time in the dark and now, with the possibility of finding out what was going on, and I could not conceive of one good question. Let me explain.

Yes, I had attended the meeting at the chapel, but what would he know of a party organised for drunken students? Also, our lady-in-black was obviously her own woman and free to do whatever she wanted, with whomsoever she pleased. That she chose to do it with my best friend, was of no concern to the Professor. What should he know, or care, of such things? What about the ceremony itself? Well, I had been drunk, or worse, drugged and, as a consequence, had no idea if the things that I'd thought I had seen were even real. Furthermore, I had grappled like a randy sailor with a young maiden and, though I had enjoyed her only briefly, it was still during an orgy. I was not proud of these transgressions and believed they were excesses of which he would not want to hear. As for the killing of my assailant, I had no wish to incriminate myself in a murder if I didn't have to. What would the poor old Professor know of such wickedness anyway?

I tutted to myself and tried to order my thoughts as we neared the church. I saw the priest welcoming his congregation one by one and prayed that my questions would arrange themselves in such neat fashion.

"Relax and it will come to you," assured the Professor, and I had a moment of clarity as the most important of the previous night's events resurfaced once again, its significance outweighing my personal plight. I knew that I must tell someone.

I squeezed my eyes shut and confessed, "I watched a man die last night after he was shot with an arrow."

He did not hesitate, not even for an instant. "I know. It was me. I killed him. He was going to murder you."

"What?" I exclaimed, inadvertently alerting the priest and his parishioners to our presence.

Annoyingly, Van Halestrom repeated himself, "I said, I know. it was me. I killed him. He was going to murder you."

"Yes, yes, I heard you the first time," I hissed, trying to keep my voice down.

"You did ask, Sebastian."

"I know I did, sir, but, forgive me…" I noticed the churchgoers staring in our direction and whispered, "I'm sorry, sir, but I'm still a bit confused. How did you..?"

"I have a crossbow, a really good one, take a man's head off at fifty paces. I use the silver-tipped arrows so they know who has done it."

Bewildered yet again, I blundered, "They? Who are... *they*?"

"The Illuminati, I kill the Illuminati with silver-tipped arrows so they know who has done it." He watched my eyes to check that I knew what he meant.

"Yes, yes, you kill them with the silver arrows so-they-know who-has-done-it - I assure you, sir, *that* is the part I understand."

We were getting much closer to the church and I did not want to cause a scene on this pleasant Sunday morning, but Van Halestrom seemed oblivious of these sentiments and fumbled around in his pocket before producing one of the lethal darts and pushing the cursed thing right in my face. "Look here's one," he noted. "See, the tips are cast extremely thin. This increases the range and accuracy whilst, of course, ensuring they know…"

This time I anticipated him, "Who has done it - yes!"

I leapt in front of him, attempting to shield the bolt from the line of churchgoers and suggested, "We should probably put that away now."

"Perhaps you're right," he conceded and came to a halt. "Look, you told me you wanted to know what was going on. so I'm telling you. I believe I owe you that much."

He replaced the projectile in his pocket and we set off again. I took a deep breath and gathered my thoughts before continuing, "So what were the Illuminati doing at the Chapel of Liebfrauenmünster?"

"Adam Weishaupt leads the Order in Bavaria and uses the ceremonies to groom his initiates. Being rightly suspicious that you are in league against him, he tried to compromise you by drugging you then indulging you in a lustful act. When you failed to perform, as it were, he decided to have you killed. That's when I made my entry."

"*In league against him*? ...What? So you're telling me that you knew I was going to that... that... orgy... and that I would be ... in terrible danger, but you let me go anyway?

"Oh yes."

We had reached the back of the queue by now but I still could not help my anger boiling over and, breaching all-known etiquette, I finally snapped, "Damn you, Van Halestrom!"

Infuriatingly, he kept as cool as an outdoor privy while I became increasingly agitated. So much so that, when we shook hands with the priest, the nervous clergyman looked at me as though I was an escaped patient from the asylum, when all along it was the Professor who was the real madman with the crossbow and the silver arrows - so *they* knew who had 'done it.'

We entered the church and took our seats near the front below the pulpit. I was still shaking my head in disbelief and attempting, with some difficulty, to calm both my outer and inner selves before the service began. Van Halestrom made this impossible by chatting away beside me, "You know erm, Benjamin Franklyn, yes? One of the Founding Fathers of America's new United States, which by the way, is also being infiltrated by the Order. He say's his favourite part of going to church is the quiet reflection before the preacher delivers the sermon. I would have to agree. It's obvious you don't need a priest acting as some sort of conduit to your God. If you *are* going to achieve spiritual union, then you're only going to do it on your own. Anyway, that's another way they control you. Through the church." He made an arc with his eyes, "They're Illuminati too y'know?"

Someone shushed him from behind as if to prove a point and, at last, he was silenced. We bowed our heads in quiet contemplation and, after a moment, another dreadful memory flashed back into my mind. It was the horrific sight of the baby in the burning crib. So much had happened the night before, most of it whilst I was intoxicated, that I had forgotten about it until then. I whispered, "So you were at the chapel, in the hall, with... that odious bird?" He nodded and, though confounded to hear this, I carried on, "Well, what about... the infant? At one point... I thought that... it was real."

"It was. That's why I hunt the murdering scum down and kill them whenever I get the chance."

"Sweet Mother of God!" Predictably, my ear-splitting outburst caused a church warden to come over and ask what was wrong. Van Halestrom told him that I had a dementia known as, "Terretsia lacrobia - a vile sickness of the mind which forces its victims to make uncontrollable calls." He assured the old man that he was in full control of the situation and that he had brought me to the church as all scientific medicine had failed me and all we could do now was throw my ravaged soul on the mercy of the Lord.

"A good Christian can never resist a challenge," he murmured, as the warden went to sit down and the priest appeared in the pulpit. The opening hymn began and the congregation was soon in full swing and, even had I screamed 'Bloody murder!' at the top of my voice, no one would have been any the wiser such was the heartiness of the singing. I stood there in a motionless fit of delirium, uselessly humming along and feeling as though I was losing my mind. Presented, as I had been, with these wild allegations which, without any other reasonable explanation, could well be true, when all around me was such innocence, was horror in itself. A sweet old lady smiled at me from the pew ahead and I gulped and stared up at the stained glass window depicting Jesus on the cross dying for our sins.

After the hymns, the priest delivered his sermon, of which I remember nothing, and soon the prayers began. A small confessional was opened ten paces away at the side of the hall. For some reason, Van Halestrom elbowed me towards it until I almost fell off my pew. I resisted at first, irritably shaking my head at him, but he seemed to insist. Eventually, I gave in, certain that, at least in the confessional, I might be able to get some peace and solitude. If I were to let the Professor go before me, I would still be there on Judgement Day waiting for him to be forgiven for his dark deeds. An old lady emerged from inside crossing her chest and I made my way over then let myself in and settled down on the bench. After a minute, the priest entered and sat down behind the screen. Another quiet moment passed before he spoke. "It wasn't really me in the chapel last night."

I yanked my head away from the screen. Not only did the priest seem to know me, but he had a woman's voice. A voice that I knew well. Though I knew it was impossible, I was sure that it was the lady-in-black's. I put my head in my hands and wondered if this madness would ever end.

There was a pause before she spoke again, "I said, it wasn't really me at the chapel last night... Well it was... but then it wasn't. Oh I wish I had time to explain. Is that you, Herr Junge-Kinda?"

How could it be her? In the church - of all places - in the confessional, impersonating a man of the cloth when the last time I had seen her she was hanging off the end of my best friend? My mind was swamped by waves of conflicting emotions. It was becoming impossible to tell the difference between my irrational dreams and my absurd reality.

I stumbled for something to say and ended up asking, "So, what are you doing here now, in a confessional, in St Bartholomew's Church?" On hearing my question, I became determined to get a proper answer and pressed on, "On a Sunday morning, two streets from my house... impersonating a *priest*? Why? ...Why? ...*Why*..?"

She whispered breathlessly, "I came to see you. To explain what happened last night."

I leaned closer, trying to see through the screen. "Well, I cannot see you, as usual, so you might as well tell me."

"There isn't time. I must leave straight away."

I sighed. "Begging your pardon, my lady, but does it not seem a waste of time? Surely, if you wanted to talk to me, why did you not come as a normal parishioner? We could have done that, like normal people do - probably - somewhere in the world." Realising that this sounded perhaps too wistful, I pulled myself together and pressed my ear against the screen, listening intently for her answer.

It came quickly and she gasped, "I could not risk being seen. The Order's agents are everywhere. You must take great care and do whatever the Professor tells you."

"I think we are already at the stage where he tells me what

I'm going to do before I know it myself. It would seem that... in many ways..." I tried to hint at my feelings for her, "...I am no longer in possession of my freewill."

I waited for a reply, but this time there was none. After a moment, I put my nose up to the screen and peered between the lattices, but there was no one there. She had gone. It was the last straw for me that morning and I fully lost my mind.

"For the sweet love of Christ! Will someone please tell me what in heaven's name is going on?"

I shouted this outrage so loudly that, when I flung open the door, the line of prospective confessors fairly jumped out of their shoes. In a frenzy of bewilderment, I went to the first and violently shook him, shouting, "Where is she? What have you done with her?"

Seeing my psychosis deepening, Van Halestrom approached and, not wanting to cause any more of a scene than we already had, he took hold of my shoulders and insisted, "We should go now, Sebastian. There is nothing more we can do here."

"What do you mean, 'there is nothing more we can do here'? We have to find her. She was here! Just now! I heard her voice speaking to me!"

Having lost control of my senses, I was unable to realise how deranged this sounded. I managed to break free from Van Halestrom and throw open the door on the other side of the confessional, only to find, to my deepening confusion, the innocent, young priest from outside, smiling up at me and adjusting his cassock. Being oblivious of my quest to find a vanishing woman, he was mortified when I hauled him up by his dog collar, screaming, "What have you done to her? What have you done to that poor woman?"

The church has its limits too, and this last particularly humiliating imposition on my behalf exceeded nearly every one.

Considering the potential seriousness of my indiscretions, I was lucky that the city's watchmen were not summoned once more. Who knows what the fine is for assaulting a priest? I'm sure it was a lot more than breaking a window and some chamber pots. We were eventually asked to leave, though I am certain that we would have been forced to go, had the Professor not dragged me out of the place kicking and screaming and shouting oaths like a Prussian troubadour.

"Perhaps a different church would be best next Sunday," mentioned the Professor with a prudent cough as we walked away from St Bartholomews and back up the avenue, "There are actually twelve churches in Ingolstadt. Or is it thirteen?"

I frowned ungraciously at him as he carried on, "Right, my lad, you probably need a proper meal and a good rest. So, if you will permit me, I shall take you back to my humble abode where I wil try to make amends for the predicament that you believe yourself to be in."

I had already suffered enough of his riddles for one day and shot him a glare to show it. But he simply smiled, regardless of my disdain and continued in the same annoyingly even-handed manner, "Do not fret, my lad. Everything will soon start falling into place. Then nothing will surprise you except what you are prepared to do about it."

He tapped his cane twice on the cobbles, whereupon an expensive, black coach drawn by a matching pair of black horses appeared from behind us. Of course, this was a total surprise in itself, thus ruining his promise and simultaneously removing any remaining credibility that he may have possessed. I sighed and ruffled my forehead as the driver opened the door below him. Van Halestrom gestured at the waiting coach and I begrudgingly climbed aboard. He followed me inside and I heard the driver's whip crack as we pulled away.

*7.

---

7. The Illuminati & The Founding Fathers of America. The extent to which the Illuminati had penetrated revolutionary American politics via the Freemasons, of which all the founding fathers were members, is unknowable. However, Thomas Jefferson, Ambassador to France from 1785-1789, knew Weishaupt and wrote sympathetically of his professed basic aim of '*making men wise and virtuous*' and contended that, unlike the new American republic, '*secretive methods were a necessity under the religious and aristocratic tyranny of Europe.*' Hundreds of conspiracy theories persist to this day concerning the Order's involvement with revolutionary America as many have noted the Masonic symbolism designed into The Great Seal of The United States and even upon the street layout of Washington DC.

Chapter 9

The Castle Landfried

The black coach slipped through the city gates and soon the walls of Ingolstadt were far behind us. We carried on travelling north at a decent rate for the next hour till the flatter farmland, typical of the Danube, slowly changed into a series of deep valleys and, presently, we took a turn at a fork in the road then made our way into the hills. After a few miles along a solitary dusty track, I glimpsed a fabulous castle for which we seemed inevitably headed. Half château, half splendid fortress, the building clung precariously to the top of a daunting promontory of rock, its turrets and pointed towers making for an impressive view set against the pine-covered valleys and distant misty mountains to the east.

The Professor nodded at the imposing fort and pointed out, "The Castle Landfried; built some four hundred years ago by a local nobleman of the same name. According to all accounts, he was a most evil man who liked to lock his detractors away in the castle dungeons, many of the poor souls never to be heard of again. Although he was a homicidal maniac, as you can see, he was also an excellent architect."

The coach swept ever upwards and passed over a spectacularly high bridge spanning a fearful canyon. My habitual fear of heights briefly stirred as we rumbled across until, with another insistent crack of the driver's whip, we reached the other side. Next, we came to a pair of black iron gates mounted with the crest of a two-headed eagle. I watched in awe as they mysteriously opened by themselves then peered back through the dust kicking up behind us to see them, somehow, close again. Amazed, I turned to gaze at the castle's magnificent towers, which reached into the sky like fingers of a gigantic armoured glove.

We rattled under the portcullis and into an outer courtyard then through a second archway leading to a large cobbled square. With a sharp, "Whoa!" from the driver we slowed at the foot of a stone stairway below the door of the keep, from which a smartly dressed old servant had appeared and was already making his way down toward us.

He was by the coach door when we stopped and opened it, greeting his master, "Good day, sir." Upon seeing me, he added, slightly condescendingly, "I see you have brought a guest, sir. Does this mean I should set the dining table for two?"

"That's right, Bacon. Herr Drechsler will be staying the night. Please prepare the Günter suite for him."

I stepped down from the coach and marvelled up at the awe-inspiring castle. The masonry seemed perfect in every detail, with splendid fortified walls surrounding the courtyard, citadel and keep and, above them all, six or seven dizzying towers soaring so high that I almost fell over oggling up at them. Van Halestrom jumped down from the coach and called out, "Klaus, my friend, you may take the rest of the day off. We shan't be needing you any longer."

The driver gave him a wry smile and steered the coach away.

After examining the exceptional architecture for a moment longer, I could not help but exclaim, "It is a truly incredible building, Herr Professor. In each and every way."

To which his older servant, who was making his way back up the stairs, answered, "Apart from keeping it warm in the winter."

I faced Van Halestrom in consternation. His servant had publicly cheeked us. Surely he should be immediately reprimanded, so as to set an example to the other staff. I had already noticed his relaxed attitude with the driver, and was determined to tell him that it would not do. I piped up, but out of earshot of the elderly rogue, not wanting to overstep my mark,

"Surely, sir, you should punish your servant for his impudence?"

Somehow the old fart still heard me from twenty paces away and rudely replied over his shoulder, "I'm a butler, sir, not a servant and he knows there's no point in complaining, let alone *punishing* me, I'm far too old to change now."

This rudeness was intolerable and I went to argue my case for chastising the scoundrel. Before I could, Van Halestrom raised a finger and plainly stated. "He's from England. Very good really. Couldn't run the place without him. Remember, Sebastian, nothing is *ever* what it seems."

I could not imagine what this had to do with letting your servant backchat you and gave up with a shrug of exasperation.

We climbed the stairs behind the old duffer and filed through the front door into a grand hallway, the walls of which were covered with stuffed animal heads, including wild boar and antelope and a few peculiar species that I did not even recognise.

"I didn't kill them," mentioned the Professor, gesturing up at the brutish, frozen faces as we passed, "Hunting animals for pleasure is not a pastime I would encourage anyone to take part in, but they do give the place a certain ambiance."

"But how is a man meant to test himself and hone his skills for the battlefield, to say nothing of feeding himself, without the thrill of the hunt?"

"There are many ways to simulate the hunting process, Herr Drechsler. There is also more important prey than helpless animals."

We turned from the hallway into a comfortable study, where he offered me one of a pair of leather chairs sitting in front of a roaring fire. He lit his pipe with a taper and went through a handful of letters from the mantelpiece, muttering to himself, "Bill. Bill. Bill." After the fourth of fifth, he sighed, "Sometimes, Herr Drechsler, I feel like old Luther."

Unsure of what he meant, I urged him to explain with an uncertain shake of my head.

"Wherever I go there's always another troublesome bill in front of me." He mimed hammering a nail into a wall.

"I think I understand. Do you mean when the Protestant reformist fixed his proclamation of religious freedom to the door of Wartburg church in 1517?"

"The very same, lad," he said with a chuckle. "You're obviously well educated, but sometimes your sense of humour reminds me of old Luther."

With this he threw the letters into the fire.

"Is that not a little rash, sir?"

"Why do you think I live in a castle?" he bluntly replied. "The truth of the matter, Herr Drechsler, is that the vast proportion of money being sought by my debtors is in fact payment for the unnecessary war fought against Austria and, as such, is a financial illusion. A monetary phantom dreamt up by economic vampires who wish to suck the lifeblood out of the country. I have spent much time and effort confiscating money from my enemies and I do not intend to give it back to them in the form of taxes."

He agitated the coals with a poker and sent a cloud of glowing ashes flying up the chimney.

"But surely, sir, the state cannot function without the taxes of the people of whom it is the master?"

"There's no master to it, my lad. The taxes merely pay usurious interest on unnecessary loans. The criminals who own this debt also control the amount of money in the system, diluting and increasing it at will, thus turning the 'people,' as you put it, into fiscal slaves. This is the hidden conspiracy behind capitalism. I believe it was somehow the reason for your foreboding dream and, also, how the Illuminati plan to rule the world."

I shuddered upon recalling my hideous nightmare and ventured, "Sir, it would seem that every theme I begin upon, quickly leads back to the Illuminati."

"That's because everything *does* lead back to the Illuminati. They are the sprawling octopus behind most that is bad on this earth, possessing the power to corrupt even international heads of state and royalty from the shadows. While one tentacle creates war and revolution, another causes stock market crashes, while yet another swoops in to collect the debt. Like a rampaging monster they will continue to ravage all until they are stopped. That's why you are here."

"I don't understand, Herr Professor. Why am I here?"

"To learn how to fight against them."

"Me? Fight against *them*? How, and with what? All you gave me was a single flintlock. How am I going to stop an international gang of murderers who can supposedly control the Kings of Europe?"

"With a little help from your friends."

He flashed an optimistic smile as his servant appeared at the door and announced, "Dinner is served, sir."

We moved to a banqueting hall overlooking the fabulous mountainside and sat at opposite ends of a fine dining table. Over dinner the Professor took pains to direct the conversation away from more pressing matters and we talked in depth on a host of different topics. These discussions lasted for so long that the sun was already going down by the time we withdrew back to the cosy study where the large fire continued to blaze. Sitting in the pair of leather chairs, we supped our brandies and digested what had been a fully comprehensive meal, with so many courses that I had lost count. I must have eaten more that day than I had done in a week back in Ingolstadt and I tried to hide a rather large vaporous fart, not wishing to offend my host.

Without taking his attention from the fire, he murmured, "No need to hold them in, my lad. There's only me here and I don't mind."

I was still finding it difficult to keep a secret from the man. Glancing at the gloomy portrait over the fireplace, I attempted to change the subject. "Who's the character in the picture, Herr Van Halestrom?"

"It is the old landlord himself: Count Theodor Vladimir Landfried the third, a thoroughly ruthless villain from Russia. During his heinous life, he tortured and murdered hundreds of innocents terrorising the local population with a series of horrific pogroms and witch hunts. Such was the blood-curdling callousness of his atrocities, that he was responsible for perpetuating the myth of the vampire throughout the area."

I shifted in my seat and stared up at the painting as another blast of wind moaned up the old chimney. "It's not the sort of painting one would normally hang in the room that they visit before going to bed, Professor."

"Ah, but mad aristocrats, and even mythical vampires, are nothing compared to the monsters that we face. For, unlike the madman they are cunning, organised, extremely sophisticated and, unlike vampires, they are real and not imaginary."

The flames threw flickering shapes across his face as a lone crack from the fire cut through the quiet. I leant in closer and murmured, "You mean... the Illuminati?"

"Yes, lad, the Illuminati." He turned to me with the fire dancing in his eyes and began, "The real vampires are an occult priesthood shrouded in mystery, but thought to originate from the very dawns of time. They claim descendance from the first murderer, Cain, and worship a demonic interpretation of the Ancient Mystery School Religion, Kabbalah. A twisted primordial philosophy which teaches the desire for power.

The desire to become God. Their heretical beliefs and wicked influence have sparked fire in the minds of men for millennia."

"This fire burned brightly in the courts of ancient Babylon, Egypt, Greece, Rome, Khazaria and, more recently, in Jacques de Molay, the Knight Templar, who was put to death by the Pope in 1314 for his veneration of the corrupting faith. The papacy had every reason to be suspicious. This monolithic creed holds that the secret of controlling the world is to set the great civilisations against each other in war. Though it is no secret, but a diabolically effective philosophy. *Ordo ab chao,* or order from chaos. The belief that Adam, God's first man, is merely a microcosm of mankind and that, as Adam was led to dissolution, so can mankind be. For, like Adam, mankind is fundamentally weak and can also be led to self-destruction."

"The Illuminati plan to achieve this by providing society with opposing flawed philosophies, funding them from behind the scenes with their great wealth accrued through centuries of criminal usury. In time, these conflicting ideologies, containing ever larger parts of civilisation, will annihilate each other until, in the end, only their form of corrupted capitalism remains. It will then be offered as the only possible solution to cure man's material and philosophical woes. Wrongly believing this to be his fate, man will accept their cult of false money and, in doing so, forfeit his true destiny. With the Illuminati controlling the world's wealth, they will become masters and mankind will unwittingly become slaves. Man, like Adam, will be led astray and secretly succumb to the doctrine of Lucifer, but, instead of being brought into the light, the world will slide into darkness and oblivion with the Illuminati ruling over all as God."

A timely crack from the fire punctuated his monologue and he stared thoughtfully into the flames. By this point the hairs on the back of my neck were all standing on end, but he wasn't done yet and, after taking another swig of brandy, he continued,

"Now Weishaupt and his disciples fan this fire, helping it to spread throughout Europe and, fuelled by the oxygen of the Enlightenment, it threatens to take hold across the world. Even as I speak, this same sinister force seeks to ferment a series of international revolutions, creating new republics in France and the Americas, to collide them against the old regimes of Europe. After endless wars and suffering, their peoples will be eventually brought to their knees under the yoke of the rancid Order."

I was struggling to take in such monstrous evil but, for some reason, the theological points seemed to sink in first, so I asked, "So, are you saying, sir, that the Illuminati… worship Lucifer?"

He stroked his beard and explained, "It is perhaps not what you might first think. The Illuminati believe that Adonai, or the Biblical God to you and me, is, in fact, the God of darkness and ignorance and that *their* God is the bringer of light and, therefore, wisdom. For it is He who bears the light, that reveals man's purest freedom is to commit sin. In the eyes of the Illuminati, light is dark and dark is light - *Deus est Satan inver sus* - or God is Satan reversed. This is the spirit of their world revolution: Rebellion against God."

Only the sound of the fire stirring in the hearth filled the silence. Though I thought that I had understood what he said, I was sure that he still had not answered my question. So, with a growing feeling of trepidation, I asked once more, "Sir, are you saying that the Illuminati worship Lucifer?"

"Of course they worship Lucifer. For *He* is the ultimate rebel."

"Good Lord."

This was definitely not what a man wishes to hear before finding his bed in an old castle. That the man who was trying to kill him along with his army of thugs, was a disciple of an ancient order of Devil worshippers. Is that what Weishaupt had meant when he had said 'God of Nature'?

Seeing my anxiety, the Professor wagged his finger. "Look, lad, whatever you believe, whether or not there is a God in Heaven and a Devil presiding over Hell, what we are really fighting against here on earth, poses a much greater threat than Lucifer, or even vampires ever could. No. The enemy we face is the most cruel, vicious, resourceful, relentless, vindictive, and determined in the world. For what we are up against is the very weakness of man himself. And remember, Sebastian, that includes me and you."

This final point was lost on me such was my rapidly increasing sense of foreboding. Thunder and lightning! Was it really true? Weishaupt and the Illuminati were Luciferians? I could not help but stare at old Theodor's frightening portrait, the whites of his eyes still terrifying after all these years. And this mass murderer was apparently *nothing* compared to the 'real enemy that we faced.' Feeling decidedly uncomfortable, I listened to the crackling fire and the wind moaning in the chimney for a while longer as the Professor slipped into quiet contemplation. It had been a long day already and, for once, my urge to discover more about my new world seemed to wane as it dawned on me that I had probably heard enough for now. So, I finished my brandy and, with a small bow, wished my host goodnight. Taking a candlestick from the next room, I recalled the directions that I had been given, and found my way to the Günter suite at the top of the remotest tower in the castle.

Upon opening the door, I was startled by the eerie shadow of a grand old four-poster bed cast by my candlelight on the wall. But after undressing, I snuggled between the sheets which, to my happy surprise, had been warmed and were of such fine quality that they caused me great feelings of comfort, especially after the unsettling stories that I had heard. I somehow knew that the incredible building could protect me from all the darkness lurking outside and, though my mind seethed with evil visions, my body yearned for rest.

I yawned deeply and wondered what new revelations were to come the following day. Whatever it was, it meant missing several lectures at university, so at least I could take solace in that. This must have been the last thought that I had before falling into a very deep and, thankfully, dreamless sleep. *8.

---

8. The Origins of The Illuminati. As S. Drechsler states occult Kabballah, the basis of The Ancient Mystery School Religion, has been the faith practiced by many secret societies throughout history including the Bavarian Illuminati. I can find no mention of Ordo ab Chao (order from chaos) earlier than 1395, when it was part of masonic philosophy, though it is claimed to have existed long before then. Coincidentally, '*Fire in the Minds of Men*' (1980) J. H. Billington, traces 'the origins of the revolutionary faith' the dream of a global secular order - The world ruled by Man as God - and explores the anti-Christian character of revolutionary ideology from the French Revolution to the present era. Jacques de Molay, known for his Kabbalist faith, was burned to death in 1314 on an island in the river Seine in Paris, not by the Pope as stated, but by order of King Phillip IV of France, for heresy and devil worship in the form of the Baphomet. His Templar Knights, the original Freemasons, are thought to have established the first international system of credit.

Chapter 10

A Little Education Can Be a Dangerous Thing

I was woken by Bacon opening the curtains and filling the room with bright morning sunshine. I put a hand over my eyes and lifted myself up on my elbow as he facetiously informed me, "Ah, Herr Drechsler. I see you are about to rise. I believe the Professor has something to show you on the main terrace."

I got up, washed and dressed then went to find Van Halestrom. Annoyingly, the butler, as I had been told to refer to him, had neglected to tell me exactly where the main terrace was, no doubt out of sheer bloody mindedness, and, such was the size of the property, that it took me a full ten minutes to find my host. In the end, it was the noise that led me to him and, whilst searching about, I heard a series of shouts wafting down an arched hallway, so I followed them outside onto a large sunlit terrace overlooking the valley.

"Pull!" cried the Professor and a small plate flew into the sky, whereupon I heard a familiar swishing sound from behind and it exploded into a cloud of pieces. I turned to see Van Halestrom armed with an extraordinary crossbow, the type of which I had never seen before. After a quick inspection, I realised that it had four bows and, therefore, I guessed, the ability to fire several bolts without having to be reloaded. 'That looks like a handy bit of kit,' I said to myself as he beckoned me towards him. I strolled over and noticed Klaus, the driver, on the other end of the terrace loading some sort of catapult with a pile of plates.

"Good morning, Herr Drechsler," greeted the Professor. "What a splendid day to begin your first class. I think you'll agree, weather conditions are perfect for the ancient and noble sport of archery."

I inspected the fascinating weapon more closely. It had what I believed must be a sight, fashioned from a telescopic monocular, mounted on the top and I was quite itching to have a go. The Professor recognised this, as would a child, and offered it to me.

"She's all yours, my lad. Remember, squeeze, don't pull. Just like a woman, eh?"

I placed the unwieldy bow under my chin and peered down the monoscope at Klaus's magnified, and very anxious expression.

"Steady, Herr Drechsler," winced Van Halestrom and advised, "Remember, we are *simulating* the hunt."

"Of course, sir, sorry." I pointed the weapon at the blue yonder. "But there is nothing else on which to focus. Not even a cloud."

"Then we shall produce a target. Now, try to follow the plate in the monoscope and shoot a little ahead of it."

"Ready when you are," I said and braced myself.

He called, "Pull!" and, from over my shoulder, I saw the plate flash beyond the lens. I over-compensated, passed back in front of it, pulled instead of squeezing, then shot my bolt too early and the arrow flew harmlessly by.

"Remember, just like a woman," he reminded.

I frowned at the crossbow. "I'm glad to see these arrows are made of wood, Herr Professor. How many shots do I have left?"

"Only two. Try not to waste the next one. Right, here we go." He paused for a second before calling out, "Pull!"

This time, I anticipated the trajectory more acurately, but still fired a touch too early and the arrow clipped the plate, slightly altering its direction before falling away.

"Good shot, lad! You're a natural!" he cheered and noted, "Had a feeling you were." He gestured at the bow which I passed back and he called, "Could we have a double in this time please, Klaus?"

Using the bow's ingenious system of levers and pulleys, he reloaded and placed a couple of arrows on their stays. After composing himself, he shouted, "Pull!" and this time two plates flew in opposite directions. For an older man, his actions were remarkably agile and, in a flurry of movement, he fired twice, successfully destroying both targets. Then, to my astonishment, he spun on his heel and fired again, this time one-handed and from his waist, neatly decapitating a stone statuette standing next to an archway behind us.

"Excellent!" I clamoured, thrilled by such murderous dexterity. Who would have thought that the old scholar would be such a deadly marksman? Armed with this weapon he was certainly a formidable opponent and I had to rethink my opinion of him yet again. As these thoughts coalesced, I noticed Bacon standing in the archway only a handful of paces from the headless statue, with a look of complete contempt on his face. Surprisingly, he did not even flinch, but simply rolled his eyes and sighed with an air of thorough disdain, "Breakfast is served, sir*s*."

The Professor went to appease the rogue, "Sorry, old friend, I didn't see you there. But you never did like that statue. Remember? Only last week you said it was an erotic piece of pot unfit for a vulgarian?"

The impudent butler had rudely turned his back on his master and was already disappearing inside, but replied over his shoulder in his excruciatingly condescending tone, "Yes, of course, *sir*."

Although his master had nearly shot him, it was still a piece of bare-faced impertinence and I could not help but complain, "Can you not condition this man of yours, sir? It seems the fellow has the upper hand in nearly all your relations with him."

Van Halestrom answered firmly, but politely, "Firstly, Herr Drechsler, he is not *mine*. And second, in my affairs, no one is high and no one is low. We are all of us employed here as equals

- If not in wealth then in favour. I believe the working man must have the same rights as all others. Anything else simply breeds discontent and eventually irreconcilable differences. Bacon is the finest of stewards, Sebastian. You will find that out in time. For now, you must get used to him. After all, it is just his way."

It seemed that the servant had enough bad manners to fill both St Mark's Square and the Bascilica, but was beyond reproach. I mulled over this unnatural social order, trying to appreciate what the Professor had said, but I was having difficulty. In his position, I would have simply sacked the insolent old rascal and brought in a more servile replacement. Then I remembered Van Halestrom's words, 'Nothing is *ever* what it seems,' and tried to reserve judgement for another time.

Over a hearty breakfast, the Professor explained to me that his plate-launching catapult was inspired by Archimedes, his favourite of the ancient Greek scholars. He told me of the great battles that the inventor had helped to win, defending his home city of Syracuse from the might of the Roman Empire, before tragically being killed by an invading centurion for refusing to stop his calculations. Also how, before his untimely death, he had produced many incredible leaps in technology and thinking which have greatly furthered the ascent of man; the water pumping screw, the lever, and the mathematical formulae for density and volume, all miraculous achievements in themselves.

Listening to the Professor speak was like being showered by a great fountain of knowledge. A constant flow which never once stopped throughout our long friendship. Even to this day, some sixty years later, I still remember the wisdom he bestowed on me across the table in that sunny room in the Castle Landfried.

After breakfast, he led me through to the adjoining room where a blackboard had been erected. Written upon it was a timetable for my week's indoctrination into his crafts which he took time to explain. I was to spend the rest of the day practicing with the quadre bow, then on Tuesday, I was to be introduced to explosives, poison, and a variety of other dark weaponry. Wednesday would be taken up by a hike through the countryside, culminating in a rock climb where I would familiarise myself with the use of safety ropes and basic mountaineering techniques. On Thursday, Klaus was to teach me 'evasive driving skills' and how to master the reins of the coach, then on Friday, I was to have a five hour fencing, knife and axe lesson. When it came to Saturday, the Professor was vaguer about his plans, suggesting that my activities for that day had not yet been chosen, but that I should expect something 'a little different.' I was to be paid ten thalers a day for my time at the castle, receiving this money at the end of the week and every night, after my lessons, I would be taught more about the secrets of the Illuminati.

I became increasingly excited as the Professor went through the week's activities. It seemed as though fate had placed me in front of a door leading to my new self and all I had to do was go through it. When he had finished, he asked me if I had any questions and I told him, "My only reservation, sir, is that my studies do not suffer as a result of my time in your service, and that my parents do not discover my absence from the university."

"Those matters have been taken care of, my lad," he said with a waggle of his pipe. "I have made the necessary communications with your lecturers, and a plan has already been made to alleviate the need for you to attend your classes this week."

I wondered what he meant by this, but guessed that he had enough influence at the university to make his claims a reality.

"There is one more thing, Professor," I asked rather sheepishly.

"Oh that, of course, I wondered when you were going to ask." He chuckled and gave me a knowing eye. "Yes, yes, Sebastian. Do not fear, you will be seeing her again very soon."

Remarkably, he had done it again. The wily old bird knew exactly what I meant: The-lady-in-black. I nodded that I understood and we made our way back to the main terrace, where a large bucket of wooden arrows lay next to the daunting crossbow. Klaus knelt by the catapult with several stacks of plates piled beside him and, along the balustrade, three straw targets on stands had been placed at differing ranges.

'This is what studying should be like,' I said to myself and walked over to the weapon flexing my fingers.

The next five days were some of the most hardworking, terrifying, and enjoyable times of my young life and, during this time, I formed a deep bond with the amiable Professor. It was hard not to. Although he was my social superior, he actively encouraged my dissension with laughter, unlike my father who was definitely not of the same disposition. Due to the nature of the training, at times, it was impossible not to exchange harsh words, but it was always in a way that left no ill feeling between us. As I came to understand this strange social order, I relaxed and began to learn more quickly. Strangely, the good Professor seemed to actively enjoy my lively backchat, which he regularly induced in me by making one of his over-simplistic remarks in regard to how easy something should be.

For, as he predicted, though I did find a natural empathy with the quadre bow, some of the other skills were a lot harder for me to perfect on such a rapid basis. So his constant over use of the word 'just,' frequently aroused my temper. 'Just' hit the target. 'Just' mix the potion. 'Just' climb the rope, while we swung around four-hundred feet above the village of Bisenhard from an escarpment that he jokingly informed me was known as, "The Fissure of Death, and responsible for the demise of many a poor mountaineer during its gruesome history," - with my fear of heights making me consider suicide a veritable pleasure.

In the evenings in front of the fire, he carried on teaching me about the Illuminati and told me of their strange accordance with occult religious practices, such as the Zoroastrian calendar which I had seen in Weishaupt's chambers. Also, he explained that, to aid the secrecy of the organisation, the leaders had chosen code names for themselves after the greats of antiquity; Philo, Cato, and Ajax, amongst others, with Weishaupt arrogantly titling himself Spartacus. They also had coded words for locations too. Munich was Athens, Ingolstadt was Ephesus, and Bavaria was Achaia.

After a while, I felt that I was beginning to understand the covert workings of the Order, and the Professor explained to me how such knowledge sets one aside from the man in the street, who is typically unaware of the sinister powers manipulating world affairs right under his nose. In turn, this great ignorance in the populous can produce a kind of madness in the recipient of the information. A feeling such as I had experienced in the church. Because so many folk are simply unprepared to believe what you know, by telling them, you run the risk of alienating yourself to those around you, so it was generally best to be clandestine about such conspiratorial theories. It was unnerving at times, but I took to the subject with a keen interest and soon found myself greatly intrigued. Although, one thing that did seem to stay a secret was Van Halestrom's obsessive will for its destruction, which, I felt, always somehow remained unexplained.

On Friday night, it occurred to me how quickly my time had passed and how much I was going to miss the lessons and the other challenges which had been so enjoyable to overcome. Another thing that I was going to miss, were the three large meals a day and a huge four-poster bed, which was inexplicably warmed for me every night and always covered in the finest, fresh-smelling linen.

I sat on the end of the bed in my nightshirt, holding up my candle and taking a look around my room for the last time. After my morning lesson, I was to leave the castle to perform my next errand for the Professor, then return back to my own lodgings and go about my normal business as I had done before. I let out a sigh, contemplating that my temporary life as a gentleman was over and grimaced at the thought of splashing cold water on my face back in my draughty little room at Frauline Warburg's.

Strangely, there was a quiet knock at the door and I made my way over to see who it could be at this late hour. It was well past midnight and the house was usually asleep by this time. On opening it, I was surprised to find Bacon there with his ghostly old face lit by his lantern. He sniffed portentously before offering me a thick folder of manuscripts and saying, in his own indubitable way, "I think you will find these all up to date, sir."

I took the packet off him and inspected it. On the first page was a résumé of my timetable at university, with a list of subjects covered, and I hastily began leafing through the papers. Though the handwriting was that of another, and the language slightly different from my own, they were copies of the essays that I had been set over the last week. When the revelation dawned on me I unthinkingly murmured, "These could be useful."

As soon as I had said this I realised that it was too much of a coincidence but, before I could explain myself, the sardonic butler pointed out, "Forgive me, sir, but that was, rather obviously, the intention." I frowned, somewhat annoyed that I had not understood quicker as he carried on, "I think you'll find these writings sufficiently robust to deceive your tutors, sir. Also, I have taken the liberty of rewriting some of your work, which you left at Frau Hoffmeister's. You were quite wrong, I believe, in your theories concerning the philosopher Aristotle and his opinions on freewill, so I have made the necessary corrections."

I stared at the stack of papers as his words sank in. Could it be true? I counted up the essays and was astonished to find that they were all there, even, as I reached the bottom of the folder, all the remaining work that I had to complete before my upcoming exams. Elation swept through me as I realised the butler's role in it. The Professor had been too busy teaching me to have written them, so he must have authored them himself. While I had been engrossed in the packet, he had quietly crept away and I peered over the balustrade as his lantern descended the spiral stairs and whispered into the dark, "Thank you, Bacon."

The light stopped for a moment and a derisive, "Yes, sir," echoed up the stairs, before it set off once again and gradually faded away. I returned to my room squeezing the bulging folder to my chest and closed the door with my back. Yes! Van Halestrom was right again. Bacon was, indeed, the finest of stewards! *9.

---

9. Adam Weishaupt's Illuminati Codename: 'Spartacus.' S. Drechsler's recollections are accurate here. The Bavarian Illuminati allocated codenames to important members and these were often taken from Greek or Roman antiquity. Adam Weishaupt's was Spartacus, after the revolutionary Thracian gladiator who led the slave uprising against the Roman Empire in 71 B.C. Other leading lights took secret titles including; Baron Von Knigge; Philo, Johann Christophe Bode; Ameilius, etc. Ancient pseudonyms were also used for cities and states. For instance; Munich was known as Athens, Frankfurt as Thebes and, as the author points out, Bavaria was Achaia.

Chapter 11

The Serpent was More Subtle

I could not have been in a better frame of mind when I woke on my last day at the castle. With the year's course work complete, a full month left to prepare for my exams, plenty of money in my purse and a week of healthy exercise and top nosh under my belt to boot, I was as happy as old Ludwig. The dreadful events of the previous week had faded from my mind, and even after my lessons in the Illuminati, their threat seemed somehow distant. I sat up in bed with my hands behind my head and casually greeted Bacon as he opened the curtains. My mood was further buoyed by the fact that I suspected another imminent rendezvous with my lady-in-black. After her pleas of innocence in the confessional at St Bartholomew's, I felt that I could enjoy the promise of her enticing sauciness once again. Yes, it was true, like the sturdy castle around me, I was on top of the world that sunny morning.

The day began well with a hearty breakfast, at which Bacon told me that the Professor would not be joining me as he had some work to complete. So, after eating alone, I made my way to a small balcony which had become a favorite place of mine, as it had a mounted telescope overlooking the winding track leading to the castle. I placed my eye on the lens and was shocked to see a beautiful young woman wearing a powdered wig and a stylish yellow dress standing by the road. I looked again but now frustratingly her face was obscured by a white parasol. Though, in an extraordinarily low cut frock, her sweet and heaving bosom was all but revealed. It seemed that the damsel was in some distress and she anxiously waved a gloved hand in my direction.

'Good gracious,' I thought, 'a beautiful woman in trouble? All the way out here, with no one around to help but me?'

This was true. I had no idea where the Professor or Bacon was. I swung the telescope to see the lady was standing a stone's throw from a driverless carriage which looked as though it had been ransacked. I rose and waved back in her direction, but as I squinted into the distance, I realised that she was too far away to see without the benefit of the lens. After taking another quick peak down the telescope at her heaving cleavage, I decided that it was time for action and ran down to the stables.

Within two taps of a tinker's hammer, I was trotting under the castle's portcullis on a fresh young filly with a flintlock stuffed in my belt, determined to rescue the woman from her dilemma. After which, I was sure that she would be inclined to let me charm her with my new sense of confidence and apparent wealth. Maybe even give me a little reward as well. After making sure that I had the key to the gate in my back pocket, having found out that only the Professor's coach automatically opened it, I rode down the path over the bridge and pushed the horse to a gallop, as the enticing possibilities revealed themselves to me.

I soon found the abandoned coach by the side of the road but, disappointingly, no grateful maiden to thank me for my trouble. I dismounted and, seeing several garments scattered on the ground, poked a black corset with the barrel of my pistol. Keeping my eyes open for the lady, I led the filly down the path with my gun at the ready in case there were bandits skulking round the next bend, and that's when I saw her. Somehow she was now standing on a huge boulder on the far side of the road, which meant there was a mountain stream running between us. I clearly remember thinking, 'How did she get there?' But there was no time to ask.

"Thank heavens above!" she squealed with excitement, obviously overjoyed to see her saviour. "A strong decent man who can come to a woman's aid. Oh, I'm so lucky you're here!"

She blew me a kiss from under her parasol, and from this close range I could see perfectly well how her young bosom heaved. Her accent was Spanish, but she had quite good command of our language and chatted away breathlessly, "I waved at the castle because it was the only place I could imagine someone would be. As you can see, I've been robbed. There were two beastly villains with guns who took everything I had, then chased my pathetic driver away. Now the coward has not returned and I am stranded here helpless."

Time to play the hero I reckoned. I lowered my voice a little to further impress the woman. "Fear not, my good lady. We shall soon make everything better. Now, the first thing we must do is remove you from that rock."

"I cannot get down. I have already tried." She fretted, "I think I will need to be carried."

There was a pause, while I looked at the stream then back at her. She seemed to share my concern and asked, "You do think you can do it don't you?"

"Of course I can," I declared, speaking proudly from my chest. I stuck the gun in my belt and, figuring that I could jump the stream to the delectable woman then sort the rest out when I got there, I took a few steps back, made a run for it and leapt onto the boulder. I landed at the woman's feet with an undignified slap, but unfortunately could not grip the rock's smooth face and slowly descended into the stream.

The temptress looked down at me with her finger on her lip and sighed, "Ooh," as the cold water chilled through my lower half. Once at the bottom, I frowned at her and, with great effort, managed to inch my way out before eventually pulling myself back to her feet. When I raised myself onto my haunches, she leant down to help me up, gasping, "Oh, thank you, thank you, kind sir," and fully enveloped my face in her cleavage.

She flustered, "Oh but, sir, when the robbers came they threw my vanity case over this rock behind me and it has my jewellery inside. Will you find it for me? *Please*?"

She was already helping me up the boulder with her hand on my waist and I tried to glimpse her pretty face under the parasol, but could only see her coquettish lips pouting, "Oh thank you, kind sir. You will be my *special* one for this wonderful favour."

Motivated once more by this encouragement, and another firm push on my backside, I carried on up the boulder and reached the top, where I quickly saw a small wooden chest banded with iron. 'That was easy,' I chuckled to myself and knelt down beside the box to give it a shake. There was certainly something inside, so I undid the clasp and lifted the lid.

'Boom!' There was an enormous explosion, or so it seemed, in reality, it was probably tiny. For had it been of any sizeable proportions, I would probably not be here today.

However, the blast was sufficient to throw me backwards and I repeated my ungraceful slide down the boulder and splashed back into the stream but thoroughly submerged this time. When I resurfaced, coughing and gasping for air and nursing my wounds, the blasted lady, if indeed she ever was one, was now somehow sitting side-saddle on my horse, twirling her parasol on her shoulder and roaring with laughter. I pulled my gun from my belt, but glared at the dripping weapon and threw it in the stream. She howled uproariously at this and I pulled myself onto the riverbank cursing under my breath.

"You've obviously still got a long way to go, Herr *Wunderkind*. It seems you have a simple face and a simple mind to match it."

Good God! My-lady-in-black was the-seductress-in-yellow. I had to look again as she blew me another kiss and held out her beautiful face, now for the first time fully apparent to me.

She put a finger to her lip and sighed, "Ooh," *again,* in a thoroughly facetious manner. This was extremely galling. She knew that she had tricked me with her womanly ways and that I had been her chump. I had even lowered my blasted voice to impress her. How ridiculous? Compounding my humiliation, the crafty wench slowly pulled the castle key from the depths of her cleavage and winked at me. Confound it! She had managed to pickpocket the damn thing off me when I thought that she was sizing up my athletic frame.

"Let's go back and see the Professor shall we? I'm sure he'll be interested to hear about this." She dismounted the horse in one graceful slide and marched off to her carriage, addressing me over her shoulder as though I were a child, "You can take me there, if you like? That is, *if* you can drive?"

And so, I had to suffer the ignominy of driving her back to the castle in her carriage then having to ask for the key to re-enter the gate. The Professor had told me that I would be seeing her again, 'very soon,' but I had not expected this. Over the past week, he had explained that the cocky woman was a most trusted member of his organisation and that they had worked together many times before. This only intensified my embarrassment, especially after the way she had duped me, and I was mortified by the willing part that I had played in my own downfall. Still hanging my head in shame, we met with the Professor in the library some twenty minutes later.

"He's not good enough and you know it," griped the lady.

"He'll be fine on the night, trust me. He always does the right thing in the end. Don't you, Herr Drechsler?"

I neither appreciated Van Halestrom patronising me, or the lady's doubt in my ability. I did not want to lose the Professor's faith in me or the job which had been so profitable.

"If you just need a messenger then I'm sure he's fit for purpose.

But c'mon, he didn't even think it was odd that the telescope was pointing right at me, yet he couldn't see me without it. And once he was down there, I could have tried a lot harder to get him to open the box. Mon Dieu! He didn't even know that I'd stolen the key. It was too easy. I don't want him around if he's going to be a liability."

I hadn't been appreciating the way that they had been talking about me since we had got to the library, and finally showed it by petulantly crossing my arms. There was a lingering pause as we all considered our positions and I could not help but watch our gorgeous ally. She had changed into a bright white shirt, riding breeches and knee-high leather boots and was indeed a beauty beyond compare. Tall, about five foot nine inches, with flowing chestnut hair and a full but athletic figure, she was as attractive a woman as I had ever seen. But there was also something else about this girl. A true grit and sheer damn-it-all attitude that I had rarely seen in any man, let alone a woman. Her soulful eyes pierced through everything they beheld and she spoke passionately through a pair of cherry-red lips that only a dead man would not desire.

She broke the silence, "So what are we going to do?"

"We carry on as planned. Sebastian will complete the task and we shall say no more about it. I need to be elsewhere and there is no one else we can trust."

Fed up with my lowly position in the proceedings, I finally snapped, "Is it fair that this person knows my name and that I do not know theirs?"

"It's Francesca and I do not care who knows it," she snorted, rearing up like a spirited filly.

"Alright you two," arbitrated the Professor and, after taking a deep breath, he began, "Tonight, Sebastian, as you may have guessed, your task will be a little different from the one I usually ask you to perform. I wish you to go to Weishaupt's secret lodge, known as The Golden Dawn, situated twenty miles west of Regensburg and, once there, steal a manuscript. This document is known as 'The Thirteen Protocols' and is of great importance to us. I haven't asked you to do anything like this before, but it is my belief that you are ready to go to the next level. As an indication of my faith in you, I will also double your wages to complete this job. We already have other agents there to aid you in your mission. They have been instructed to leave a window open for you, and we believe there will be no one else there to hinder your progress, so your safety will be assured. You will gain entry into the lodge after the papers are stored and Weishaupt and his cronies have adjourned to a meeting elsewhere in the building. When you have secured the manuscript you will take it to Frau Hoffmeister's safe house whereupon you will be instructed what to do next."

'Sounds easy enough,' I thought and wondered what all the fuss was about.'

He leant closer, his eyes filling with grim determination. "Remember, Sebastian, we cannot afford any mistakes tonight. This manuscript is of the utmost importance. For, within its pages, are contained the devilish scheme to divide and conquer the great tribes of the earth and lead them into eternal slavery."

"Right then," I said, looking between their serious faces. Maybe that *was* a bit different after all. [10.]

---

10. Weishaupt & The Lodge of The Golden Dawn. It is amazing that S. Drechsler recalls these details as mainstream historians have always argued that this sect was started by William Wyan Wescott in England circa 1887, but speculation has always existed that Weishaupt was at least partly responsible for its establishment in the 1700's, and even that the order was an ancient satanic cult which provided a meeting place for those with designs of spreading the Luciferian doctrine throughout the world.

Chapter 12

The Spear the Axe and the Arrow

The weather had turned as bad as the atmosphere between me and Francesca as we rode back to Ingolstadt on that stormy Saturday evening. The rain beat down harder with every stride of our horses and we had not exchanged a single word since leaving the castle. When we at last reached the city's northern gates, she pulled up her mount and said coldly, "This is where I leave you, Herr Blunderkind, but I'm sure I'll have the misfortune of seeing you again somewhere soon."

She cantered away and I watched her go with an unhappy sigh. Absolutely beautiful but, like most women I had met, totally impossible to understand. Though there was never another who had quite the same effect on me as Francesca Nicola Kropotkin. I trotted into the city and went to the stables to exchange the horse that I had borrowed from the castle for my own Petrova. Next, I visited my rooms around the corner as I wanted to get my satchel, my lucky hat and, most important of all, the pistol the Professor had given me. I tied Petrova outside and dashed up the stairs into my room. After picking up my hat and satchel from the dresser, I noticed a piece of paper wedged in the mirror. I stared at it for a moment before grabbing it and opening it out and my heart filled with dread, for drawn upon it was the spear the axe and the arrow.

How was this here? Who had done this? I turned round half expecting to see Adam Weishaupt standing in the shadows. I screwed up the paper and threw it away before flying down the stairs, bursting out of the front door, jumping on Petrova and galloping off. This frightening invasion of privacy had introduced a new level of threat to my life and unsettled me to the core. Things were getting personal. Now they were not only trying to kill me in the street, they were coming to my house -

maybe to do it there. This fright also caused me to make my first mistake working for the Professor. In my haste to leave, I forgot the gun. It may seem stupid now, but I was so rattled by the note, that I neglected to find the pistol in my drawer. What a fateful error that was to prove. All I could think about at that moment were the atrocities at the chapel and everything the Professor had told me took on a sharper focus, but unaware of my foolish mistake, I went on my mission without a weapon. I leaned over Petrova's mane and squeezed my heels into her flanks, urging her on, on to Weishaupt's Lodge of the Golden Dawn.

I arrived at the rendezvous a little early, as was my habit, to check the lay of the land. At least, I believed it to be early. I had not bothered to bring the star clock as the weather was so abysmal. Looking up into the driving rain, I could hardly make out the procession of black clouds filling the sky, never mind the stars. Not only was it pouring down, but a tumultuous wind had risen and it howled through the trees under which I sheltered so fiercely that I had to hold onto my hat. I peered into the darkness, trying to make out the two flags marking the lodge's location behind a thicket up ahead. My instructions were to wait there until seeing a lantern flash, whereupon I was to move in and find the window that had been left open for me. At this point, I would enter the building, grab the manuscript and make my getaway.

Van Halestrom had assured me that, while at no time would I see my accomplices, so as not to compromise their identities, they could all be relied upon to complete their tasks. This was comforting, but I was certain that my lady Francesca would also be there in some guise or another, no doubt, wearing lewd attire and draped over some poor unsuspecting fool to trick, deceive or simply insult them as part of the plan. Though I was glad that she was on our side, I hated the thought of her licentiousness, however feigned it was.

I stared towards the lodge and wondered exactly what *was* going on in there? The Professor had been unspecific about the details of the meeting, mentioning only that the manuscript was to be discussed by the assembly at the beginning of the evening before the party moved to another part of the building and this was to be the moment of my action. I waited nervously for the signal and huddled from the rain under the row of trees.

After what seemed like an age, I saw the lantern flash up ahead. It was time to move. I led Petrova through the short meadow leading up to the thicket, keeping my eye on the flags thrashing about in the gale. As I got closer, an icy shiver ran up my spine when I saw emblazoned upon them the same emblem, which I had seen most notably two hours ago on the note stuck to my blasted mirror, of the spear the axe and the arrow.

For the first time, I was scared. What was I doing here? Was I really sneaking through a field in a storm in the middle of the night to steal something off my own lecturer, a man of great importance, who could not only ruin me academically but, on good authority, had also tried to kill me, and especially after I had received a mysterious warning note?

I squatted down, the seriousness of the situation seemingly forcing me to the ground. I took a swift breath of damp night air and tried to bolster myself. 'C'mon Sebastian, the bastard did try and kill you. You at least owe it to him to ruin his party.' Also, if I was successful, it might shut up the high-and-mighty, two-faced *Princess* Francesca, whilst proving my real worth to the Professor. Then, who knows what I might achieve within his organisation? Though the bigger conspiracy was on my mind, at that moment, I was more motivated by the respect that my heroism would engender in my colleagues, particularly Francesca. Also, the small matter of the money had to be considered. I bounced on my haunches as my thoughts coalesced into those of action.

I had come this far, all I had to do was walk into a room, pick up a piece of paper and leave fast. I could definitely do the last part. I pictured myself nonchalantly leaning against the fireside in the Castle Landfried reading the document to a fawning Francesca, who I imagined in a ridiculously alluring frock to give me extra impetus.

That did the trick, and I rose with fresh determination. I led Petrova to the edge of the thicket where I tied her to a tree, before making the rest of my way through the soaking undergrowth. The Professor had been right, as usual, and sent me on the correct course. For, although the foliage was so thick that I momentarily lost sight of the flagpoles, when I appeared on the other side, I was directly facing the lodge.

The storm had been worsening by the second but, as I gazed at the dark silhouetted building, a huge flash of lightning lit up the scene as clear as a summer's day. I shuddered upon seeing a dozen ghoulish figures in strange hooded robes in the driveway attending to a queue of coaches. I gawped at the unearthly vision for a moment before instinctively ducking down as the proceeding thunderclap roared overhead. As far as I could tell, there was no one else around the rest of the place and I strained to see the window where I was to make my entry. Sure enough, through the driving rain and tangled black branches, I spied a dim light shining between a pair of open shutters near the rear of the house.

To my dismay, the window was on the first floor, which seemed a disastrous oversight. But after closer inspection, I saw that, because the lodge was built into the side of a hill, the thicket around the back was the same height. I pushed my way through the bushes and came up to the building. As I had thought, the bank was level with the window, but the wall was at least six feet away, leaving an alarming gap in between, maybe twelve foot deep.

After inspecting the various dimensions, I realised that I was going to have to jump for it. The leap would be difficult, but not impossible, as the window had a broad ledge on which I could land. I shuffled round trying to make enough room for a run up, but it was very difficult because the plants were in all the wrong places. I checked to see if there was another option. There wasn't, and I crouched down to peer through the opened shutters. Inside the room lay a long polished table surrounded by a dozen or so chairs, and, as I looked to the far end, I spotted a parchment resting on a scroll box. It had to be the manuscript. I pulled myself up. This was it. All I had to do was complete this jump. The rest was simple. If I got this bit right, I would be riding away from here in ten minutes another hundred thalers richer into the bargain and no one would be any the wiser - except me.

I took a deep breath and flexed my knees, whispering, "You can do it Seb," and clapped my hands to gee myself up. I steadied myself, leaned back into the bushes as far as I could, put my head down and went to make my leap. *[11.]

---

11. The Spear The Axe & The Arrow. While I can find no record of this particular combination of symbols being used by the Illuminati, the seperate insignias go back to antiquity. The spear mounted with the Phrygian cap has held revolutionary symbolism for centuries. Since ancient Roman times the cap has represented those who seek liberty as it was worn by slaves who had won their freedom and made infamous during the French Revolution of 1789, with the red of the cap also being linked to Bolshevik and other communist emblems. The axe surrounded with the bundle of birch rods, or fasces, also has its roots in ancient Rome and was the symbol for strength and authority, the birch to whip and the axe to wield the ultimate capital punishment. In the context of the story, it is interesting as these insignias were to be used by opposing political ideologies; Communism; the red cap. Fascism; the fasces and the root of the word 'Fascist.'

Chapter 13

The Lodge of the Golden Dawn

I landed on the window ledge with a grunt. Pleased by my athleticism, I decided to congratulate myself. After all, it *was* an impressive jump. "Well done Seb," I whispered and, of course, that's when I lost my balance. So confident had I been that I was safe, I had not thought to hold on to anything and, to my horror, I started to fall backwards desperately flailing my arms around but, at the last moment, threw out my hands and grabbed the edges of the shutters.

"Concentrate Seb!" I gasped and awkwardly pulled myself inside, a feat in itself for the shutters swung about on their hinges as I went in through the window. I landed as softly as I could then took a few tentative steps into the room, but saw that I was leaving a trail of muddy footprints across a beautiful Persian rug similar to that in Weishaupt's office. I tiptoed round the chairs doing my best not to foul the carpet and approached the head of the table where the rolled parchment lay on the scroll box tied with a red ribbon decorated with arcane hieroglyphs.

"Here we go Seb," I said to myself, but as I leaned over to pick it up, a blast of wind slapped the shutters against their stays with an almighty crash. I snapped my head round and suddenly heard voices, lots of them, approaching fast. I hesitated and glanced at the manuscript then back at the window. Could I make it? I scowled at my filthy footprints as the handle of the door at the side of the room started to twist. "Not now! Not now!" I fretted and, turning around to find a pair of cupboard doors set in the wooden panelling behind me, flung them open and leapt inside as the voices entered the room.

My heart was banging like a skeleton pleasuring itself in a biscuit tin - *'Dang! Dang! Dang! Dang!'* I made sure that the doors were safely closed in front of me and tried to control my panting. It was pitch-black inside the cupboard and I stood frozen like a statue listening to the men muttering and milling around before they gradually took their places. After a while, a silence fell over them and I squatted down to find a keyhole and, putting my eye to it, this was the amazing sight that I saw.

Around the table sat thirteen mysterious figures wearing black robes with pointed hoods and slits for eyes. I thought that this was convenient as it might prevent them from seeing my filthy footprints covering the floor. To my dismay, I heard someone complaining about the draft and the sound of the shutters at the far end of the room being closed. Then, with a sinking heart, I heard a bolt being brought down to lock them in place.

"Capital!" I whispered and let out a silent groan. Everyone settled in their places, leaving a few red robed sentinels standing round the edge of the room, whom I guessed were of a lower rank as they did not sit. Now there was only one empty place left, the chair directly in front of me at the head of the table with the document beyond it on the scroll box. I heard the door from the hallway open as the last of the mysterious bunch arrived and, when this particular individual entered, even from inside the cupboard, I felt that a presence had come amongst them.

He sat down barely six feet away with his golden robe almost blocking my view and, after a short pause, addressed the meeting, "Good evening my Brothers." It was Weishaupt. The blood chilled in my veins as he carried on, "This is a great night for this esteemed lodge, and for the whole of our glorious organisation. Since the modern inception of our order in 1776, we have directed our labours towards this moment which we will look back upon in centuries to come as a pivotal point in the quest to reach our goals. Seven years ago, you tasked me to revise the document here in front of us: The Thirteen Protocols.

The sacred text handed down through the ages by our sect's holy bloodlines, citing the methods by which we will rule over 'die hörig.' Tonight we shall accept these new directives as law into our mighty fraternity and we will do this in the usual way."

'Who's *die hörig*?' I wondered and, convinced that I was about to hear the secrets in the document, shifted about to get a better view. However, much to my frustration, it soon dawned on me that Weishaupt was reading it to himself. "[12.]

My suspicions were confirmed when, after a couple of minutes, he passed it to the man next to him who began to clumsily read it through his slits. Thunder and lightning! I grimaced in the darkness realising that there must be some solemn vow of silence. I calculated; two minutes each, thirteen of them in all. Damn it! This is going to take an age. Trust my blasted luck.

And so it was. I watched and waited as the parchment was slowly passed around the table in virtual silence as the men coughed, belched, farted, and scratched themselves, until eventually the protracted ceremony was over and Weishaupt broke the silence, "Brothers, now that we have familiarised ourselves with the sacred text, we shall move downstairs to the altar to sanctify the rite.

Finally, the 'brothers' got up and filed out behind Weishaupt, followed by the red sentinels with the last of these closing the door behind him. "Thank God for that," I gasped and let out an extensive sigh of relief.

---

12. The Illuminati & Die Hörig (The Subservient or 'The Slaves'). It is unsurprising that S. Drechsler did not recognise this word as it would have been antiquated, even when he heard it two-hundred-and-fifty-years ago, and originates from Middle High German (1050-1350) which explains why it was not familiar to his ear. *Hörig* translates as 'in serfdom' (of a peasant: bound to his lord's land and required to work for him) and as 'unfree' or subject to any form of 'bondage.' Within the context of this story, it would seem quite obvious that what is meant here is 'slave.'

I waited for a moment before slipping out of the cupboard, grabbing the document and, at last, throwing it in my satchel. Now I was more than ready to leave and dashed over to the shutters only to find, to my nightmarish terror, a huge padlock now holding them in place. I shook them to make sure, but it was useless. They were locked tight.

No! Surely I was done for. Curse the stupid Professor. Curse this bit of paper. What difference could it make anyway, apart from removing me from the rest of a life that I had planned so hard to enjoy? I desperately tried the shutters again, but it was no good. They were immovable. I would have needed an axe to break out. What was I to do? I prowled round the table like a rat caught in a trap. How had I let this happen to me? I was about to drown myself in self-pity, when I spotted some black robes hanging in the cupboard in which I had been hiding. My heart leapt as I realised the chance that they might give me. I pulled open the doors revealing three robes in all and I took the first. After checking that I had no other option, which was obviously the case, I pulled the strange garment over my head.

A minute later, I peeped from behind the door and checked up and down the hallway. By the looks of it, there was no one around, so I sneaked along the corridor to the top of the stairs. Hastily descending towards the front door, I asked myself 'Where is everyone?' when, to my eternal displeasure, one of them came out and told me. As I reached the bottom of the stairway, a hooded brother appeared from the shadows and grunted, "Hey. Where have you been? They're all waiting for you in the cellar."

I stood fixed to the spot, not knowing what to do.

"Well, what are you waiting for?" he demanded.

I shrugged inside my robes, which I was starting to realise were perhaps a size too big. He thrust a tiny purple cushion at me, which I involuntarily took from him. He waited for a second before impatiently gesturing at a doorway behind me and, without thinking, I ran over to it stupidly calling out, "Thanks."

I went through the door and down a flight of candlelit stairs, holding out the cushion like an idiot. Upon reaching a pair of curtains at the bottom, I sensed that this might be a good opportunity to turn back but, when I heard footsteps coming down from above, I cursed my luck, took a deep breath, held out the cushion and went through the curtains.

Seeing a room full of grown men in hooded robes with slits for eyes all turn to face you when you have broken into their secret underground ritual, is a sight that never leaves you. It is the sort of scene that has the potency to still be burnt onto your mind's eye long after other memories have faded. Believe me.

Although utterly terrified at that moment, somehow I did not pass out or go down on my knees, begging them, "Make it end! Make it end!" The robed men formed two lines before me as another came over and placed a horrible curved knife on the cushion. Remembering not to say 'Thanks' this time, I slowly made my way between the rows of men. Out of the shadows ahead, Adam Weishaupt appeared in his golden costume and went to stand behind an altar.

He bade me to approach and, with my heart pounding like a cannon at Waterloo, I wondered in what possible way this abhorrent set of circumstances could be any worse? I immediately found out when two red sentinels emerged next to him dragging a beautiful naked woman along with a black bag pulled over her head.

And me carrying a sacrificial knife! I nearly screamed inside my hood and barely managed to control myself. When I reached the altar, the woman was put down on her knees and I prayed 'Sweet Jesus save me from this horror,' as it suddenly dawned on me that this poor girl might well be Francesca.

Maybe she had been caught and was now to be slain for her deception. I simply did not know. Weishaupt took the knife and uttered some rot about divine spirits, but I could not concentrate on his words as the girl's head was tipped back by one of the hooded devils.

I could not bear to watch anymore and shut my eyes. God forgive me for not stopping that evil ritual, but if I had reacted then both the girl and myself would have been lost. What could I have done? By thunder! I was so scared that I nearly wet myself.

Perhaps I could have knocked Weishaupt over, even got the knife off him, but there were thirty others who would have rendered any lone struggler useless. Anyway, it was already too late. There was a gruesome slitting noise, a subdued gasp, the sound of ruffling robes, and the soft thud of a slumping body. Then the vilest detail of all. Even with my eyes closed, I could feel the gawping, perverted pleasure of those who had witnessed this disgusting act.

I felt the weight of the knife return to the pillow and squinted out of my slits to see Weishaupt washing his hands in a golden bowl on the altar. There was a group sigh and the sound of footsteps, followed by the voices of a small choir reciting a medieval chant. I turned back the way that I had come and walked towards the door holding out the blood-stained knife on the pillow. By the grace of God, no one tried to stop me. Lord knows what I would have done if someone had? I went straight between the curtains, up the stairs, through the door at the top, placed the cushion on a chair by the front door and stepped outside into the storm which was raging so hard that it almost blew me off my feet.

I glanced uneasily at the sentinels loitering round the driveway and my heart sprang into my mouth when I spotted one of them who had removed his hood and was vainly stroking back his bright orange hair in the gale. Holy Christ! It was Jan Kohler or I was the Mayor of Ingolstadt! What in God's name was my best friend doing at this depraved ritual? Something told me that this was not a good time to ask. So I ducked my head, wrapped my hands in my sleeves like a monk and darted round the side of the building.

I quickly found a convenient tree root under the window where I had broken in and frantically hoisted myself up the bank. Finally free from the dreadful lodge, I tore through the undergrowth ripping off my robes and throwing them away. I floundered on at full pelt, not caring about the branches slapping me in my face, or the sting of a thorny vine in my hand. The pain did not matter. The only thing that mattered was getting away from that evil place and those murdering Satanic fiends as quickly as possible.

Moments later, I was galloping Petrova through the black Bavarian countryside and the driving wind and rain as if all Hell itself was coming up behind me and licking so close that my heels were starting to smoulder, all the time encouraging her with my calls, "C'mon, girl! Let's fly tonight!" while the lightning flashed and the thunder roared around us.

It was all true. Everything the Professor had said. I was living in a tragic play of terror. A fantasy world, more nightmare than reality, in which even my friends were characters in the horrendous plot. I prayed that God would let me be the hero of the piece and that I might live happily ever after. Now that I had the documents, I figured I must be halfway to understanding my new crazed reality. Had I known how far I had left to go, I might have given up right there and then.

Only one thing was certain, and I shouted out to confirm it, "I take it all back Van Halestrom!" Because it appeared that the one consistent thing in my new life, was that he was right again.

Chapter 14

The Four Horsemen of the Apocalypse

I had already suffered enough horrors on that perilous night to last me until the grave. To say nothing of horrid cupboards, terrifying rituals, traitorous friends, and evil sacrifices. So, as I fled the lodge begging God to help me amidst the raging storm, I considered that He must be busy elsewhere when my nightmare intensified still further. For, as I picked up the road back to Ingolstadt and pushed Petrova to breakneck speed, we came across four of the devilish red sentinels on horseback travelling the other way.

What they were doing riding four abreast down a narrow country road at night in a storm I will never know? What did they expect? They were lucky that I did not run them down. It was only my riding skill and Petrova's instinct which prevented a major collision and we barged into the line of horsemen knocking them asunder. Perhaps it was this that made them suspicious, or the fact that I gave them the finger when one of them called out, "I hope you can ride your mother better!"

If there's one thing that I cannot abide, it's someone insulting my mother. Not that I was about to return and demand satisfaction by slapping the biggest one of them round the face and insisting that he get down from his horse so I could thrash some respect into him. Anyway, that was unimportant now because, to my utter dismay, they were going to give me a chance to have a fight with them whether I liked it or not and came chasing after me.

"No! No! No!" I cried. What could I do? Of course! I had the pistol. It was then that I realised, as I felt for the gun in my bag, that it was back in the drawer, in my dresser, in my blasted room. All I had to protect me was my stupid *lucky* hat, my riding crop, and a bag full of this murderous gang's stolen documents. Shit!

This was turning into another seriously bad night and I tried to think of what I, Sebastian Drechsler, humble, foolish student would normally be doing on a Saturday evening. It certainly wasn't this and I banged my heels into Petrova's flanks once more, urging her away from the wall of red robes and snorting black stallions coming up behind us.

For, though we were hurtling along, somehow my pursuers had managed to catch us up. Sweet Mother of God - they were quick. I could not help but glance behind as a flash of lightning illuminated the terrible vision further and the bridles of the four horses glinted in the unearthly light. Even with their hooded robes masking their faces, I could see their determination to catch me. It was the four horsemen of the apocalypse incarnate, three lengths behind and closing in fast. But damn it! The cocky swine still rode four abreast as they tore down the lane with the black mud splashing up from their pounding hooves.

This was my advantage and I knew how best to take it. When another burst of lightning lit the road ahead, I swerved Petrova towards a narrow dip in the hedge and, knowing that they could not all follow at once, asked her to jump for me. As I had hoped, they faltered at the hedgerow while we landed with a solid thump in the field and sped off.

I glanced behind to see that I was now being pursued by only one red-robed horseman. The others were nowhere to be seen and I thanked God that the odds had been made a little better in my favour. But after tearing on for another mile, and through a little hamlet, I considered screaming for help at the shadowy buildings because the red demon was gaining on me with every stride of his powerful black stallion. I glanced over my shoulder once more, to see the human phantom barely a length behind and, even in the darkness, I was certain that I could see his eyes glaring through his hooded slits.

Petrova was tiring fast and, as the hooded sentinel inexorably closed in, I finally realised that I would have to fight him. It was the only way. The moment that he caught up, I would try and strike him down with my riding crop. I desperately geed Petrova on and raised my arm, hoping beyond hope that something would save me when, to my complete and utter astonishment, amongst the furious wind and rain, something did. For incredibly, at that very moment, an almighty bolt of lightning shot down from the heavens and struck my pursuer squarely in his chest then lifted him from his horse and propelled him backwards in a screaming fireball of cinders and death. I rode on for a full furlong staring back in pure disbelief at his galloping rider-less horse as the rumbling thunderclap subsided around us. Up to then, God had never needed to intervene in my life in such a momentous way, but despite his obvious protection of me, I suddenly flung my satchel into the road.

Why I did it, I will never know. Surely, if I was being looked after, I could have made good my escape along with the papers. But, that very second, I saw a cluster of glowing lanterns amongst the approaching shadows and, certain that the other cultists had circled me and were coming back to avenge their fallen comrade, I turned Petrova into a small copse by the side of the road. Shaking, soaked and panic-stricken I dismounted and, trying to keep us both as still as possible, heard a shout as the pack of riders pulled up where I could see them. Despite the atrocious weather, they had spotted the bag and one of them lifted it up then inspected its contents. I was relieved when I realised that it was not the three surviving red devils, but another group of men. Although they too looked tough and purposeful so I squatted down further, not knowing what to think.

After a short discussion, the horsemen rode off towards the immoliated cultist and I stayed there quivering in the darkness for a moment longer before pulling myself together and setting Petrova in the opposite direction. Now I wasted not one minute getting away. I have honestly never ridden faster in my life, but if sheer terror could have propelled me along that road then I would have reached Frau Hoffmeister's safe house even quicker. I flew up the driveway where I was spotted by the stable lad sheltering from the rain under the branches of a tree. He whistled up ahead and, when I reached the farmhouse, the kind old lady was waiting outside with a glowing lantern.

She busied the stable lad to attend to Petrova and I entered into the warmth of the house. I gasped with relief as I came in through the door, only to be thrown back onto my heels by a familiar voice asking me, "What took you so long, my lad?"

Sitting by the table in the dappling firelight, I was amazed to see Professor Van Halestrom and the shock fully stunted my reply, "How... on... earth?"

Without taking his eyes off me, he lit his pipe and continued, "I see that you don't have your satchel. So I presume the papers are lost too. But, judging by the look on your face, our enemies are not in possession of them. Am I right?" He was always blasted right. I didn't know why he bothered asking. "Am I right, Sebastian?" he repeated.

I hung my head in shame, furious with myself for discarding the documnets and muttered, "I threw the bag and the papers in the road, sir. Some riders came and picked them up."

He shot forward in his chair, demanding, "How many riders? Were they serious looking men?"

Surprised by his intensity, I held up the fingers of my gloves to show him, mumbling, "Five... maybe six."

He thumped his fist on the table, scaring me out of any remaining wits and cried, "By Jupiter! Then we may be the luckiest men in Bavaria."

"But surely, sir, I have failed you. Tonight is a total disaster."

He sprung from his chair and grabbed my shoulders, assuring, "On the contrary, Sebastian. By the grace of good fortune, I think we still have the advantage."

"But how can this be, sir?"

"Tonight, Sebastian, I believe that we have been party to a remarkable turn of fate. You see, I think it was the sheriff's men that you saw find the satchel. They had been out patrolling after receiving reports from a concerned privy councillor of sinister *ghouls on the prowl*." He gave me a knowing wink to indicate his part in this deception, before carrying on, "If so, then the authorities have the protocols which, after all, was our main objective. It would seem serendipity, in this case, is the mother of good fortune. Well done, Sebastian. Well done."

My bewildered spirits soared as the news sank in. If he was right, as usual, then somehow my honour had been saved by this extraordinary coincidence. Good grace indeed. It was a blasted miracle. But suddenly recalling Francesca's possible plight, I could not help but gasp, "But maybe, sir, everything is still lost."

"Relax, lad," he replied, obviously misunderstanding me and tapping his forehead, "I managed to memorize the papers before you stole them. See, I have made a copy."

I followed his eyes to some parchments lying next to an ink pot and quill on the table. My scrambled thoughts raged for a moment until I asked, "Please, sir, tell me how is it possible that you managed to *memorize* them?" I looked about the room reconsidering his presence at the farmhouse, before eyeing him with some suspicion. "And how are you here at all? Explain this to me. Are you somehow... omnipresent?"

"No, my lad, I was there."

This was impossible! What was he talking about? I confronted him, "Where? Where were you? Inside my blasted hat?"

"No. I was in the room, in a robe at the table, disguised as an elder. I saw your footprints on the rug. I guessed you were hiding in the cupboard behind Weishaupt." He slapped me on the back and chortled, "I must say, I felt for you when they bolted the windows, but I knew you would get out of there and, in the end, get out of there you did."

It was as though he had been watching me wherever I went. "But... how? How were you there in a robe at the table? How is it possible?"

He raised a finger, insisting, "Everything is possible, Sebastian. Even to attend the evil ritual of the Golden Dawn as we both did tonight and get away undetected."

"You mean you saw me! You were at the ritual too?"

"Yes, Sebastian, I was at the ritual too. After reading the protocols I was trapped in the procession with the others and forced to adjourn downstairs, where I was also waiting for the moment to escape."

"But... but..." I stammered, my thoughts roiling like the contents of a butter churn worked by a hysterical dairymaid.

He stroked his beard and went on, "Now I can explain. You have just taken part in a vital mission planned ever since we discovered that Weishaupt's revised version of the protocols was to be revealed at the Lodge of the Golden Dawn. This document is incontrovertible proof of the Illuminati's diabolical plans for world revolution. Therefore, it was imperative that we got the original to show to the highest authority. It had initially been our plan to intercept one of the elders, as I did tonight, and for me to use his personal effects to gain access to the protocols then, hopefully, steal them. But this was a risky strategy at best, as it meant I would have to be the very last to leave the room. As you saw yourself, it would have been impossible without putting up a serious fight. Then, a couple of days ago we found a servant who was prepared to leave a window open, but who wouldn't risk removing the documents himself, even for a price. This is where you came in - so to speak. I was sure that one of us would be able to seize the protocols and this meant that we could still get our man. I knew that one way or another we would succeed, and one way or another we did."

Incredulous to hear of his elaborate scheming, I could not help but blurt, "But surely you couldn't have planned it all?"

"No. Of course not, but my liquidation and impersonation of Herr Franz Lange did prepare the way for you as his inadvertent understudy, as it was Lange who was supposed to be carrying the cushion. Do you see, lad? Your unintentional heroism saved the day twice. Once, ensuring the sheriff obtained the protocols then, again, by playing the part of Lange. For, as his imposter, I should have taken the cushion. I was simply unaware of it and might have been discovered had you not entered when you did. I must say, I was most surprised to see you walk in wearing those robes. They must have been two sizes too big. I thought you were going to trip up and bring us both to shame. I left moments after you then Klaus brought me here in Lange's stolen coach. Simple."

"Simple?" God's breakfast. This man needed a dictionary. "So, you were there, posing as them? Killing them?"

"I was hunting."

"Killing, hunting. It's all the same isn't it?"

"Councillor Lange was a very evil man, Sebastian, a head of one of the Illuminati bloodlines. His ticket had been marked for a long time. He had to go."

Shocked to hear of another unsettling murder, and remembering the evil scenes at the ritual, I begged, "Then, sir, why did you not kill them all?"

"You were there, Sebastian. There were nearly thirty of them.

What could we do? It would have been hopeless and you know it. Like you, I also closed my eyes."

He *had* been there. He had seen me close my eyes, even behind my slits. I watched him with frantic apprehension and beseeched, "Well if you know all, sir, then please tell me. Was it... Francesca?"

He put his hand on my shoulder and solemnly replied, "No. Francesca is safe." I gasped with relief and finally the stress and anxiety overwhelmed me and I collapsed into a chair. The Professor pulled up a stool and Frau Hoffmeister came in to put a couple of tankards of beer on the table. Such was my need for a drink that I grabbed one of them and half emptied it in two enormous gulps, before wiping the foam from my mouth and going to drink again. After taking a goodly swig himself, Van Halestrom muttered, "It was her sister, Montarese."

"Holy Father!" I blurted and spurted out my mouthful of beer.

He frowned and carried on, "I'm afraid there was nothing we could do. We tried our best to rescue her from the Chapel of Liebfrauenmünster last week, where you saw her with your friend. Unfortunately, we failed and I believe her fate was sealed. Though Francesca tried valiantly to find a way to save her, alas, it was all in vain. Montarese had been involved with the Illuminati for many years. She was a tortured soul, my lad. In the end, I fear it was inevitable."

"Good God." I shook my head in astonishment remembering the events last weekend at the chapel, and also Francesca's deep preoccupation on our way back to Ingolstadt earlier that evening. Overwrought by these shocking details, to say nothing of my alarm at the danger in which my own life had been placed, as the entirety of the night's events became apparent to me, I could not help but jibe, "Professor, I cannot help but feel that I have been used as a pawn in your lethal game of chess."

He leaned back in his chair, sucking on his pipe and musing, "Given your movements tonight, Sebastian, maybe not a pawn, but a knight."

Having my evenings' horrendous and death-defying deeds likened to a parlour game was the last straw for me and I finally lost my temper. "A confounded knight, sir! I was almost killed. *More* than once. Why did you not tell me of the mortal danger that I faced?"

He leaned across the table and pointed his pipe at me. "You might not have done it if you had known of the peril."

"Of course-I-might-not-have-done-it-if-I-had-known-of-the-*peril*! Surely that goes without saying. Imagine suggesting to me that I should steal Weishaupt's protocols but that, if I was caught, I will definitely be killed and then me agreeing to it? You said nothing of sacrifices or crazed cultists. You lied to me. I thought you were against the lies and the treachery of our enemies?"

"If it was a lie, Sebastian, it was a small one and employed to defeat a falsehood of much larger proportions. In terms of morality it is a fair transaction."

"A fair transaction? It is a miracle that I am still alive! Four of the red maniacs chased me I… I was nearly struck by lightning."

He held up his hands, granting, "You have obviously been through a lot, Sebastian. I can see that, but it is over. Things may seem a little confusing now but, if I am right, in the future we may well look back on tonight as a great victory."

Francesca's sister had been murdered, and nearly me too, and I had found out that my best friend was working for the bastards who had done it. As far as I was concerned the night was teetering on catastrophe.

"If it is a victory, sir, then please tell me what we have won?"

He pushed the papers into the middle of the table and fixed me with an earnest stare.

"As I have said, I'm sure the sheriff has the original and, for our own benefit, I have made this copy so we may know the details of their scheme. Now we understand their plans, we can understand how to fight them. For now, Sebastian, we too are the Illuminated ones."

He turned his attention to his documents and puffed away on his pipe. Although scared, angry, and thoroughly confused, I could not help but wonder, 'Perfect memory, assassin, imposter, mind reader, is there anything this wizard cannot do?'

I took another long draw of beer and wiped my mouth with the back of my glove. It was over. I had lived to tell the tale of the incredible night of the lightning strike when others had been far less fortunate. Sitting there dripping wet and trembling with fear, it would have been impossible for me to know the implications that my inadvertent heroism was to have on the future. No one could have. Except for the Professor of course. Looking back, I realise that he knew very well what to expect and the profound effect the robbery would have. For did the wise old bird not cleverly predict, 'We may well look back on tonight as a great victory'? Prophetic words indeed.

As I played out the evening's unforgettable events in my mind, I could not help but think that somehow God had been watching over me, guiding and protecting me through the ordeal. I prayed that He would keep up his vigil, but worried that I might not be able to count on his timely intervention forever.

After watching the Professor studying the papers for a while longer, I took the opportunity to find out some more of the riddle and asked, "So when can I read them, Herr Professor?"

"Soon," he murmured. "Very soon."

*13. *14.

---

13. <u>Illuminati Agent Jacob Lanz Struck by lightning.</u> Incredibly, though there seems to be some conjecture about the precise timing of this amazing <u>event</u>, according to one of the most notable sources, '*<u>Pawns in the Game</u>*' (1958) by William Carr, this top ranking Illuminati agent was struck by lightning and killed on 10th July 1784 near Regensburg Bavaria. When the authorities discovered his body they mistakenly concluded that he had been carrying the incriminating documents himself. <u>Now</u> it has become widespread belief that Lanz was, in fact, on a mission to deliver the papers to Paris where they would be used to aid the French revolution and that the papers were sewn into his robes. If we are to believe S. Drechsler's version of events, it is fascinating to discover the real truth behind what is already an incredible but, little-known, historical event. Either this is the event chronicled by so many historians and <u>conspiracy</u> theorists alike, or we are party to an <u>absolutely</u> extraordinary coincidence.

14. <u>Franz Lange; Councillor of Eichstatt & The Bavarian Illuminati.</u> S. Drechsler's recollection of this character's gruesome death would seem to explain an anomaly from the official stories. This member of the Bavarian Illuminati is often confused with <u>Jakob</u> Lanz (very similar to 'Lange') who, it would appear, after being struck by lightning, also perished on the same night. Interestingly, I can find no official date for the obituary of F. Lange, so it is certainly possible that the author's version of events is true.

Chapter 15

The Thirteen Protocols

I read the Professor's copy of the Protocols on Sunday morning back in Ingolstadt in the park near my lodgings. Afterwards I went straight to a church and prayed for some time. I did not go back to my rooms, but sent someone round to pick up my things and I moved into new lodgings that very evening. I no longer felt safe at Frauleine Warburg's and neither would you have.

It is not possible for me to relay the whole document within the pages of my story, as time will not allow. However, to give you an idea of the evil venom which lay in the fearful passages, I have recalled one of the protocols that struck me most forcibly. I am not surprised that Van Halestrom had remembered them, perfect memory or not. Seventy years on, parts of the text are so frightening that they are still seared onto my mind. This is number twelve entitled, 'Tyranny of Power.' As I recall, it went something like this;

'...While the peoples of the world are still stunned by the accomplished fact of our revolution, still in a condition of terror and uncertainty brought about by the chaos that we have created, we shall restore our own order by destroying all the other mechanisms of their inferior civilisation;

Aristocracy: Family: Property: Government: Nation: Religion.

Once these obstacles are removed, the people of the world will be forced to recognise, once and for all, that we have seized everything we wanted and that we are so super-abundantly filled with power, that in no case, shall we take any account of them, and so, far from paying any attention to their opinions or wishes, we are ready and able to crush with irresistible force all expression or manifestation thereof at every moment and in every place. Then in fear and trembling they will close their eyes to everything, and be content to await what will be the end of it all.' [Protocol 12].

I spent the rest of the day in a daze staring into a tankard of beer at a local tavern. Not only had the ominous protocols crushed my spirits to a pulp, but now the other monumental events of the previous night began to weigh heavily on my mind. Three gruesome deaths, the lightning strike, the sacrifice, the chase and, to top it all, Jan, my oldest friend, an Illuminati servant. Not even he could joke his way out of this and I wondered, with much angst, what we would say to each other next time we met. Altogether, it was impossible not to let these thoughts drag me into a whirlpool of dark machinations and I spent that night tossing and turning on the bed in my new rooms unable to sleep.

Monday morning was no better and I walked into university like a ghost with my mind in a turmoil. From out of nowhere, a sharp voice snapped me from my stupor, like no other could, "Herr Drechsler!"

It was Weishaupt. His cold blue eyes glared at me from behind his spectacles and his harsh voice fired off the words, "I wish to see you in my chambers after your morning lecture. You will be there."

I was too scared to run off and stood transfixed to the spot (which, by now, had practically become my modus operandi). He stormed off with his black gown billowing behind him and passed a couple of students who dodged out of his way and ducked their heads for fear of catching his eye. I was convinced that I was done for and that he knew that it was me who had stolen his precious documents. This was certainly not your typical Monday morning at university, to be killed by your lecturer in the free hour before lunch.

Understandably, it was hard to concentrate throughout my next class and then, almost without knowing it, I was standing in front of Weishaupt's door three hours later in a blind funk.

'You can do this,' I tried to convince myself, unconvincingly. He could not prove anything, and even he was not mad enough to kill me in his rooms. Or so I hoped. Finally, with my heart in my mouth, I found the courage to knock.

"Come," wafted a gentle response and, dreading what was to come, I shuffled inside.

"Ah. Young Herr Drechsler. Please take a seat."

Confusingly, he had reverted to his ingratiating style which threw me even further off balance. I closed the door and lowered myself into a chair as he eyed me up and down from behind his desk.

"How is everything going, Sebastian? Getting on all right?" He put a finger on his chin, continuing with a hint of insincerity, "Exams coming up soon. I suppose you're ready for them all, aren't you? Fine student like you will have no trouble passing. No. Not you, Herr Drechsler. Which is good. I'm sure your parents would be terribly disappointed if anything were to prevent you from completing your studies here at the university. To say nothing of drunken antics, being locked in the city gaol, and bad timekeeping." There was an unsettling pause before his demeanour darkened and he growled, "I've got my eye on you, boy. And remember, my eye sees everywhere." Without taking his off mine, he nodded at the door. "Now go. I have two funerals to arrange."

Having been given the chance to leave, I nearly fell flat on my face in my haste to get out the door and I hurried away from his rooms nervously going through everything that he had said.

"First he is fearsome, then polite, then fearsome again," I chattered to myself. It was enough to send me mad. At least it had been brief which, thank God, had not given me the opportunity to condemn myself out of my own mouth.

Damn him and his all-seeing eye. I wondered if one of the funerals was going to be mine. Then I remembered the Professor's assassination of Councillor Lange and the lightning strike 'Hand of God' that had sent someone, or at least what was left of them, straight to the grave. Surely Weishaupt must have known these people, but I still could not tell if he knew of my involvement with the robbery. Would he have confronted me about it if he had, or would that have meant that he risked exposing himself? This game of cat and mouse had too many permutations to consider all at once. It was like playing a hundred games of chess simultaneously with the Professor.

Whatever The Doctor knew, he was certainly suspicious and he had already tried to kill me before. So I resolved to stay as far away from the faculty as possible and to study for my exams in my new basement room on Spitalstrasse, about which I had not told a soul.

Later that week, I reported the meeting to Van Halestrom, but he simply laughed it off and said, "He's just playing mind games with you, my boy. Remember, lad: *Ordo ab chao*. The means with which the weak usurp the strong. Otherwise known as the old wive's trick, blowing hot and cold. Ha ha. Don't worry, Sebastian. Stand firm. You have nothing to fear from that creature whilst in the confines of the university. He cannot prove anything, so do not concern yourself with his threats. Mark my words, we will see to it that you complete your exams legitimately."

"And, what if I don't complete them *legitimately*, sir? What then?"

"Why then, my lad," he cheered bombastically, "We shall cheat."

He gave me a hearty slap on the back and I thought him quite the rogue. I knew that if Van Halestrom said he could do something then I had every reason to believe him. So I tried to relax and let his positive words reassure me. Though, to be truthful, deep down inside, I was still absolutely terrified about what was coming around the next bend. *15.

---

15. The Original Writings of The Illuminati. The original documents found with Lanz's body after the lightning strike have not survived, so unfortunately, there is no record of the text to back up Drechsler's account. Although other papers seized from agents of the Bavarian Illuminati on later dates bear strong similarity to those the author describes and clearly cite the abolition of all; Monarchy, Government, Property, Patriotism, Family and Religion. These documents were reprinted and released by the Bavarian authorities in 1787, to warn foreign countries about the Illuminati and their revolutionary intentions. Interestingly, the text bears a strong resemblance to the mother of all conspiracy documents, '***The Protocols of the Elders of Zion***' (1903) a book published in Russia and proved, beyond doubt, to be a hoax, produced for political ends. Though it is an inexplicable coincidence that the document S. Drechsler recalls, bears such a close resemblance to this text released over a hundred years later, forged or not.

Chapter 16

Tribulations and Examinations

So it was settled. I was to study in my basement, trying not to twitch whenever someone went past the window and keeping my head down until my exams. This was made easier as Bacon had already completed my coursework, removing my need to visit the university altogether. So I threw myself into my books and seldom left the house for two weeks. In this time, I saw no one but my untalkative landlord and sorely craved any company at all, especially that of the Professor and, of course, the mysterious but tragic Francesca, of whom I dreamt frequently.

Then, as with all periods of waiting, the day eventually came when it was at an end and I paced down the lanes to the university, busily going through the facts that I had crammed into my aching head. My exams were to be conducted over three days, history on the first, philosophy on the second and, on the third, the one that I was really dreading, canon law.

It wasn't only because my examiner was a murderous Luciferian maniac with designs on taking over the world, though it was hard to keep these salient facts from my thoughts entirely, it was because the subject itself was as complicated as Byzantine bureaucracy. Which, come to think of it, is exactly what it was. The endless lists of statutes and over-complicated laws would not settle in my mind as I had no care of what one priest had to facilitate for another, nor how their infernal bishop would feel about it if they did not. It was not like history, where the dates and events were naturally fixed in the memory by the drama of the story they told. History, I could do. So, I was not wholly unsurprised to find myself sneaking out of the university a few hours later, quietly content at the way my first exam had gone and much relieved that the initial part of the ordeal was over.

However, something that did surprise me was the sight of the Professor's black coach parked in the street outside the gates. Klaus spotted me and signalled with a discreet nod, that I should carry on down the road. Presently, the pair of black horses appeared at my shoulder and I heard Van Halestrom offer, "Hop in, my lad. We can give you a lift if you like?"

I pulled myself up through the open door and sat down opposite him as the whip cracked and the coach rattled away.

"That went well, didn't it?" he said, reading my mind as usual, and continuing to do so. "You'll probably be all right tomorrow, as you rightly expect, but the third exam looks as though it might pose a more significant obstacle."

"Why is that, sir?" I asked, fully expecting another horrid complication approaching which, of course, it was.

He answered unceremoniously, "Weishaupt plans to destroy your papers before they are marked, so you will not score at all, thus placing you in abstentia and making your expulsion from the university a certainty. My clerk overheard him boasting about it with one of his cronies at the faculty."

"What!"

He held up a finger. "Do not worry, Sebastian. A plan is afoot to foil his scheme, but it relies entirely upon two significant points which are directly under your control."

"What... what must I do?"

"As you know, the exam is to take place in the old cloister rooms. Once there, you must occupy desk number seven and, as soon as Weishaupt reveals the questions on the blackboard, you must write them down immediately then leave them where they can be seen. Otherwise, our plan fails and, along with it, your university career."

My mind was still too stuffed full of dates and names to keep up and I babbled, "But... but...why?"

"It is unimportant, Sebastian. Just do as I say and everything will be fine."

There was that infernal word 'just,' again, but I let him go on.

"Now, we shan't take you to your house as we don't want to give away its location, and there are matters of great importance to which I must attend. I have not wished to concern you with these because of your studies." He flashed a grin then balanced it with a look of stern resolve. "Although this much I *can* tell you. Due to our recent endeavours a number of Illuminati dignitaries, including the influential Baron Von Knigge, have chosen to distance themselves from the Order. Also, an edict has been sought in the high court against Weishaupt, by none other than His Majesty Karl Theodore, after the documents you stole were handed in as evidence to the Prosecutor Royal. So, if we are successful, my lad, it will be, in no small part, down to you." *[16]

He tapped his cane on the ceiling, bringing the coach to a halt and put his hand on my knee. "Now I'm afraid we must leave you, my friend. Just remember, desk number seven. Alright?"

I dismounted and heard him call out, "Farewell, my boy. Good luck now. Don't give up," and the coach rumbled away.

I scuttled back to my basement and locked the door behind me, reflecting how the complicated things in life were now even more so. I wondered, with much trepidation, if this meant that Weishaupt had found out that it was me who had stolen the protocols? But then surely he would haved killed me if he had?

---

16. The First Edict Against The Illuminati. In summer 1784 the first edict banning secret societies was issued by Charles Theodore Elector of Bavaria. Though these measures were seen as half-hearted, tellingly the authorities' suspicion of the Illuminati continued to mount around this time, which may well be explained by the author's exploits. Baron Adolph Knigge was a prominent aristocrat highly influential within the order, who notably fell out with Weishaupt during this period and official records agree that the academic had suddenly become unpopular due to growing disquite over his organisation.

Unsurprisingly, that night, I had a terrible dream. In this nightmare I was sitting at my desk in the exam looking at a blank sheet of paper, when Weishaupt appeared beside me brandishing the curved knife from the sacrifice. The other students did not see him but kept scribbling away and, though I tried to scream, I could not because of the strict rule of silence during the test.

To my credit, even after these nocturnal hauntings, I did not buckle and the following day's philosophy exam went as smoothly as the first. That evening, I lay in bed praying for the swift completion of my final test and that I could get to the correct desk. With these worries churning in my mind, I hardly slept a wink. Exams were bad enough already, but this was ridiculous.

Then the most awful of beginnings. After spending the whole night listening to the chimes of St Maria's slowly drawing closer to the moment that I had been dreading for so long, when seven o'clock at last came round, half an hour before I was meant to rise, I finally fell asleep. I awoke minutes before the start of the exam in a state of absolute delirium and ran so fast through the streets that I would have flattened anyone unfortunate enough to get in my way. If the sight of a wild-eyed student charging along with his night shirt flapping over his breeches was not enough to stir the townspeople from my path, I resorted to shouting at the top of my voice, "Move, you blasted idiots!"

I bolted down the colonnade of the old cloister rooms then erupted with fear upon seeing the students already going inside. "No! No! No!!" I blabbed, envisioning my disappointed father shaking his head while my mother openly wept behind him and the old man gravely pronounced, "Boy, *you* are a failure."

I hurled myself into the queue and barged my way through then burst in the room to see everyone selecting their prospective seats. Quickly getting my bearings, I spotted desk number seven bathed in sunlight falling from an adjacent window, but noticed portly Grubber only a few feet away and closing in fast.

I nearly screamed at him but, remembering the strict rule of silence, which should I break would mean instant expulsion, I flew towards the desk, coughing as loudly as I dared then kneed him in the back of his thigh. A technique that I had been taught by the Professor when wishing to incapacitate someone from behind. And incapacitate him it did. For, in my haste to get into the chair before my ample colleague, I used quite some force and left the ill-fated Grubber writhing on the floor in agony. Weishaupt appeared at his door, eager to see what all the fuss was about, but I innocently shrugged my shoulders and pointed at my throat.

His eyes filled with suspicion before he pulled his crocodile grin, obviously contemplating his deceitful plan. Little did he know, that I had a plan of my own and I secretly scoffed, before realising with a start, 'What *was* the blasted plan?' I had no idea at all. I had had neither the time, nor the straightness of mind even to consider it.

Feeling suddenly sympathetic, I offered Grubber my hand, but he anxiously pulled away and went to find another desk. Glancing around, I now felt completely helpless in the bright morning sunshine and gazed at the blank sheets of paper on my desk. Weishaupt looked out over us before signalling the start of the test then removed the cloth from the blackboard to reveal the questions. I picked up my quill and, as instructed, wrote them down before beginning my own work as I had intended.

Well, I am not going to tell you what happened over the next two hours, for its very mention would probably bore you to death as surely as cataloguing every grain of sand in the world would, then doing it all again, thrice. Suffice to say, that, in the end, I thought it went quite well. Not a stunning account of canon law by any stretch of the imagination, but probably enough to get me through. Or so I thought.

When the bell sounded, Weishaupt came round collecting the papers and then dismissed us. Being the furthest from the door, I was the last to leave the room so I was alone with him when, to my utter horror, I saw him locate my paper then, with a look of pure devilment in his eye, stare me straight in the face and remove it from the pile.

"Pig dog!" I cursed under my breath. But how could I complain? He would simply deny his intentions and he knew that I could not speak as the conditions of the test were still being observed. He left through his own entrance, clearly putting my paper inside his robe and giving the others to the waiting clerk to be taken to the adjudicator. The frustration was maddening. I wanted to turn the bastard round and smash his damnedable teeth in. I stormed out of the cloister rooms in a furious rage, swearing that someday, in some way, I would get my revenge, however long it took. For now I was definitely ruined.

I marched into the courtyard, planning many gruesome acts of violence where Weishaupt was the screaming, blood-covered victim, but was amazed when I saw someone that I had not expected to see in the slightest. In fact, so stunned was I to find him there, that it momentarily stopped me from considering the outrage which had befallen me. Although he had his collar pulled up unusually high, and the brim of his hat suspiciously low, I could tell that it was snooty old Bacon slowly making his way along with the crowd of students. He stood out like a sore thumb amongst the throng and turned the other way out of the gates. I ran up behind him, bursting with a mixture of intrigue and anticipation and softly asked, "Herr Bacon? Is that you?"

He acknowledged me with a tip of his hat and answered in his usual considered drawl, "Ah. Herr Drechsler. How pleasant to see you, sir," but continued walking, seemingly as unsurprised to see me as if he were back in the castle drawing the curtains.

I wondered, desperate with hope, "Pray, sir, what have you been doing here at the university?"

After inhaling for an unforgivably long time, he announced, "I believe, sir, that I have had the rather dubious privilege of coming here and fighting my way through herds of malodorous students in order to sit in a dusty room all morning peering through a telescope writing your exam paper on canon law."

Of course! That was why I had to be at desk number seven, because it was the only one that could be spied through the window. He carried on in the same grating monotone, "I understand, sir, that the clerk is our man, so to speak, and will place my manuscript in the pile where it will be marked with the rest. Weishaupt suspects nothing so will not check, as he believes that he has destroyed the original."

While he delivered this life-changing news, the black coach pulled up next to us with trusty Klaus at the reins. In a deceptively graceful movement for a man of his age, the old butler hopped aboard and closed the door behind him then leant from the window, cordially tipped the brim of his hat and wished me, "Good day, sir."

Klaus gave me a friendly wink as he roused the horses and the coach trundled off up the street. I watched them bumping away in joyful rapture and yodelled as loud and high as I could, "Yaahoo! Up yours Adam Weishaupt!"

That was a good day from then on in. Horrid exams completed, the last of which by a veritable genius, the sweet smells of summer filling the air, pretty girls everywhere making themselves available for the crowds of young students celebrating the end of term and, above all, the sweet thought of Weishaupt's angry face distorting with apoplexy as I confidently strolled past him on my way back into university for the first day of term next September.

"Hurrah!" I cheered to myself and supped the head off a frothy tankard of beer. It had been a long time coming, but that evening, for the first time in ages, I did finally relax. Although, as was becoming my habit, completely on my own. For, due to my enforced self-incarceration in my new lodgings, and the solitude which moving to a new town had already brought, compounded by the fact that I no longer saw Jan, I had become quite alone in Ingolstadt. Though it was not a concern at that precise moment, I had noticed it happening generally in my life, and reflected that this was because no one else seemed to have the allure of the new band of twilight folk that I was coming to know.

Chapter 17

Summer Holidays

The summer holidays passed happily without incident. After gratefully receiving the confirmation of my successful examinations, I proudly returned home to Tuffengarten for three weeks during August to spend some time with my parents. Mother was overjoyed to see me and instantly began fattening me up, complaining that 'the food of Ingolstadt was only good for townspeople, but not for a country boy like you, who needs more energy than those idle city folk.' Which was the utter irrationality of my French mother that I had missed so much.

Father, on the other hand, was his usual abrupt self. Having become used to the relative informality of university life, and especially my new brotherhood of friends, I found it hard to remember to bow to him, in the morning, before and after lunch, and even before going to bed. It started to make my back ache in the end, but it was nice to see him anyway. Although he tried his hardest to cover his real feelings with those of piety, worry, concern, and much stern contemplation, I was sure that somewhere deep inside the old man, there was a glimmer of pride that his only son had survived his first year of university. Heaven knows what he would have thought, had he even an inkling of the life that I actually led.

I spent much of my time fishing at my usual spot by the river and noticed how sorely I missed my old friend Jan. This was the first summer that we had spent apart since we were boys and I worried that the different paths we had chosen toward manhood would mean that we would never talk to each other again. Since seeing him at Weishaupt's wretched lodge, I had been making a lengthy detour to avoid walking past the moneychangers and his lodgings on my way home from university.

These distractions aside, I was in good spirits and five pounds heavier when I returned to my basement room in Ingolstadt and saw a note pushed under my front door. It was from Van Halestrom who wanted to meet with me. This was, of course, not what the message said, because as usual, it was in code and read, '*Game of chess. Monday six o'clock. My chambers.*' My heart leapt at the news and the possibility of seeing Francesca again.

I was in fine fettle that fresh September morning as I strolled back into university for the first day of term. Such were my spirits, that I was not daunted when I saw Weishaupt dressed in his black gown lurking in his usual place in the corridor and watching the year's new undergraduates filing by. Of course, he could not hide his shock upon seeing me return and threw me the most malevolent of stares. To my eternal pride, I did not cower, but strode proudly past, even braving a whistle, an act of defiance which clearly infuriated him. It was even better than I had pictured. What was he to do? Send me down for whistling? Much as he would like, even he couldn't be that strict.

One of my colleagues beside me, a morbid but insightful lad called Frankenstein or some such, witnessed the exchange and wittered under his breath, "You don't want to get The Old Doctor upset. He might *literally* have your guts for garters."

I laughed off the comment but, through the day, it dawned on me that my hiatus from danger was over now that Weishaupt knew that I had thwarted him. Even though he would only be lecturing me once a week, and I could always hide at the back, having him creeping round the university and head of the law department was enough to set my mind whirring through a series of dark machinations. Now he would surely be planning his revenge. By the end of the day, my fine mood had dwindled considerably and I consoled myself with my up-and-coming meeting with the Professor.

At six o'clock sharp, I entered Van Halestrom's room, noticing that the pieces on his chessboard were prepared for a game. 'No need for code,' I thought as he offered me a chair and, after drawing white, he made the first move.

"Good to see you, Sebastian. I hope you have your wits about you, for there is much for you to know. Firstly, work is still carrying on in the courts to bring about the trial of Weishaupt and his organisation. This is excellent news as we feared that they may have already managed to sieze control of the judiciary. Though, whether the courts are successful or not, at the end of October it seems there will be another opportunity for us to further bring about the Order's downfall. I will tell you more about this when it comes to pass. In the meantime, I have another job for you. Are you interested?"

I moved a knight into play and replied, "Of course, Professor. What is the task?"

"Not so much a *task*, but a spot of extracurricular activity. Something for the weekend, if you will?" He moved a pawn into attack and repeated, "That's right. Just a spot of extracurricular activity."

It was that word 'just' again, but I missed it this time. What was to happen on my next mission was a proper shock indeed. A real eye opener for sure. Extracurricular activity my Bavarian arse. *[17.]

---

17. Frankenstein & The Illuminati. This must be Drechsler's little joke, though possibly an insightful one. He would, of course, have been familiar with Mary Shelley's novel '***Frankenstein***' (1818) set in Ingolstadt University around the same time. So maybe it was a nickname given retrospectively to one of his more morbid fellow students. He may have also been trying to be cryptic, given the context of the story, as there is much agreed symbolic connection of the Illuminati and '***Frankenstein.***' Mary's husband, Percy Shelly, certainly admired the secret society and there are many fascinating allegorical connections between the romantic Gothic masterpiece and Weishaupt's order.

Chapter 18

Life, Liberty and the Pursuit of Happiness

So, the next Saturday morning I was huddled behind a frosty blackberry bush on a freezing hillside, rubbing my hands together trying to keep warm. I poked my head over the brambles for the dozenth time and spied up the high forest pass that wound all the way from the near horizon back up to our position.

"Here they come," whispered the Professor and ducked down behind a bush a few yards away. Soon, a large covered wagon pulled by two white horses rolled over the brow of the hill with three hardened looking characters on the footplate. Their breath clouded in the cold morning air as they scanned the surrounding scenery, but with their collars turned up and their hats drooping over their eyes, I could hardly see their faces at all. I glanced over at Van Halestrom only to find that he had vanished and my heart began to thump like the fist of a man who has woken up in a coffin. As usual, he had not told me what to expect, but we had travelled a fair distance to this place and I was pretty sure that he had not come all this way to deliver these brutes some flowers. My worst fears came true when I heard him fiercely command, "Halt or I shoot!"

I peeped out from behind the bush to see him standing twenty feet in front of the wagon with his menacing bow pushed under his chin. The three ruffians looked at him then amongst themselves as if doing some mental arithmetic. Finding the result in their favour, they chuckled before the biggest brought up a massive blunderbuss and fired off a thunderous blast.'Boom!'

The shot ripped huge splinters from a silver birch where Van Halestrom was standing as the explosion rang out through the forest. Having expected to see my friend struck down in mortal agony, when the smoke cleared, I was startled to see him ten paces nearer the carriage. Before I knew it, a hail of silver-tipped bolts spurted from his bow and sliced through the air before hitting their targets, 'Zut! Zut! Zut!' I watched aghast as all three men fell from the wagon then thumped into the icy ground where they stayed, lying perfectly still but grotesquely contorted.

Van Halestrom inched over, all the time whispering to calm the frightened horses and keeping the bow trained on the bodies. When he was sure that the brutes were all dead, he called out, "Come here, Sebastian!"

I crept over to the carnage as a plump old gentleman emerged from behind the canvas at the front of the wagon with his hands held high above his expensive wig. He regarded the Professor with abject terror in between glancing at his hired help who were now obviously no help at all. I came up behind Van Halestrom as the quivering man stepped down from the footplate. He was about sixty-years old and wore a fine blue coat with brass buttons and large fancy cuffs over a pair of gleaming white breeches stretched tight around his bulging midrift.

The Professor spoke clear and earnest, "Martin von Speer, I accuse you of the heinous crimes of slavery, murder, piracy, kidnapping, and the wilful violence you have committed upon thousands of unfortunates whose lives you have ruined. On behalf of those individuals and for freedom and liberty throughout the world, I, Peter Van Halestrom, sentence you to death by firing squad and may God have pity on your pathetic soul."

I could not bear to watch and looked away for a split second but heard the click of the trigger and the punch of the arrow then turned back to see the man staring at us in horror. He glanced down at his stomach, expecting to see the arrow but, incredibly, it had disappeared inside him. He stared back at us in disbelief as a large bloodstain spread across his breeches then he fell to his knees, a position that he held for a moment before collapsing face down on the frozen ground with one final deathly gasp.

"Right, that's that," said the Professor offhandedly and, without batting an eyelid, went to the back of the wagon and started unfastening the canvas. "Would you help me here please?" he asked politely and, though still in a state of shock after the violence that I had seen, I joined in. We removed four heavy strongboxes from the wagon and placed them on the roadside, whereupon the Professor produced a sturdy, silver-handled knife and prised them open like oysters. Though the treasure, in this case, was a huge haul of coinage piled to the very brim of the boxes which we loaded into our saddlebags.

After moving the wagon and the four corpses from the track, we freed the horses and walked our own from the forest. Once into the open, we cantered for a couple of miles before slowing to preserve our mounts as the weight that we carried was of such burden. We did not return to Ingolstadt but travelled north to Nuremberg. Van Halestrom had told me that our mission would last the whole weekend and that I should be 'prepared for all eventualities.' But this was difficult, to say the least, when on a day out with him. After half a mile or so of bumping along through the pine trees, I finally plucked up the courage to ask, "Sir, would you now please tell me what the hell is going on?"

"Of course, my lad. I'm sorry that that had to happen in the way it did. I would also like to promise you that there will soon be a day when these nasty surprises become a thing of the past. It is in the nature of the training that they are performed in such a manner, to ensure they have the right impact."

"Well they certainly had *impact*," I replied sardonically.

"Herr Speer was an important member of the Illuminati who was being groomed for inclusion into the elite level. He supplied many of its members with slaves throughout Europe and the Americas. Had I not killed him, in two months' time another six hundred men, women, and children would have gone missing from the coast of West Africa or some other brutal, impoverished part of the world. Two hundred of these would die, maybe more, depending on the conditions of the crossing. The rest would suffer the endless humiliation and degradation of a lifetime's enforced servitude at the hands of a master who possessed limitless capacity to further their woe and suffering. I am simply not prepared to stand idly by, knowing that these disgusting crimes will continue, when I could have stopped the perpetrators of this evil myself. The courts will do nothing about these men, so I have taken it upon myself to become their judge, jury and executioner."

He sighed and solemnly continued, "Slavery is one of the most abhorrent crimes of all and anyone who even considers it a possible career has already negated their right to be treated like a human being. There is nothing that can be done about such people and that is why they must be destroyed like dogs that have gone mad. In life, there are opposing sides of good and bad. All inherently evil systems rely on there being a host, i.e. the good, and a self-appointed parasite which feeds from it, i.e. the bad. When a man becomes as bad as Von Speer, he is doubtless a murderer, a pervert, a liar, a cheat, and a total immoral deviant who should not be let near normal gentlefolk, who credulously project their own peaceful qualities onto him. Historically, the problem of the good is that, unlike the bad, they dare not strike first. This reluctance of the good to act, creates the symbiotic cycle of their own suffering and, in turn, produces creatures like Von Speer. That's where we come in. To strike first. To hunt down these evil doers and redress the balance. This is the big lesson, Sebastian. In order to save lives, sometimes it is right to kill. I call this moral calculus and you need to embrace the concept before you can advance to the next level."

"Right then," I remarked, somewhat dismayed at this bleak assessment of the human condition and wondered out loud, "What level am I at now, Herr Professor?" calculating the further horrors that I would have to witness to achieve the next levels of 'understanding.'

"When you no longer need to ask what level you have attained, you are sufficiently initiated and, of course, it no longer becomes a priority to know. You will come to understand this."

'More paradoxical thinking,' I thought, somewhat unsatisfied by this circular reasoning and still troubled after seeing such unprovoked assassinations. I could not fathom the justification for the slaughter of these men who were, after all, merely going about their lawful business, however cruel. How could this be right?

You may find it shocking, but I was to come to see these acts of violence as not only fully justified, and more than necessary, but a necessity. These stark conclusions were brought to the fore by many things that were to happen in the future, but especially the events of the following day, when I was to witness one of the most remarkably uplifting experiences of my life. Although, as usual, the Professor had not forewarned me of his plans, so there was much for me to ponder as we journeyed down the road to Nuremberg.

We reached the city at sunset and found suitable lodgings whereupon the two of us turned in early, as the ride, along the the other events of the day, had been of such a testing nature. We woke early, breakfasted heartily then rode into the centre of town and to a large storehouse next to the river. Van Halestrom left me looking after the horses and, as I wondered why we had come to this place, I noticed a sign hanging over a door that read, '*Slaves for Sale.*' Shortly after, Van Halestrom returned with a most incredible crew in tow.

To my complete astonishment, he had used Von Speer's papers to collect the slaves belonging to the freshly deceased merchant and was marching them out of the building in full view of the other traders. This demanded no small act of valour on the Professor's part as there would have been hell to pay if someone had realised what was going on. So we quickly lined up the slaves, with one of us on either side, then marched the poor souls away from the market and off through the streets.

What a strange sight we made, thirty men, women and children of all colours and origins, young and old, with me and the Professor showing them the way. We came to a haberdashery where Van Halestrom raised the shopkeeper and, after allaying his concerns about working on the Sabbath by offering him too much money to refuse, so help me God if we didn't clothe every single one of the hapless folk using more of our ill-gotten gains. There was much happiness amongst our brigade as they started to relax in their more hospitable circumstances. They had been cold in the autumnal weather, having nothing about them but rags at best, so these clothes were greeted with much relief.

Next, I was sent to buy food and using the same technique of bribing the local store owners though, to be truthful, not that much was necessary, I collected such a quantity that I had to bring it back in a wheelbarrow before dishing it out to the throng.

With our new friends now fed, watered, and clothed in decent fashion, the bizarre parade continued down to the docks where the Professor troubled himself for some time arranging and paying for journeys with the boat captains. He handed out hastily drawn maps and more money and tried to divide our troop into parties which could travel together, with some sort of natural leader who would understand what best to do. In some cases, he even booked guides and companions, warning these people that if any harm came to the individuals put into their care he would be back to prosecute terrible punishments upon them all.

After several long hours, with the last of our abused individuals either booked on a boat, or already travelling down the river, the Professor and I cantered away from the docks. There had been several earnest and emotional farewells at the riverside as the liberated people thanked us for what we had done. Van Halestrom left the city without a penny left of the money that we had stolen and I calculated that this generosity had made some of our freed charges very wealthy indeed. There was a small but solid community of mulattoes at Mainz, a day's sail east along the river Pegnitz, where I believe that many of our group had settled and their descendants are still living peacefully today. And God bless them all. Each and every one of them.

"We have made some people very happy this day," ventured the Professor.

"And others slightly less so," I noted. Sarcasm aside, the events of that weekend and seeing the different looks in the eyes of the murdered merchant and that of his freed slaves, would not leave me and, I might add, are still there to this day. Van Halestrom may have had unusual teaching methods, but his lesson in moral calculus was unforgettable. And what an important lesson that was to prove.

Chapter 19

The Art of War

The next few weeks were very busy for me, as the Professor's demands on my time increased. At the weekends, I visited the Castle Landfried and was given more combat lessons in various disciplines. Van Halestrom taught me how he had moved so quickly in the forest and how to use the awesome quadre bow with devastating effect. After much practice, I became able to cut one of the large straw targets in half with a series of shots placed close together in a line. The Professor roared with delight to see this destruction and commented that I was becoming 'a veritable William Tell.'

In the castle gymnasium I learned many acts of brutalism; how to break an arm with a twist, and how to kill with a kick, or a punch, and even how to slit a man's throat. I worried that I would not be able to carry out such extreme acts of violence. Of course, I had fought before. Yes, in a tavern brawl, once or twice, but never with any real conviction, and always in self-defence. So this was all very serious stuff and I looked with growing concern to the future when these skills would be called upon to order. Needless to say, the Professor understood this and told me that if I felt uncomfortable at any time, we could call a halt. But this never came to pass and the training carried on and on.

I was sure these lessons had something to do with the event the Professor had told me about which was to take place at the end of October. It was already nearing the end of the month and brown leaves were piling up against the door of my basement room on Spitalstrasse. As the nights drew in, I became both apprehensive and excited in equal measure, for I had also been told that Francesca would be deeply involved with this mission.

I had not seen her for so long that it made her memory induce a painful longing in me, but it was impossible for me to gauge what she would do when I saw her next. Would she embrace me and tell me that I was a hero, as I dreamed, or ridicule me as a pathetic fool as she did in my nightmares? Though profoundly unbalancing, I resigned, in the end, to envisage the possibility of both outcomes simultaneously.

By now, I had taken to avoiding Weishaupt's lectures completely. Despite there being scores of other students in the hall, I could not stand being near the man. Van Halestrom assured me that he was under far too much scrutiny to attempt revenge, especially on a student of the university. But a couple of times, I caught him glaring at me and, knowing what he was capable of, it was too much to bear. I knew that not attending was risky, and something that I would not always be able to do, but I sensed that somehow things couldn't stay the way they were for long. There was much gossip round the campus about Weishaupt, the Illuminati and the courts. Also, a sordid rumour that the supposedly authoritarian professor had had an affair with his sister - of all people - and, like a late summer storm brooding over the mountains, something had to break. I could only pray that it would not be me.

On the last Friday of October, I went to stow my hat and scarf in my locker and found a note stuck in the crack of the door which read, '*Chess match, six o'clock.*' Suspecting that I was about to receive news of my next mission, I found it impossible to concentrate on the day's lectures and, as soon as they were over, I was hurrying down the busy corridors towards the Professor's study. A moment later, I was sitting before his desk brimming with anticipation as he greeted me in his usual affable way.

"Tea, Sebastian?" He set out two cups of the steaming brew and, after lighting his pipe, rummaged around in a drawer for a moment then produced a medallion and tossed it on the desk where it landed with a clunk. "Have you ever seen this before?"

I picked it up and instantly received a fearful jolt of déjà-vu. For, embossed on the face, surrounded by some Latin phrases and floating above a capless pyramid, was the ominous eye from my dream. The precursor of all the life-changing events that had befallen me over the past six months and I almost threw the thing down in revulsion.

"It is the vision from your dream, is it not?" probed the Professor. What to say to a man who has asked you to agree with the thing that you had already thought, but had not yet the chance to mention, was still an annoying mystery to me. I tilted an eyebrow and muttered, "You know it is."

As usual, he carried on regardless of my displeasure, "This symbol has recently been selected by the American Congress for its great seal, proving the Illuminati's rot is spreading into the highest offices of that land. Notice that there are thirteen layers to the pyramid. This is a metaphor for our society. The bottom level is you and me and every other uninitiate in the world, '*die hörig*,' as they like to call us, or 'the slaves.'"

So that was what it meant. I was most displeased to be referred to as a slave and remembered Weishaupt using the word when I was hiding in the cupboard at his beastly lodge. The Professor continued and pointed his pipe at the medallion, "As we go up the pyramid the bricks indicate the layers of Weishaupt's vision of civilisation until, the penultimate level, representing him and the elders and, crowning it all, The Eye of Horus, the Egyptian God symbolizing the underworld and Lucifer, by whom all in the society are ultimately controlled. Note the date at the bottom: 1776, the year of the Order's most recent incarnation under the oversight of our good friend, Adam Weishaupt, or Herr Spartacus to you and me. Now the Latin, if you would translate please?"

I read out the phrases, "Annuit Cœptis Novo Ordo Seculorum. He approves of our undertakings and new order... of the ages?"

"Yes, lad. Very good. In this case 'He' is Lucifer and seculorum means the world, so, 'New Order of the World.' How's that for coming right out and saying it? This technique of publicly flaunting occult symbolism is called 'hidden in plain sight.' It is indeed their plan to have a new order for the world: Their order. And this is what we intend to do about it."

He rolled out the plans of a building on the table and explained, "This All Hallows' Eve at the Temple of Eleusis in Munich, the most important meeting of the Illuminati will be held since its modern inception eight years ago. At this rite, attended by the entire oligarchy, including the heads of the family bloodlines, the magic Eleusinian Mystery will be performed, summoning the spirit of their faith to aid them in their battle against the authorities.

Things are coming to a head. The Order are running scared, but are going to perform this rite anyway whilst mounting a coup d'état before the state can move on them. They already have many top officials under their control, and also a dignitary of extremely high office who is part of their scheme to take over the realm. It is no coincidence that there is another meeting in Munich that night at the state chancellery where the high court sits to pass judgement on Weishaupt's organisation. *[18]

---

18. The Pyramid & The All Seeing 'Eye' of Providence (The Eye of Horus). This symbol, with its intriguing Latin inscriptions, remains perhaps one of the most famous conspiracies of all time, though the engraving described here would be slightly different to the one we are familiar with today. Interestingly, an earlier version of the symbol had already been accepted by the founding fathers in 1782, as The Great Seal of America. Perhaps its most celebrated expression is on the reverse of the US one dollar bill, first printed on the notes in 1933 under the oversight of President F.D. Roosevelt. Speculation about this esoteric symbol and its usage, meaning and history would appear to be almost endless and a great deal of time would have to be set aside to research this one topic alone, such is the volume of literature written about it. Good luck!

The Illuminati plan to wipe out all who attend this meeting then fill their places with their own men, thus becoming the rulers of the nation. Ergo, ordo ab chao."

I struggled to comprehend such treason and blundered, "...And how do they intend to achieve this miracle, sir?"

"Ah, that's the most interesting part of the plan."

He sipped his tea and, annoyingly, at the moment I felt he was about to elaborate, forcing me to ask, "...Which is?"

"Blow up the chancellery building with them all inside."

I looked around for a sane person to confirm what I thought I had heard and gawked, "I beg your pardon, sir, I thought you said..."

"I did. Blow up the building with them all inside."

"Yes, yes, Professor, that is the part I heard," I flustered. "It is the act of demolition itself that sounds a little far-fetched to me."

"On the contrary, my friend, it is simple. The explosives are already laid deep within the building's foundations but are so well hidden that they cannot be found. Therefore we must lie in wait for the conspirators to arrive and attempt to trigger them." Noticing my stupefaction, he raised an eyebrow. "Is it so surprising, Sebastian? Remember, a similar plot has been tried before. In 1605 Herr Guido Fawkes the English Catholic planned to blow up the Houses of Parliment in London. Though I fear the Illuminati may be more successful than old Guido. That is, unless they are stopped."

Was this possible? My mind was whirling like a dervish.

He surveyed the plans on the table and carried on, "During the mission Klaus and I will be across the city at the chancellery ensuring it isn't destroyed, while you and Francesca will lead the ground assault at the temple. She will infiltrate the gathering using her particular skills to seduce the aforementioned dignitary then extricate him from the ritual before the arrival of the magistrates who have also been informed of the plot."

"He is of such significance to the state that his exposure as an Illuminati disciple could mean the overturning of our entire monarchy. Although morally problematic, we must help him flee before the authorities get there. Your task will be to look over Francesca and her charge during their time at the ceremony. You will break into the temple and maintain a vigil over the pair making sure no harm comes to them and that she escapes with our target, whereupon you will also leave and we will meet at a safe destination. Any questions?"

Quite understandably I had several, so I tried the first, "What... should I do if someone tries to stop me?"

"Of course, it would be better to stay in the shadows throughout the mission but, if you must, you can kill as many as you wish. We only need to catch a handful of the leadership alive to secure a conviction. Although, if they are already dead, my friend, then maybe we need not trouble the courts at all."

I felt my fists clench at the idea of killing for the first time as he went on, "But you'll have your work cut out achieving such innumerable slaughter. Over two-hundred members will be in attendance. Oh yes. The whole kit and kaboodle will be there. And this is our chance to catch them *red-handed*."

I understood his irony recalling the gruesome sacrifice that I had witnessed at the last of their demonic rituals, and shuddered at the thought of seeing such horror again. He picked up his cup of tea without taking his eyes of the plans and I grasped the opportunity to get some more detail.

"Tell me, sir, how were the Illuminati able to achieve the positioning of the explosives in the chancellery?"

"They infiltrated the Masons charged with constructing such government buildings a long time ago. It is the reason that I left. I used to be a Grand Master myself, but the Illuminati's influence over the fraternity forced me to leave. For many centuries, the Masons have been a fine tradition, but now they are manipulated from within by a few crazed radicals. I fear their hidden hand will besmirch the organisation's good name far into the future. Anything else?" He finished his tea. *[19.]

I was surprised to hear that the Professor had been a Mason, a Grand Master no less. He was still full of surprises. I tried to focus on the task at hand for which I had been training so long. Surely, I could not go back now? Perhaps, if I could manage to '*stay in the shadows*,' as the Professor recommended then, hopefully, I would not have to kill anyone at all. Still, if I was going to play my part in guarding Francesca, I wanted to be able to do it properly.

I stuck out my chin and, trying to appear as confident as possible, I mentioned, "I might be a little low on hardware for such an adventure, sir. All I possess in terms of weaponry is the single flintlock pistol you gave me three months ago, and I haven't fired that once yet."

"Ah yes, that reminds me." He went to his bookcase and pulled back the worn spine of '*The Art of War*' by Sun Tzu. I was bemused when a hidden door cut into the shelves swung open to reveal a secret cupboard filled with an incredible haul of weapons, sufficient to start a small war - even arming both sides!

"Is it really safe to have all this... *equipment* here?" I asked,

---

19. Freemasons & The Illuminati. The commonly held belief that the tradition of Freemasonry provides the Illuminati a host in which to conceal itself, has existed for hundreds of years and been speculated about endlessly. This claim is given weight by the official ratification of the two organisations at the Congress of Wilhelmsbad in 1782. It is said that the leaderships' true goals are only revealed to adepts at the higher degrees while the lower members are unaware of these plans and naturally defend the integrity of the institution. It is interesting that S. Drechsler recalls his mentor describing its influence as a 'hidden hand' - a term which has now become commonplace.

counting at least twenty muskets, an entire rack of blunderbusses, several caskets of shot and powder and even a tiny quarter pounder cannon.

"Of course, Herr Drechsler. Surely it's the last place anyone would think of looking."

It wasn't exactly what I had meant, though he was certainly right. Who in their right mind would expect to find such a deadly arsenal hidden in a lecturer's bookcase?

Sometime later, I shuffled away from the Professor's study lugging a huge and very suspicious looking black bag. A series of palpitations swept through me as I considered its contents; one quadre bow, forty silver-tipped arrows, sixty wooden ones, two daggers, two flintlock pistols, a short sword, four grenades, a file of poison, a knuckle duster, one bandolier, forty feet of silk twine, a long black cloak, and my own detailed floorplan of the temple. Such was the haul, that there were several boxes that I had not even had the time to open. Altogether the bag, which was made from thick heavy canvass, weighed at least sixty pounds.

I struggled under its weight and bulk so much that even getting it out of the university and through the gates was a task in itself. Though my new basement room was not far away, the bag was so heavy that I worried I could not complete the journey without doing myself a serious injury. Also, there was the further complication of the detour that I had to make to avoid Jan's lodgings. I stopped next to a tree by the road and pulled up my collar to keep out the murky fog which hung like a cloak over the city that night. I rubbed my hands together and blew on them, wishing that I had a nice warm coach to take me home.

Well, sometimes in life you have to be careful what you wish for, especially to avoid hard labour, or difficult confrontations, because many moments of indolence and reluctance have led to a fall. And oh, how far we have to fall.

Chapter 20

Pearls before Swine

When the coach that I yearned for *did* materialise out of the fog and pulled up beside me, I could hardly believe my luck. Certain that it was the Professor coming to my aid, I had already half-opened the door and was about to drag my bag aboard, when I heard Adam Weishaupt exclaim with feigned surprise, "*Ah, Herr Drechsler*. Fancy seeing you here. Why don't you join me? I'm sure that we can take you wherever you want to go."

I stood there dumbstruck with the open door in my hand and peered into the compartment. Weishaupt emerged from the darkness like a ghoul rising from a grave and suggested, "Surely, it would be ungentlemanly to turn down a lift from your lecturer, Sebastian."

Though he was on his own, except for his wizened old driver, and I was carrying enough weaponry to slay a whole platoon, I still felt uneasy.

He forced a smile. "Jump aboard, my boy. To show there are no hard feelings. Eh?"

What could I do? Social etiquette prevented me from slamming the door in his face and telling him to go to blazes. After all, as he had said, he was still my lecturer. Feeling the reassuring weight of the bag once more, I took a deep breath and heaved it onto the opposite seat.

He raised an eyebrow when it suspiciously clattered down, but overlooked it and, as I pulled myself on board, he asked, "Where to?"

I may have got into the coach, but I was not stupid enough to reveal my proper address and I called outside to the driver, "Take me to the convent on Donaustrasse."

We set off with a jolt and he regarded me with a baleful smile. "I'm sure that you don't live in a convent, Sebastian. Though it's a shame you don't trust me enough to tell me where you live, at least you'll share a coach with me. So, I think this marks an improvement in our relationship, don't you?" He eased back into the darkness, smirking from ear to ear and condescending, "Now, I know we didn't get off to a good start..."

'You can say that again!' I nearly shouted, but bit my lip and let him carry on.

"I also know that you are somewhat, aware of my situation, as it were, and I yours. But, instead of this being a problem, I think it could lead to a greater sense of understanding between us."

As he said this, he pushed a small box toward me with his shoe. I peered at it for a second before he chuckled and prompted, "Take a look. It won't bite you."

I could barely see his untrustworthy eyes amongst the shadows and, remembering what had happened the last time I opened a box such as this, I leant over to examine the casket more carefully. It was the size of a large brick with an elaborately carved lid and I ran my finger over the intricate patterns.

"Go on, open it," he tempted, "You know you want to."

Not sure what he was up to, but certain that it was not a trap, I gingerly lifted the lid then heard my gasp reverberate around the coach. For inside, lay five luminous pearls softly glowing in the dark. As it dawned on me that I was expected to take this treasure trove, enough to buy my mother and father a huge house and provide me with wealth far beyond the dreams of the most hopeless romantic, I almost fainted. The women, the clothes, the splendour, my own coach. Wait, not one, but two. why not three? C'mon Sebastian. Enjoy yourself. You can afford to. I fell back in the seat with my heart a flutter, prospecting that the life of a gentleman, which I had tasted so briefly at the Professor's castle, could be mine forever. Then it occurred to me that, paradoxically, it would have no Professor in at all. Weishaupt butted into my thoughts, "I'm sure there's enough there for a man of your tastes to have everything you could ever wish for."

"How do you know what I wish for?" I sniped, finally finding my voice.

"I see it in your face, Herr Drechsler. I see it when you look at my coach. I see it when you look at the pearls. And when you look at my maid. You know, you could simply say the word and I could have her sent to your rooms? I'm sure you'd appreciate that. Wouldn't you? I can promise that she would be more than willing to accommodate your every whim. All these things are within your grasp, Herr Drechsler." He tapped the box with his toe and finished, "All you have to do is bend over and take them."

"Why don't you stick your blasted pearls up your evil arse?" Was what I should have said. Alas, to my never-ending shame, I did not and the coach pulled away leaving me with my bag of guns, and bombs, and knives, now all rendered completely useless because I had been bought off by my mortal enemy. Even after he had tried to kill me, and ruin me, and terrorise me, he had been able to shut me up by simply paying for my contrition. I felt every emotion at once; revulsion, joy, rage, sadness, calmness, anxiety - everything from one extreme to the other - to the point where my ideas became a spinning wheel of confusion with me at the hub watching them blur past, baffling me with their polarity.

To add insult to injury, I now had to carry the enormous bag, *and* the box, back to my basement room several streets away. After an exhausting trip, during which I sustained several minor injuries, some of which I'm certain I still suffer today, I finally barged through my front door and almost jumped out of my skin when Bacon greeted me from the shadows, "Good evening, sir."

"What on God's Earth! How the hell did you get in here?"

I could make out his wiry frame sitting on my bed.

"I see that you took the bribe, sir. The Professor told me you would. Well, I suppose that it is academic now. At least Weishaupt thinks that he has bought you off."

I dropped the bag and glanced down at the box under my arm. "How did you know?"

"It is not important how I knew, sir. Call it good timing. I merely saw Weishaupt pick you up and then got here before you. You were, I believe, quite some time with your baggage."

I was not at all happy to find Bacon in my quarters spying on me. Now my secret was out, when all I had wanted to do was be alone with the loot and work out what to do next.

I inquired with some annoyance, "Well, if your master knows all, *sir*, then why has he sent his *servant* and not come himself?"

"To be perfectly honest about the matter, sir, he does not know that I am here. Also, I feel it only fair to tell you that, in reality, I am in fact the former and he the latter, sir, and not the other way round."

I tried to untie his knotted sentence and, releasing the bond, I realised what he was insinuating. This was ridiculous. The man was merely a servant. Van Halestrom was the master and the true heir and guardian of the castle. It was he who had the job and the reputation and the distinctions. How dare the *butler* make such a claim? I went to put the cad in his place, once and for all but, as I did, I recalled the Professor's words, 'Nothing is *ever* what it seems,' and how he had let the servant speak back to him and it slowly dawned on me, 'Could this be true? *As well*?'

It was at that moment, as I stared at Bacon's inscrutable old face half covered in shadow, that I realised it simply must be. In exactly the same way that everything else that I had once believed to be one way was, in fact, the other.

As was becoming my habit, I let out an immense sigh and, preparing myself for the inevitable revelations, I wearily begged, "For goodness sake, man, just tell me the truth."

He took a measured breath and began, "The truth, sir, is that I was once the Professor's mentor and, before that, someone else mentored me. When the Professor's turn comes then another will replace him, and so on. That is the way our system works. And I can tell you, sir, we were offered the bribe too. It is something that happens to us all. In the end." He gave me an oddly good-natured smile then pushed himself off the bed and went to leave.

"But what happens now?" I asked, unsure of my next move.

"Now, sir, I believe we are at the point that the Professor has told you about, where nothing surprises you except what you are prepared to do about it." And, with this last confounding remark, he opened the door, bade me, "Good night, sir," bowed, then left.

Damn the impertinent, unfathomable, unpredictable Bacon and his blasted riddles. Thunder and lightning. This bunch were an infuriating gang of constant liars.

I flopped down on the bed and opened the box, wondering how long it would take Weishaupt's buxom maid to get there. Hell's bells. What was I to do? If I took the pearls and fled, as Weishaupt obviously wanted, wouldn't the Professor or Bacon come after me? What a nightmare that would be. Even if I *was* armed to the teeth with a bag full of military hardware, I still wouldn't fancy my chances against Van Halestrom in his undergarments with his hands tied behind his back. No thank you. Anyway, I would miss him terribly. Inconsolably - and the rest of them. Especially Francesca. The prospect of a life without her was unimaginable. And what would I do? Wander round aimlessly, a member of the idle rich, but one who must always look over his shoulder. And how would I explain it to my parents? My mother would get the truth out of me in a minute and my father even faster than that.

Really, of course, I knew what I should do, or else I wouldn't have been sitting there looking at the pearls in the first place but galloping Petrova to the jewellery quarter in Augsburg to exchange them for good old hard cash right away.

Added to this, was the complexity that, as I understood it, I was seen as Van Halestrom's apprentice and heir. Perhaps I had fantasised about such things, but I had kept those most fanciful notions firmly at the back of my mind. Now, after what Bacon had said, this seemed more like an impending certainty, rather than a distant possibility, especially if I didn't get killed in the meantime. Though the responsibility of this inheritance was so overwhelming that, at that precise moment, I could not even consider it. I closed the box, but not before taking one of the pearls - for my old age you understand. In case I lived that long.

The following morning, I received a letter from my mother who wrote;

'It was so good to see you recently. You know that your father and I both trust you to be good, but that, whatever happens, we will always be proud of you. You are forever in our hearts and minds. Your loving Mother & Father.'

I am not ashamed to say that I cried for some time after reading this. It was profoundly touching to be reminded of the tenderness of my loving and decent parents, especially after all that I had been through recently.

The very next day, I was galloping Petrova through the city's southern gates but, instead of Augsburg, I was headed for Munich. For I had decided to carry out my mission and help my friends thwart the evil Illuminati. And, with these thoughts at the front of my mind, I began to forge a steely resolve to carry on to the next level of understanding, because I knew, deep down inside that, whatever it entailed, it was there that I would find my new self.

Chapter 21

The Eye of Horus

All Hallows' Eve 1784 was a strangely balmy night but, as I hunched behind the parapet on the roof of the Imperial Exchange in the heart of Munich, I could feel the cold hand of fear on my shoulder. Twenty feet below me, lay the Temple of Eleusis and I watched the dignitaries being greeted at the entrance through my crossbow's monoscope. My nerves were as taut as the strings on my bow, as I waited for my Lady Francesca's appearance at eight o'clock sharp along with her new mysterious friend. Despite having no idea who he was, I already despised him enough to punch him in the face - knowing that that face was probably being pushed into her heaving bosom in the back of some expensive carriage even as I thought it. I tried to shake off the disturbing image and concentrated back on my mission. The Professor had said that he would, 'Let me know,' when he was in place at the chancellery, but I could not understand how he was going to perform this miracle as it was well over a mile away.

While I considered this, there was a loud bang in the sky from the direction of the chancellery and I watched a firework brightly fizzle out. I peeped back through the scope as the distant chime of a church clock struck eight and, exactly on time, Francesca appeared in my lens with her new, and extremely diminutive companion in tow.

Good God! The scheme was like the workings of a clock. I realised that they must have done this hundreds of times before, then prayed that they had not when Francesca stuck her lips to the mouth of her tiny cad like a starving leech. Such was the intimacy of their embrace, and the size of the scrawny swine's feathered hat, that I still could not see his face. I told myself that she would never fall for an idiot who would wear such a thing, only to see them clutch each other with even more ardour then wobble unsteadily into the temple. Damn it! The other guests had looked similarly *relaxed* and I wondered if they had all been drinking the same sickly potion with which I had been drugged at the Chapel of Liebfrauenmünster a few months before.

But there was no time for such ponderings. It was time for action. I hoped that my training had prepared me for what was to come and aimed my crossbow at the raised porch on the temple roof then fired an arrow with the silk twine trailing behind it. The bolt found its mark with a resounding thud and I tested the line, giving it a hefty tug, as it had to bear my weight as I slid across to the other side. I had practised a similar rope slide back at the castle, but this would be the first time that I had done it in earnest - on a mission, at night, fifty feet from the ground. I tried not to think about it and to get the better of my vertigo which was erupting inside me like a volcano.

I tied the other end of the twine around a chimney and reloaded the empty stay of my bow, as trained, then slung its strap over my shoulder. After making sure that the rest of my weapons were secure, I took a deep breath, put a loop over the twine, grabbed it with both hands then prepared to do the most foolhardy thing that I had ever done in my life and threw myself off the tallest building in Munich.

I could not have been more pleasantly surprised. Maybe it was because of the intense worry that I had suffered beforehand but, once I got going, I positively enjoyed the brief mid-air ride and slid down towards the temple roof at exactly the right speed with my black cloak fluttering heroically behind me.

What I enjoyed a lot less, was the unmistakable sound of the chimney collapsing over my shoulder. The line suddenly slackened, barely staying tight enough to let me land safely, and I turned around to see the entire chimney stack come crashing down in an immense cloud of rubble and dust.

I watched in silent anguish as the masonry poured down into the street and stupidly put my finger to my lips, as if telling the tumbling stonework to make less noise, because it was very noisy. Very noisy indeed. I cowered down on one knee, certain that the terrible racket would give my presence away and waited for the alarm to be sounded as the last brick came to rest.

To my great relief, none was forthcoming and I hurriedly pulled in the twine, trying to retrieve as much of my stealth as possible. I stashed the line and crept across the roof collecting my bearings. Having been over the temple floor plans a thousand times, I knew exactly where I was going and quickly found the door leading downstairs. Finding it open, I wasn't surprised. Who would expect someone to come in from the roof? I descended the stairs and arrived, as planned, in a corridor running the length of the top floor. The Professor had told me that the dignitaries would retire to individual chambers in the basement to continue imbibing and change into their robes, before attending the main ceremony upstairs which would begin at nine o'clock.

I knew that there was a service ladder at the end of the corridor leading to the cellars where the chambers were located. So, I ran down the hallway and found the door of the shaft then clambered inside. After mounting the ladder, I closed the door and breathed a sigh of relief. So far so good. I had penetrated the lion's den and hadn't had to kill anyone, yet. I climbed down the shaft hoping to find Francesca fast, so I could check to see that nothing untoward was happening to her. Whatever that meant - on this strangest of nights.

I reached the bottom then dismounted the ladder and saw that I was in the corridor running behind the dressing chambers. As I stalked down the passageway, I realised its real purpose when I noticed spy holes drilled through the walls. Some of the holes even had stools under them where I presumed the spying had become so constant that the Peeping Tom needed support.

I put my eye to the nearest hole and -Good Lord!- I got a shock when I did. For inside was a naked young woman straddling a man in a chair and passionately riding him away whilst, rather whimsically, wearing his hat - a bishop's mitre! I pulled my eye away but quickly put it back, thinking, 'lucky old sod,' before realising, with a fright, that my good lady might be up to something similar. I rushed to the next hole and peeped through, then instantly wished that I had not, for two men were having the most strenuous of physical intimacies with each other, which to me was a purely repellent thing to behold so I yanked my eye back. The exuberance of the sexual acts certainly seemed to prove my theory that the guests were drugged. The Professor had explained that this Dionysian celebration used alcohol and other intoxicating substances to heighten the level of pleasure and excess, signifying Persephone's unholy descent into the underworld.

Two hoots to Persephone! I wondered if I actually wanted to see what was going on in the next room. My decision was made by the sound of voices coming around the corner, so I ran back to the ladder and climbed up into the shadows as two men passed right under my feet. There was some dirty laughter as they spied through the holes themselves and my jealous mind sprang into action, producing a vivid scene of intense sexual paranoia that only one's conscious can create. The perverts stayed there sniggering and muttering for at least half an hour until, eventually, I feared that I must go back upstairs as the time was fast approaching for the ceremony to begin.

I hung in the dark for a few more agonising minutes before reluctantly scaling back up the ladder, furious with myself for failing in my mission to keep watch over Francesca. Trying hard not to imagine what she might be up to, I closed the door of the shaft then tiptoed back along the corridor to the end where I skulked behind a column above the central staircase.

Below me stood a solitary sentinel guarding the archway leading to the balcony which ran all the way around the central hall. I did not want to do away with him unless absolutely necessary, so I waited a further five minutes trying to avoid the grisly act. But, when a tremendous booming gong announced the start of the ceremony, and the idiot had still not moved, I unsheathed a dagger from my bandolier and prepared to do what I had been trained to for so long.

I took a deep breath, held out the blade and took three ninja-like steps towards him but, when I got two paces away, the bastard casually strolled off. I turned tail and flew back behind the column like a startled pheasant with my heart pounding louder than the blasted gong. After a moment, I peered round the column and the guard was nowhere to be seen, so, after one more glance up and down to check that the coast was clear, I replaced the dagger and dashed through the archway.

The balcony was exactly as I had pictured, overlooking the domed hall which was steadily filling with cultists. What I had not pictured was a large capless pyramid standing in the middle of the room, exactly like the one on the Professor's medallion but almost as high as the balcony. I stooped down and sneaked along behind the balustrade, until directly above the pyramid's open head then peeped between the stone pillars. The last of the cultists filed into the room all wearing their identical hooded robes and I suddenly realised, 'How the devil am I going to see my lady when she's dressed in the same fashion?'

I found out instantly and almost swallowed my tongue when she came out of the shadows at the back of the hall supported by two red-robed sentinels with her head swaying as if in a trance. Now, for the first time, I properly saw Francesca all at once because, apart from her groin which was covered in a skimpy piece of black material forming a 'V,' she was completely naked.

I say this now, but despite my overwhelming fear at that moment, I could not help thinking how incredibly beautiful she was. Indeed, more beautiful than anything I had ever seen. I gasped at her gorgeousness before bringing myself under control.

I wondered why they had afforded her the dignity of letting her wear this smallest of garments and not placed the same terrible bag on her head as her poor sister. My question was promptly answered - they didn't, and one of the sentinels pulled a black bag over her head. She swayed languidly as he tightened the drawstring, convincing me that she had been drugged for, if not, she would have kicked him in his potted potatoes so hard that he could have eaten them mashed for his supper. The sentinels pushed her through the crowd towards the base of the pyramid where another figure had appeared. I recognised his golden robes and arrogant striding posture straight away. It was Adam Weishaupt and one of the sentinels forced Francesca to kneel at his feet as a silence fell round the hall.

He raised his arms and called out at the top of his voice, "Tonight my Brothers, for we are all brothers on this mystic eve, we have come together to celebrate our spirits' return to the underworld for the winter! Though, this is not a time of decline or death for us. For death becomes our life, as night turns into day, as darkness is illuminated by light, and order follows chaos. Tonight, we shall perform the Eleusinian mystery and its power will be passed down through all levels of our brotherhood, from the ultimate one, our celestial master, to us, the bearers of his light. Now prepare to behold his awesome and eternal majesty!"

What the blazes did that mean? I was half-inclined to leave right then having such little wish to find out but my sense of duty, and the fact that I was absolutely scared rigid, kept me exactly where I was. Droning incantations began with the emergence of four Kabbalist priests who were all wearing jewelled breastplates.

Somehow, I thought their necklaces should've had twelve gems, not nine. But God knows why? This was not the time to remember.

The shamans took up their positions at the four corners of the pyramid, swinging bowls of smoking incense around their feet. Then came the next terrible shock. Twenty paces behind Francesca appeared the devil with the purple cushion and, already on it, the curved knife. I rolled onto my side, swung the crossbow off my back and took aim down the monoscope at the cluster of men surrounding her then got ready to take the head off the first son of a bitch who lifted a finger.

What in hell's name was I going to do now? The situation was desperate and getting worse by the second. I had thirty arrows in my quiver and there were at least two-hundred deviant lunatics downstairs, all capable of murdering the woman of my dreams and, occasionally, my nightmares. One thing was certain, I would have wagered the box of pearls back in my room that she was in no fit state to run away, or do anything else for that matter, as she knelt helplessly swaying form side to side in front of Weishaupt.

My mouth became dry and my trigger finger started to sweat as I took up the tension in the bow. Making things even worse, Weishaupt was becoming increasingly shrouded in the smoke from the priests' ceremonial urns and I almost lost sight of the cushion in the swirling fumes. *[20]

---

20. Kabbalist Priests' Breastplates. Kabbalah is an arcane form of mysticism of unknown origin which has many different interpretations, some of them quite peculiar, though this ceremony would have been unusual to say the least. According to ancient tradition, these priests would have worn ornate robes and breastplates decorated with twelve precious stones, representing the twelve tribes of the Old Testament. Interestingly, when Satan was banished from Heaven, it is said that he was also given similar gems but, tellingly, only nine. Kabbalah speaks of nine spheres, or dimensions, existing in the universe and some terrifying prophecies eudure as to what is contained within these.

He called out to the top of the pyramid, his voice barely audible over the priests' climaxing chants, "Come to us, Oh Holiest of Ones! Come to dine with us, and feast on those who have stood in our way! Oh glorious Horus, I exhort thee, create yourself for us now!" Despite all this ludicrous mumbo jumbo, I was astonished when the pyramid shuddered so violently that the first few rows of the congregation all took a step back.

"What is this energy?" I murmured, for the vibrations were so powerful that I found it impossible to concentrate on my target and, for a split second, I took my eye off the lens. As I did, I saw a mysterious spark burst into life over the pyramid. I tried to ignore it and focus back on the knife, but its brightness amid the darkenend room forced me to look again and I witnessed the small point of light become a furious spitting ball of fire which glowed incandescently under my line of sight.

Weishaupt's voice echoed from below, "Oh mystic night we hail thee! Come to us and show us thy glorious illumination!"

As this oath ended, another intense rumble emanated from the pyramid, accompanied by an unearthly crackling noise. The glowing ball magnified further still and rapidly became too bright to ignore. Such was its power, that I knew that no one in the hall would be able to look at anything else and, in one awful moment, the ball metamorphosed into a monstrous blazing eye.

Unable to believe what I was seeing, I gawped as the dreadful apparition blinked to reveal a huge iris which gazed down upon the startled crowd, bathing them in a terrifying white light. The cultists gasped deeply at this sight, which was Hell itself right there in the room. and I envied Francesca who could not see it, because the second that I did I knew that I would never be able to forget it again. My body shook, my teeth chattered and my hair truly stood on end in that horrid moment that I first beheld The Eye of Horus!

I was so shocked that I had pushed myself against the wall at the back of the balcony with my crossbow in my lap and my trembling hands over my face. Who would have behaved in any other way after seeing that, I do not know? But if they claimed that they would have acted any differently then they are a liar.

Weishaupt beseeched again, calling out amongst the smoke and blinding light, "You have come for the flesh that is your tribute Oh Mighty One! We are moments away from that instant!"

There was a slight pause while the dastardly eye blinked again and then - Holy Mother of Christ! - the thing actually spoke.

"Bring her to me!" It cackled, or at least that's what I thought it said. It was strangely muffled and I wondered whether there was a problem with the entity's voice. That was when I thought, as it hovered below me, 'You odious shit! Coming all this way for my beautiful Francesca then you get here and start shouting.'

My dislike for the phantasm was growing, no doubt helped by the fact that it was not staring directly at me, for, had it been, I would probably have run all the way home. Though nearly blinded by the light, I pointed the bow between the pillars and the cushion fell back into my sights. Weishaupt must have been waiting for the moment that the bombs were set to go off at the chancellery and I sensed that it was only seconds away as I heard him order, "Prepare the girl!" and another rumble shook through the hall.

'Christ make these arrows fly true,' I prayed and nearly screamed as Francesca's head was pulled back to reveal her long neck. I knew that it was time for action when the man who was to complete the murder picked up the knife. I waited for him to raise the blade above his head. That was close enough and I pulled the trigger. The arrow tore off and hit him in the face, ending him right there and then. And he was the first that I ever killed.

Of course, he did not know what had hit him. Neither did any of his friends. The room was so smokey downstairs that it must have been impossible to tell what was going on. He flailed backwards into the startled audience and dropped the knife, sending it rattling across the floor.

"Find that you bastards!" I cursed as the idiots ran round constantly having to adjust their hoods to see what they were doing. But out of the corner of my eye, I noticed one cultist who could see exactly what he was doing. For he had removed his hood to show off his bright orange hair again, but this time he was only two feet away. Good God! It was Jan Kohler insanely smiling down on me.

"Sorry, old chum," he said in a chillingly conversational tone and stabbed me with his rapier, then pulled a face that I had only seen once before when he was beating up a smaller boy at school. But, by a million to one chance, his blade deflected off the dagger in my bandolier and pronged into the floor. I kicked him in the balls for that. He wasn't playing anymore, so neither was I. He howled in pain and clutched his testicles but fell on my chest and knocked the wind out of me. I tried to push him off but he managed to get his hands around my throat and started to strangle me. His straining face lit up in the dazzling, crackling light as he gasped, "You're out of your depth, college boy! You should have come with us when you had the chance. They will win in the end. They're too powerful to resist!"

His big hands tightened round my neck as though the power he spoke of was in his very fists. He was still as heavy as an ox and I felt he was going to win as he had done when we were boys. He punched me in the face then pinned my arm down with his knee and picked up his rapier. My position was hopeless. Surely I was going to die. Killed by my oldest friend, I began to weep as he lifted up his blade.

'Thud!' A silver-tipped arrow shot into his forehead, forcing his eyes to bulge open wide and a fountain of blood to splatter from his brains. Though shocked beyond belief, I was suddenly overcome with the great power that a mother possesses when its child is in peril. I pulled myself from under his writhing body and hoisted him onto his feet, then leant him against the balustrade. I looked into his dying eyes one last time and said, "Goodbye, old friend," then, shielding my face from the burning light beneath me, I released my grip. It was half instinct, half horror that made me let go, and Jan tumbled from the balcony. I had not meant to do it. It simply happened that way. I watched him fall into the blazing eye and, with an enormous explosion of ectoplasm and a mighty thunderclap, the apparition disappeared.

I took a deep breath and instantly coughed up the obnoxious gases filling my lungs. Looking down amongst the bedlam caused by the explosion, I saw Francesca still kneeling in the same place and I glanced across the hall to the shadows from where the arrow had come. Van Halestrom! It must have been. There was no sign of Jan's body below me and I shook my head in wonder. Though wondering was not the thing to do at that moment and I knew it. It was time to fight. I picked up the bow and, sticking a finger up at my fear of heights, spectacularly gate-vaulted the balustrade. I smacked into the side of the pyramid then slid to the floor and jumped up with my bow at the ready.

Weishaupt was nowhere to be seen amongst the raving cultists, who were all charging about like headless chickens in the alarm. But one of them, much cooler than the others, had somehow found the knife and was creeping up behind Francesca. He spotted me and charged over, thrusting out the blade, but he did not stand a chance. Now that I had killed once, I was thoroughly prepared to do it again. I almost cut the fool in half with my three remaining bolts and he fell to the floor in a mangled heap.

Looking about, it seemed that he was the only one putting up a fight, so I quickly put down the bow and took off my cloak to cover Francesca then pulled myself close, whispering softly in her ear, "It's me, my lady, Sebastian."

There was a vacant murmur from inside the bag but, as I tried to remove it, I felt a tap on my shoulder and whipped my head round to see another, much smaller, hooded devil standing over me imperiously resting his hand on his hip. I sprang to my feet as the idiot tried to foppishly slap me with the back of his hand, but I dodged him and punched him right between his slits. He reeled backwards and I went to punch him again but, before I could, his hood was whipped off from behind. Well I knew *this* man! His face was on half the statues in town. It was Joseph II Emperor of the entire blasted Holy Roman Empire with Professor Van Halestrom standing behind him holding his hood and yelling "Not in the face! Not in the face! He's got to have his portrait painted next week!"

I pulled back in disbelief as Van Halestrom, resplendent in black cloak, tricorn hat and neckerchief, supported the regent's fall and, in a swift manoeuvre belying his years, swept the tiny unconscious man onto his shoulders and proceeded to carry him like a butcher lifting a slaughtered pig. "Good work, Sebastian!" he cried, "Now get Francesca and follow me."

I immediately obeyed and pulled her up along with my bow then removed her bag. My heart flew when she squinted at me and slurred, "Junge-Kinda?" and I clutched her round the waist and guided her through the surrounding pandemonium. The Brother's tiny slits were not helping matters and they kept running into each other as they tried to escape the smokey hall. It seemed that the sight of the Devil appearing then blowing up in front of them was enough to make even the most unrepentant Luciferian run around screaming in delirium.

We weaved through the mayhem as another sentinel approached looking suspiciously between our human cargoes. He unwisely went to stop us and the Professor let him have it with a one-handed shot from his hip, 'Zut!' Because of the short range, the silver-tipped bolt almost cleaved the bastard's head in two and flashed out the other side with a blast of crimson matter. I hissed, "Happy All Hallows' Eve to you too, you bastard! That'll teach you to go round raising Lucifer, won't it?" and spat on him as we ran past to prove a point.

In the general panic, everyone was making their way to the front of the temple, but I knew that there was another way out at the side. I gestured at Van Halestrom to follow me and led us through a door into a large empty room which reverberated to the sound of our hurrying footsteps. From here we fell into an outer corridor, at the end of which we came up to a door that I knew led into a side street.

I tried to open it, but this one was locked as I had expected and I turned to the Professor not knowing what to do. He nodded and, still carrying the little Emperor across his back, managed to produced a short blunderbuss from under his cloak no bigger than a baby's arm. I flung my bow's strap over my shoulder and he tossed me the gun. Putting myself in front of Francesca to protect her from the blast, I fired at the door from point-blank range. 'Boom!' An explosion of splinters rained down on us and I raised my head to see the door half destroyed and the lock blown to pieces. I finished it off with a well-placed kick and led us outside to an iron fence. Luckily, we were only a few streets away from the alley where I had left Petrova. I gave her a little whistle and, within seconds, my faithful beauty appeared round the corner and came to stand by the railings. This made our next task much easier, because it allowed Francesca to be placed on top of her while I sat astride the fence. Then with the Emperor -

of all people - we did the same, until I finally had them both laid across the saddle. I could hear the fierce calls and running boots of the magistrates from the front of the temple, but fortunately there was no one down our side of the building. I thanked my lucky stars for this, as it sounded like there was a sizeable riot going on between the hordes of startled cultists and the arriving forces of the law. I turned Petrova in the other direction and nodded to Van Halestrom who pulled himself up on the railing.

He glanced towards the ensuing commotion and murmured, "I must help them. I will see you in an hour at the meeting place."

He pulled up his neckerchief and jumped down from the fence, warning me, "Stay in the shadows my friend!" and, heeding his own advice, disappeared into the darkness. I led Petrova away as the shouts and the cries faded behind us and we found some secluded lanes to walk through to our prearranged destination, a deserted square on the outskirts of the city. I waited nervously in the gloom for an hour or so until, as promised, the Professor reappeared along with Klaus in a small cart. We placed Francesca and the Emperor onboard, tied Petrova behind and, at last, made our way out of the city. Sticking to the back streets, we saw not a soul and were soon rattling through the countryside.

Amazingly, throughout all this our charges had not stirred once despite being bundled about like two sacks of corn. Francesca was still in a trance and, every now and then, giggled, "No. I don't want anymore." Whatever *that* meant? I dreaded to think and hoped that she might not remember. The Emperor, and I constantly had to keep reminding myself of that - the Emperor of Holy Rome was in the back of our cart - and still resolutely unconscious.

"I didn't hit him that hard," I tutted and concluded that our mighty regent was either a milksop, or had drunk as much of the poisonous grog as rambling Francesca.

It had been convenient that they both slept before while we needed them to be quiet but now, as we swept along, I wished for her to wake up urgently so that I could point out how truly heroic I had been. I asked Van Halestrom if he had any smelling salts, but he said that he had not and gave me a wry smile knowing what I was about. He was right of course. I did not give a fig about that pathetic Joseph, but that woman I wanted to wake up right there and then and so much that it hurt.

"There will be time for that later," reassured the Professor and cleverly changed the subject, explaining how, with Klaus's help, he had foiled the plot to blow up the chancellery by catching the conspirators in the act, and quickly enough to come to my aid at the temple, with the shot that saved my life, and ended Jan's.

I had to fight back the tears when he asked me to forgive him for slaying my best friend. Even though he had tried to kill me, Jan's death was a terrible blow and, along with the shock of the night's other events, I soon found myself gabbling senselessly beside my comrades, "I can't believe Jan is gone... and Lucifer... He is real. You saw him *too*, Professor. The evil eye appearing above the pyramid. God help us all."

To my astonishment, he stoically replied, "Yes Jan is gone, Sebastian, but as far as the Devil's concerned, I believe that tonight we have witnessed a display of 'Deus ex machina,' as the Greek playwrights called it: The use of machinery to put the gods upon the stage. I suspect this performance was the work of a master illusionist, employed to achieve much the same effect."

"Master illusionist!" I cried, confounded by his scepticism.

He raised a finger to keep me in check and carried on, "I believe the dramatic light, explosions and crackling noise were produced by a mixture of phosphorous and gunpowder. That's what you noticed when Jan fell from the balcony."

He nodded at my coat, suggesting, "Smell your clothes, Sebastian. Is it not the scent of hunting?" I gave my sleeve a sniff. Though I recognised the odour of gunpowder, I had fired the blunderbuss at the door, so I was still unconvinced. But before I could argue, he said, "And the *evil eye*, as you put it, was not sent from hell, but made by a man, and the laughable voice from inside the pyramid belonged to a human, not a devil. Remember, Sebastian, mindless religion has done much of Weishaupt's hard work already. People's willful ignorance and superstition, will always led to their suffering and manipulation - whoever they are. This is precisely the same fear that the master illusionist employs to achieve control, even over his own cult. Though I feel it would be fair to say that tonight's performance did not go entirely according to plan. Especially after our interventions, eh?" He winked and went on, "After all, do you honestly think *Lucifer* would be sent back to hell by a single body falling into *His* aura like that? Think about it. It makes no sense at all."

Unable to control my peevish bluster any longer, I finally managed to interject, "But, sir, tell me then, what about my dream? You said it yourself, you had the same one. Remember? We both saw the eye at the top of the pyramid. You told me that it was 'Lucifer himself.'"

"In the end, my lad, a dream is only a dream and originates from the same collective consciousness that produces all dreams. As far as the Devil goes, I'm sure the Illuminati believe that *He* is real. I just don't share their opinion, that's all."

This was insufferable and once again I went to argue my case, "But surely, sir, it was the blackest of magic. Right there in front of us. You saw it too."

"Ah, but what is magic, Sebastian? It's not a burning bush, or a statue of Christ weeping blood. Or a visit from an angel, or a ghost, or even the Devil. But the simple and everyday, the movement of a bat at night, the birth of a child, the earth-shattering power of nature." He smiled hopefully and finished, "Even the depth of feelings we have for others. Eh?"

I glanced at Francesca, knowing what he was insinuating and turned back to find him ruefuly chuckling to himself. At that moment, in my youthful ignorance and armed, as I was back then, with a fertile imagination, I was convinced that I had fought the very beast from Hell and sent him back from whence he came. Thus, I was thoroughly unprepared to have the wind taken out of my sails by theories of make-believe devils, blasted phosphorous and collective consciousness - whatever *that* was?

Of course, in time, I realised that Van Halestrom was right and that I had not seen the dark secrets of the world revealed, but in the heat of battle, and perhaps because of my Christian upbringing, I had been deceived into believing that what I'd thought I'd seen was real. Though, one way or another, it could not be denied that it was still an extraordinary night and, once again, I could not help but think that somehow God had been protecting me. I bit my lip in pain-filled anguish and prayed that He would also protect Jan's soul when it came to Heaven.

After a long six hour journey, throughout which we never once stopped talking of our nights' adventures, we eventually reached Frau Hoffmeister's in the early morning. The stable lad haloed up ahead as we rolled by and the old lady was waiting for us at the farmhouse door when we pulled up outside.

Despite all the night's extraordinary revelations, the peck on the cheek which I received from Francesca who was pretty much herself by then, was the most magical of all. I grinned with pure delight when she wished me, "Goodnight, sir," with a sincere but saucy smile as Frau Hoffmeister escorted her inside and the Professor and Klaus followed behind, pushing the disorientated Emperor before them.

I was still finding it hard to believe that this frail little man was our Lord and Sovereign. Maybe because Klaus had put a sack over his head, which led poor Joseph, who was obviously still slightly groggy, to bang his head on the door as he went in. I laughed and sniffed the wet autumn air then let out a deep and most lengthy sigh.

"That was a day and a half," I reckoned, if not in actual time, then certainly in what had been achieved. As this notion sank in, I made my way inside too and was soon enjoying a deep and very restful sleep and, happily, having not one bad dream at all.
[*21.]

---

21. Joseph II, Holy Roman Emperor & The Bavarian Illuminati 1784. S. Drechsler's seemingly outlandish claims to have seen a pyramid at this ritual are given credence by the existence of an almost identical structure at the Staatspark Hanau estate in Wilhelmsbad in northern Germany, which E book readers can see here. Coincidentally, this was the location for several meetings of the Bavarian Illuminati and the Freemasons (see footnote 19). While there is no official record of a plot to destroy the Bavarian chancellery, or proof that Emperor Joseph had sought Illuminati membership, there is every chance that they both may have happened. Joseph, very small and frail, historically known as one of the 'Enlightened Despots,' and also the brother of Marie Antoinette, was definitely (though secretly) a Freemason, belonging to a lodge called *Zur neugekronten Hoffnung* (New Crowned Hope), and a member of 'many other' secret societies at that time. Interestingly, before this point, he had dealt favourably with Weishaupt's organisation but, as S. Drechsler's account may explain, at the end of 1784 his relationship with the Illuminati definitely deteriorated. As the memoirs suggest, any other stance may have posed him insurmountable political problems. The Old Town Hall in Munich, which I believe is the building S. Drechsler is refering to here, was abandoned by the government exactly one hundred years later. Historical examples of the destruction of buildings for political ends include, as the text mentions, Guy Fawkes' failed attempt to destroy the Houses of Parliment in 1605 and also, the more successful, torching of the Reichstag by the Nazis in 1933.

Chapter 22

Celebrations and Frustrations

A few days later, Van Halestrom, Lady Francesca, Bacon, Klaus and I, stood round the banqueting table in the Castle Landfried, joyfully bringing our glasses together and toasting as one, "To our great success! Hip, hip hurrah!"

There was much handshaking and backslapping and general celebration and the Professor took time to separately thank each one of us. Next, we eagerly took our places to enjoy the stupendous feast which lay before us and, after copiously dining, relaxed round a blazing fire in the adjacent music room.

While the Professor and Klaus discussed something called '*evolution*,' and Bacon sat in the corner quietly quaffing the remaining champagne, Francesca and I, after much steady flirtatiousness from us both, at last, came together for our first real intimate conversation.

Her beautiful eyes twinkled in the candlelight as she spoke, "I am truly thankful to you, Sebastian Drechsler. You know that, don't you? And no jokes, or tricks, or fingers crossed behind my back."

She pulled out two crossed fingers from behind her back and giggled as she undid them to show that she was teasing. It worked of course, but then everything she did worked to increase my romantic feelings for her. I smiled back, happy to share this natural moment where we could behave like normal folk.

"Tonight you are more beautiful than I have ever seen you before," I said, admiring her refined yet haughty features and her gorgeous hair, which trailed over her pale white shoulders.

"What? Even more beautiful than at the temple?" she joked, provoking me further with a seductive grin.

"Yes more, because tonight you are yourself, and that is the person that I have always wanted to meet. And now that I have met you, you are more beautiful than I ever could have dreamt."

Her demeanour changed to one of sincerity. "You really are charming, aren't you?" She tried to smile, but her lip quivered and in her eye appeared a tiny tear.

I read her mind and ventured, "I'm so sorry about your sister."

She resolutely stuck out her chin and sighed, "It seems that we have both suffered a loss recently. Though, in my case, I had expected it for a long time. It was a course Montarese had chosen for herself many, many years ago. She had become very unhappy. We were separated as children when my mother ran away from our father and took Montarese with her. I had only recently met her again. Although sadly, we were never close, it made it worse to know her, if only for a little while, before she died." She sniffed away her tear and perked up, asking, "But enough of these sadnesses. How are your studies going? The Professor tells me you're an excellent student of everything you attempt and quick to learn at *most* things." She chuckled and beamed her fabulous smile. "But, from what I've seen, it seems you know a great deal already. Which I like a lot."

And how I liked this? Of all the nights of good pleasure at the castle, this was one of the best. The stunning Lady Francesca, for she *was* a real lady, from Russian nobility no less, but educated in France, talked with me for a whole hour as we chatted happily between ourselves. We joked and laughed, even touching sometimes like courting couples do, and in the most pleasing of ways. It was exactly what I had wished for since the very first day that we had met.

She explained that Jan had been seduced by Weishaupt's agents, who had met him through the moneychangers where he worked, and that it was he who had followed me home the night when I had sensed someone behind me on the road from Stuttgart. That was why she had been sent to gain his confidences at the Chapel of Liebfrauenmünster. But she had lost him in the orgy and her sister, who was under the Illuminati's influence, had lured him into performing the carnal act. On hearing this, I felt sure that it was him who had left the note on my dresser to scare me away so that we would not end up having to fight. After all, he was my oldest friend.

With these intricacies explained, I felt as though a great weight had been lifted from me and, after the pain of a friendship lost, found great happiness in the thought of a new and, hopefully, much deeper one beginning.

After a while, Klaus played the harpsichord and the two of us danced with such merriment that we encouraged the Professor to join us. There was much joy and laughter as my eyes constantly met with her's, both of us exploring each other's real thoughts, which were obviously those of tenderness, as we all joked and sang into the smallest hours of the night.

The next morning, after descending from our lonely rooms, I was once again by her side. While I escorted her to breakfast, she asked, "Are you always up this early, dear sir?"

"There was nothing else to do after dreaming of you all night, but to be with you in the morning to see if my dream was real."

Feeling the moment was right, I stopped her and placed my arm around her waist. She smiled at me with perfect truth, fully reflecting the care that I felt for her, and we kissed for the very first time. And it was a kiss that I shall never forget. Not too fast, not too slow, her wet lips slid provocatively over mine as I heard her eagerly inhale. My heart beat like a savages' drum and I pulled her neck towards me as her young bosom heaved against my manly chest. Feeling my hand start to...

"That's quite enough of that you two," called the Professor, ruining the moment and striding past with his regular grin. "Especially before breakfast. Come on. Bacon has a message for us."

We parted from each other and laughed again before sharing another moment of tender embrace, then quickly followed after him. In the dining room we found Bacon who did indeed have a message for us which had only been delivered half an hour before. He coughed portentously before reading it out and, though the message contained the best possible news, such was his style of oratory, that this was a soliloquy of such utter tedium that its repetition now would sully the pages of this fine manuscript. So, for the sake of the story, and you my dear reader, this is basically what it said - We had succeeded in exposing the Illuminati to the authorities who were now preparing to ban membership of the society altogether and to exile some of it's most important and high-ranking members.

We howled with approval and congratulated one another deeply. It would not have happened without our efforts and the clever extrication, then quick restoration, of our pathetic Emperor Joseph to his throne, after a damn good telling off behind the scenes, leaving him in a position strong enough to let his more reasoned state officials clear out the nest of vipers altogether. Court rumour had it, that the little idiot was being coerced by the Order to drag Bavaria into another unnecessary war with Austria, so we had possibly saved the lives of thousands in the process and, perhaps, even the country too.

"Hurrah!" I cried at the top of my voice, only to have my hearty bonfire promptly flushed away by a huge bucket of horse's piss. For the lofty Bacon had, in fact, received *two* messages, the latter of which informed us that Lady Francesca would have to leave that very day for Russia to see her father, a Grand Duke, because there was business there of 'great importance.'

Not now! Not now! I stewed inside, fighting the urge to bang my fists on the table like a spoilt child. Not when everything had been finally resolved. Surely, this was the time for us to go walking in the forest and to kick leaves over one another and to spend long evenings together in front of the fire like young lovers do. The business was of such insufferable importance that she could not delay her journey one moment. And so, to my utter blood-churning annoyance, the woman was disappearing yet again before we could do what we both had obviously been thinking of the previous night. I was not a virgin. I was a man and more aware of it than at any other time in my life. So to see Francesca wave goodbye from the coach window as she left through the castle gates that day, was the epitome of frustration for me, as she was the person to whom I wished to show all my bottled-up manly ambition.

"She'll be back soon," persuaded the Professor, putting his arm around my shoulder and walking me up the stairs to the castle's keep. I got over my lady's absence with a lengthy session of target practice on the quadre bow, ruthlessly destroying several targets and, two days later, I was walking through the university gates with my head held high - a young man with a lot to look forward to. Oh, and how right I was to think such a thing. How right indeed.

Things were easier at university then because, after our daring exploits at the Temple of Eleusis, Weishaupt never taught me again. One freezing cold day in December, I saw him arrive at the university in his coach. He had supposedly come there for a dressing down by the principal, Herr Vacchieri, because of the ongoing investigation of the Illuminati. But this man had been given the job by Weishaupt's Godfather, way back when he was university director so, it came as no surprise that The Doctor only received a slap on the wrist from the university board.

Though, I was shocked to discover, at a later date, (Sweet Jesus - were they *all* at it?) Vacchieri was Illuminati too! *[22.]

There were no other missions planned so, for once, I could focus properly on my education, with only the thought of that gorgeous woman taking my mind off my studies. I still kept up with my training at the castle and received an excellent Christmas gift from the Professor, who told me that he had invented the thing himself.

I lugged the huge package, almost the size of a coffin lid and wrapped up in a blanket, all the way back to Tuffengarten where I was to spend the holiday with my folks. Van Halestrom had told me that I was only to unwrap the surprise on the day of Christmas Eve, as he was a stickler for this tradition. And some surprise it was. I could not work out what it was at first, even when I had taken off the blanket. My father and I stood looking at it for half an hour before he suggested, "Are you meant to get *aboard* it?"

Whereupon, he was correct. The thin, tapered plank was a vehicle, a 'board' to ride down a hillside covered with snow. It had a curved end at the front and straps with which to tie it to your feet. The machine was incredible, at least, when I finally mastered its control and the best way of directing it through the snow which lay in abundance that Christmas of 1784.

---

22. The Illuminati & Ingolstadt University. Herr Vacchieri is mentioned in a book called '*Little Tools of Knowledge*' (2001) by P. Becker and W.Clark (pages 104-134) and seemed to occupy a role at the university similar to that of a 'school inspector,' though I can find no proof that he was a member of the Illuminati. S. Drechsler also mentions Adam Weishaupt's Godfather, though not by name. Johann Adam von Ickstatt was the Curator of Ingolstadt University up until 1778 and probably instrumental in getting Weishaupt his job. There also seems to be doubt about his membership of the Illuminati though it is hard to believe that he did not know, somehow, about the details of his godson's organisation.

I could, after a while, attain great speed and also carve out long turns in the thick banks of snow, scattering the powdered flakes in waves of shimmering iridescent particles. Even my father was impressed, though did not try it himself as he was worried he would cause himself great personal injury, but commented that, "This Professor of yours is a remarkable talent." Finding it easier to complement a man who was hundreds of miles away, rather than his own son who was standing right there beside him. He was right though, it was pure genius and such a simple craft in all its technologies. That's what real genius is, as Van Halestrom used to say, 'Genius is not complexity mused, but simplicity used.'

My father described it, "As revolutionary as Thomas Paine," and, like all revolutions, it was conspicuous. I was soon spotted by some locals as I flew about on the slopes and once slid by them with a happy, "How d' do," while they toiled in the same direction on an old cart, making little headway themselves and eyeing the board with extreme suspicion. Then, a few days later, I heard at the local tavern that some of the more backward regulars had proclaimed it 'Black Magic!' and gossiped that, 'it must be dark forces that make the thing travel so well.' But only fifty years before the Tuffengarten 'locals' had burnt an old woman to death for being a witch in the village square because she had cured someone of the sickness brought on by a bee sting. So I guess that it was hardly surprising.

Of course, this time of year also brought back memories of Jan. Though it was still hard for me to come to terms with what had happened, I tried to remember him as well as I could, and often reminisced about the happy times that we had spent together at Christmas as boys. His family had left the village some years ago so, at least, there were no awkward confrontations for me to endure.

The New Year came and went, and I waited for news of Francesca, which eventually came in February and I burst into life when 'Lord' Bacon, as I was jokingly referring to him, confided with me in the castle's drawing room, "She will be back this month, sir. I believe that you have a mission of some importance to complete with her and that the Professor will tell you about it soon."

And so it was. My following meeting with the Professor was to mark the beginning of the next chapter of my incredible tale in which, like Persephone, I was to descend into a mysterious underworld where my life was to take a series of bizarre twists and shadowy turns, each more extraordinary than the last and, every one, more terrifying and daunting than anything that I ever could have imagined.

Chapter 23

The Eyes Have It

The snow piled deep on Professor Van Halestrom's windowsill as I stared from his office over Ingolstadt's icy roofs on that cold February morning in 1785. My heart was in a flight of fancy because of my up-and-coming rendezvous with Lady Francesca and I gazed into the distant clouds wondering exactly where in the world she might be.

"Drink, Sebastian?" offered the Professor, bringing me out of my longings and passing me a goblet of steaming mulled wine, before encouraging the coals in the fireplace then making himself comfortable back in his chair.

"Well, my lad, looks like you're off to meet her. Let's hope you make a better job of it than your last game."

I glanced over at the chessboard, where many white pieces surrounded a lonely black King and considered, with some annoyance, the way he had hummed to himself, 'I knew you were going to do that,' after every move that I had made.

"Yes, Herr Professor. As always, after my visits with you, I'm inclined to work on my ability to conceal my thoughts."

"Good thinking, lad. Always an excellent technique to have mastered, particularly when it comes to matters concerning the fairer sex." He mused philosophically, "I'm sure if women were able to conceive the central thought that men held about them then they would be compelled to run away screaming and never come back again."

I wondered, as I had done on many occasions, about the absence of amy woman in the Professor's life. Seeing as he had told me about so many other things, I felt it strange that he had never mentioned this subject which was of some significance.

But I did not pry and left those matters for another time. Anyway, I was on the very edge of my seat, waiting to hear of my next meeting with Francesca. So my heart filled with glee when Van Halestrom finally confirmed, "You're going to meet her in a little place called Pettendorf, just over the border in Regensburg. There she will give you a set of papers which you will return to me. These documents contain details of the plot to overthrow the Russian Empire, and others too, toppling them one on another like dominoes, so the Illuminati can control the outcome of the tumultuous epoch."

'Typical,' I thought. 'Nothing's ever trivial is it? Not with this band of brigands. They never went to rob the postmaster or the greengrocers.' They certainly had a sense of grandeur. You could not take that away from them and I asked, with some exasperation, "How can this possibly be achieved?"

"There are many ways to start a revolution, Sebastian. We will have to wait and see. But in the end, all profound change has the same origin. Remember how Weishaupt tried to put you off balance, to destabilise you? First one way - then the other? *This* is the very essence of *ordo ab chao*. From chaos comes order and I believe that, on a much larger scale, the same principle will be used to overthrow Russia."

I tried to grasp his point, as I had many times before. The way that he put it, it sounded so simple, but what did he really mean?

He saw my confusion and, as usual, attempted to enlighten me. "Try to realise that what is effective on a personal level can be just as powerful on the larger world. To attain the next level of understanding, Sebastian, you must realise that the microcosm - is not *like* the macrocosm - but it *is* the macrocosm."

Expecting him to elaborate at this point, I was further mystified when he merely wiggled his nose and regarded me with an esoteric look in his eye.

While I wrestled with this concept, his clerk burst in speaking so rapidly that I could hardly understand a word that he said. "He's going now. It's happening this very moment. He's been given his marching orders by Herr Vacchieri, with all that '*I don't want to but I have to*' rubbish. The viper has been told he must clear his things out immediately. You must hurry if you want to see him go."

Before I realised what was going on, Van Halestrom leapt from his chair, urging me, "Come on, my lad. We must see this."

We ran up the corridor towards Weishaupt's chambers where, upon reaching the corner, we disguised our haste to a stroll and emerged at exactly the right time to see The Doctor exiting his room, accompanied by two servants carrying armfuls of books.

He noticed us watching and returned our gaze with even more than his usual glare. Unsurprisingly, he was angry to see his tormentors come to revel in his downfall, but this was a look of such unadulterated wickedness that all the hairs on the back of my neck stood to attention. Indeed, had the English phrase 'stared daggers' been taken literally, then we would have both been stabbed to death for sure. He gave us one more furious scowl before striding off with his toadying staff lugging his clobber behind him and we watched as Adam Weishaupt finally left Ingolstadt University for the very last time.

When he and his lackeys had disappeared around the bottom of the corridor, I half-whispered, "Do you really think it is over, sir?"

Van Halestrom slowly shook his head and ominously muttered, "Oh no, my friend, it is not over. Not by a long chalk."

Right! Right! Right! That's all he ever was - Blasted right! I cannot think why I never thought to ask him what would happen at the end of my life, because he was bound to have known and therefore have removed all subsequent mysteries from my mind.

Because he *was* right. It was not the end. Not by a long chalk. In many ways, it was merely another beginning. *[23.]

---

23. Adam Weishaupt Sacked from Ingolstadt University Winter of 1785. S. Drechsler's claim to have witnessed the academic's departure are accurate here, as Adam Weishaupt finally lost his position at Ingolstadt University on the 11th February 1785, amidst continuing controversy surrounding his 'not so' secret society. The authorities' first decree in July of the previous year had been quite mild, but both official and public suspicion of the Illuminati was certainly growing around this time, making it impossible for distinguished institutions such as Ingolstadt's university, who enjoyed the patronage of the state, to employ members from its ranks, never mind its prominent leader and figurehead. As S. Drechsler also mentions, as well as other competing rumours of illegitimate relationships, as strange as it may sound, most official histories record that Weishaupt was known to be having an affair with his sister-in-law.

Chapter 24

Incognito? No! Audacity, audacity!

My heart was beating like a Frenchman's fist at the door of a brothel on payday, as I played out the night's upcoming activities. I was scrubbed, shaved, dressed to the nines and speeding along in the Professor's coach, or was it Bacon's, or the Castle's?

At that moment, I didn't care. I was simply brimming with excitement to be on my next mission, and more than happy to be reclining in the comparative warmth of the plush interior while Klaus and Bacon rode on the footboard amongst the blustering sleet of a harsh winter's day. To my great surprise, and delight, I was posing as notable dignitary Count Wolfgang Faber Castell, and enjoying the deception greatly.

Van Halestrom had devised the plan to aid our uninterrupted passage with the secret papers, predicting that our high-profile would, "Counter-intuitively, provide us with safety," and boldly declaring, "Audacity, audacity. That is the best way to proceed. No one will bother you believing that you are aristocracy."

It was certainly capital fun pretending to be. I was not sure if Van Halestrom had intended it, but he must have known that it would be a hoot for me. I wondered that if, in some way, it was reward for services rendered, because being in charge, or at least apparently so, was excellent sport indeed. I endeavoured to make the most of it by pulling down the window and calling out, "What's the weather like, boys?" when only a dead man would not have known.

"Cold, sir," came back Bacon's snotty reply.

"Never mind!" I sang back and closed the window, enjoying a mischievous chuckle. This was going to be a great night. Nay, a marvellous night. Besides the opportunity to play the role of a man of great privilege, with fine clothes, the coach, servants, money, and all the other accoutrements of a nobleman, I was to meet the tantalising Lady Francesca at the finest of inns, where we were to enjoy a meal, after which, we were to retire together, in one room, with one bed, the two of us - it had been promised to me. I had even seen the letter confirming the booking. She was aware of these sleeping arrangements, as we were to appear as esteemed dignitary and courtesan, and had not complained about them, so I had every reason to believe that we would be fully together on that very eve. My pulse began to pound like a busy blacksmith's hammer once again as I considered her wondrous delights which would now, undeniably, be in my hands in only a few hours time and my head almost came off at the thought.

We reached Regensburg in the late afternoon and, as expected, the border guards lazily waved us across the gated bridge as soon as they saw our false flags and insignia. A couple of miles down the road, we rattled past a sign for Pettendorf and, not long after, pulled up outside a grand old inn - a most splendid house built in the style of a traditional Bavarian hunting lodge and pleasantly dusted with snow. I dismounted with an air of refinement and, while Bacon unloaded my heavy bags, I spotted a pair of elegant young women returning from a constitutional winter's stroll.

Eager to impress them with my supposed authority, I shouted at poor old Bacon, "Hurry up there you old boot!" like a proper aristocrat should. After all, should not everyone believe that we are who we say we are?

But the annoying scoundrel replied, "*Yes, sir,*" with such grinding derision, that it was like listening to a nail being dragged down a blackboard and the playful titter that it induced from the ladies was not worth my trouble, so I resolved not to do it again. Klaus stabled the coach and horses and met me inside the front doorway, saying with a wink, "You're all set, sir. She'll be here at seven. Enjoy yourselves."

He flicked the brim of his hat and jauntily strolled off to his quarters. I liked Klaus. He was a good stick. I liked them all. They were an excellent lot, Klaus, the Professor, even pompous old Bacon and, of course, the delectable one herself. My spirits soared once more at the thought of our certain union and, after measuring all the other luxuries surrounding me in the reception hall of the charming old inn, I contemplated with some certainty, 'What a night this is going to be. What can possibly go wrong now?'

If I'd had a million years to work it out, I would still have needed a million more, for the sheer madness that was about to occur could only have been predicted by the inmate of an insane asylum, or maybe Professor Van Halestrom. Although, surely not even he could have foreseen the things that were about to happen, because they were of such utter and complete inconceivability in each and every way.

I bathed in a soothing hot tub, before Bacon helped me change into my evening wear; a fabulous silver cutaway tailed jacket with matching satin waistcoat, black velvet breeches over bright white hose, a superb pair of fine buckled leather shoes and, to top it all, a grandiose pearl silk cravat. Regarding my refection in the mirror, I was impressed to say the least. Dressed in such finery, I certainly looked like a man of distinction and struck a pose to prove it.

"Not a bad looking chap at all," I remarked, revolving one last time in the mirror, before bidding Bacon goodnight and making my way downstairs to find my table. Passing through the reception hall and into the dining room, I was aware of the effect that my new appearance was having on those around me. Several refined characters respectfully acknowledged me as I took my seat and the waiter almost tripped over himself to bring me my first bottle of wine.

I had barely begun the second of these when, at last, Francesca arrived and, in that moment, I was so excited that I nearly ripped a hole in my new velvet breeches with my increased manly proportions. For never was there another woman such as her. Good God. What had I done to deserve this? Quite a lot actually, but it was all worth it now. For standing there before me, was a Venus of pure delectation. A waiter removed her fur cloak, whereupon she was revealed in all her shining glory and sauntered towards me in a glamorous low-cut gown that could barely contain her heaving womanliness. She had put her hair up to show off her slender bejewelled neck and was wearing a seductive beauty spot upon her cheek. I had forgotten just how beautiful she really was and almost spontaneously combusted with desire as all the wonderful déjà-vu came flooding back. I stood to meet her by the table and kissed her hand.

"Good evening, my lady. May I say, you look ravishing?"

"Yes, *you may*, kind sir" she purred, like a cat that wants to be stroked, "I have missed such pleasantries, Count Wolfgang. Russian men are not as charming as those of Bavaria."

"I was hoping that you had not the chance to find out much of Russian men, my lady."

"Their company only made me realise how lucky I was to come back to a real Bavarian man like you, sweet sir."

What further guarantee did I need of my inevitable union with this exceptional beauty than this type of flirtatiousness? I gave her a chair before sitting down myself and summoning the service to begin. This was the stuff of dreams. Maybe not everybody's, but definitely mine. Dining in the swankiest of places, being waited on hand and foot, at the most expensive table, with a woman so attractive that waiters, and guests alike, kept walking into the furniture as they gazed at her in awe and, knowing that, after this fabulous meal, we would adjourn upstairs, to the ambassador's suite, where I was going to rip off her dress and corsets and throw her on the satin sheets of a scented bed, then bite and lick and fondle every single part of her gorgeous naked body in the most carnal of ways. Then I would put my…

"What are you thinking, Wunderkind?" Her eyes twinkled like diamonds and her jewellery tried to keep up but failed dismally.

"Oh nothing." I coughed, "Perhaps how happy I am tonight."

"Go on," she prompted.

I attempted to elaborate, "Being here with you, in all this splendour and opulence. The feeling of tenderness… even love."

She smiled happily and squeezed my hand, so I continued expanding my feelings in the same hopeful way.

"My thoughts are of the future, of peace and normality, a home, where two people can live. A house filled with children…"

"Whoa there, Wunderkind," she interrupted, "This world is far too turbulent a place for those thoughts to become a reality if they are to include me. The things that I know are happening right now are so extreme that to have a child, and leave them facing a future of such inconsolable pain and suffering, would be impossible for me to bear."

"Surely things cannot be *that* bad, my lady?"

"Of course they are. You must understand by now the fate of the world has but one outcome, and that is of civilisation's fall."

"By what process? How will this apocalypse come to pass?"

"Surely the Professor has told you of the Illuminati's plans. It is proven, beyond doubt, that the scheme is inescapable. For it aligns itself with the fateful prophecy predicting the fall of man. He must have kept it from you because he didn't want you to give up the struggle."

"The *struggle*? What are you talking about?"

"I speak of 'The End of Times.'"

I shrugged in ignorance and she forlornly began, "It is the belief that man can only inherit the destiny that he deserves. For the masses are weak and selfish and can only think of themselves, and this immorality, in itself, produces the Illuminati who, in turn, foster the decline. Finally, being so inherently corrupt, as predicted in the holy bible, man's descent is irreversible. Ultimately, this malignancy, harnessed by the dark forces that we fight, will create three enormous wars covering the earth, after which, a single world dictatorship will be formed mirroring the antipathy of its spiritually broken people. The end will come in that moment and a social cataclysm will be born from which civilisation cannot return. As written in the Book of Revelation."

"Right then," I sighed. She was obviously not your average dinner partner.

"Take a look around you. Isn't everyone the same - soulless creatures interested in only what they can get for themselves?"

I followed her eyes to a waiter slyly pocketing another's tip.

She carried on, "The world over, you cannot stop it. The only thing that man possesses is envy, greed, and fear and lust for his own power. That's how he will be destroyed in the end. You're just a foolish boy to think of it any other way." She regarded me rather condescendingly and finished, "I thought that you looked to the future with too much happiness for your own good."

Seeing that I was hurt by these ridiculous sounding remarks, she took my hand and reasoned, "I feel for you, Wunderkind. I really do. But planning ahead, knowing of this terrible future, especially in our business, is an extravagance that I can ill-afford."

"All of a sudden I fancy another drink," I concluded, rudely taking my hand from hers and downing my glass in one.

"Don't be like that, Sebastian," she begged, reaching out to me, but I defiantly stood up and announced that I was going to the privy.

Emptying myself in the water closet, I cursed her over-seriousness. It was only one waiter scrounging a tip for pity's sake. It didn't mean that the rest of civilisation was about to explode in flames. I convinced myself that she would come round to my way of thinking as soon as she had sampled the twelve stones of manly vigour that I had been saving for her. I bravely contemplated taking on the hordes of enemies contriving to make this ominous prophecy come true, even calculating the amount of ammunition that I would need to wipe them all out in order to persuade her to make a life with me. So it was with a renewed sense of purpose that I returned to the dining room, and that's when the nightmares which I had thought were behind us started all over again. *[24.]

As I approached our table, two waiters suddenly pulled her from her chair and dragged her from the room. Before I could react, one of them whipped out a flintlock pistol from his waistcoat and fired it at my face. The bang nearly deafened me as the shot whistled by my ear and smashed through something behind me made of glass. I uselessly ducked after the round had gone as the other guests shouted and screamed around the room.

---

24. Illuminati & 'The End Times' Prophecy. Illuminati speculators have long contested that the Order wish to instigate a social cataclysm mirroring the fateful prophecy predicting the armageddon of civilisation, as described in the Bible's '***Book of Revelation.***' This ominous forecast recalled by S. Drechsler, also sounds strangely similar to extracts from a mysterious letter once rumoured to be kept at the British Museum which, it is claimed, was sent by the then head of world Masonry Albert Pike to Giuseppe Mazzini in 1871. If S. Drechsler's account is to be believed, then it is incredible to think that this frightening prediction for the world was even being talked about as early as 1785.

"Not now. Not now," I grunted as I sprinted after her. "What is wrong with this blasted woman? Is there no one else that can be kidnapped but her?" But when I ran out of the front door, she was already being bundled into an expensive lanterned coach.

"Get off that woman!" I yelled and was shot at again for my trouble. This round, fired by another shadowy henchman on the top of the coach, tore a hole in my coat tails. As I came up from my stoop, affected to avoid the shot, the coach sped off and I vigorously gave chase but could only keep up for a moment before it pulled away. I slid to a halt in the frosty road and stood there panting for a second before sprinting back to the inn, where a crowd of guests and staff had gathered outside shocked to have seen such violence and mayhem.

I dashed into the stables to find that Klaus had heard the shots too and was already harnessing up our horses, greeting me with a, "Be with you in a trice, sir." Moments later, our carriage burst from the stable doors with me hanging out of the window and bellowing, "Follow that blasted coach!"

To which he cheered, "That's my favourite sentence, sir!" and stirred the horses into such action that I was fairly thrown back in my seat. Good Lord! That man could drive a team of horses and was a veritable master of his trade. Though he slid the coach so wildly along the icey road that I thought we were bound to crash, he was actually in full control of these crazed manoeuvres, once or twice, even clipping our rear wheel against the snowbanks before rebounding and flying back off down the lane. I stuck my head out of the window, eager to see how we were faring and felt the whip of cold sting my face. Fifty yards ahead, I could already make out the glowing lanterns of the abductor's coach.

"Go on by thunder!" I shouted, seeing that we were catching our quarry at a prodigious rate. Feeling a rush of blood at the prospect of beating the living daylights out of the gang of thugs and getting that woman in my arms once-and-for-blasted-all, I opened the door and went to get in the front seat to aid the chase. I quickly realised how impetuous this decision was when Klaus swerved into a corner with a horrifying drop over its side and, from my perilous position, clutching the *wrong* side of the coach, I watched the snow-covered trees hurtling by hundreds of feet below. I tried to control my fear of heights by taking my eyes off the daunting canyon and, as we slid violently round the bend, I heaved myself up on the corner of the cabin then landed next to Klaus with a gasp.

He gave me a wink and whipped the reins to pull us within range, shouting out loud and clear, "C'mon, my beauties!"

'Crack!' And we were definitely in range. I ducked down as a shot zipped overhead and desperately looked around for our own firearms.

"One step ahead of you, sir," called Klaus, thumping the headboard behind us which unfolded into a tray containing a pair of shining muskets. My eyes widened with approval and, needing no further encouragement, I picked one up and cocked it then, after quickly finding my target, released a shot. 'Crack!' causing the dark silhouette firing at us to cower down in fright.

"Take that pig dog!" I cried, picking up the other gun and bringing it to bear. I considered my next shot more carefully, as it might be our last, and waited for the bastard to get up again. Then, when he did, I took my chance. 'Crack!' This time, I got him and he fell screaming from the coach and we promptly ran him over. As he went under the wheels, I could have sworn that he was wearing one of the Illuminati's red-hooded robes and I roared with a newfound rage, "Damn that blackguard to Hell!"

"They must be heading for Wolfsegg Castle!" yelled Klaus, ominously adding, "I'm sure Weishaupt has connections with that place."

"Him again! That would explain Little-Red-Firing-Hood." Enough was enough. If Weishaupt did have anything to do with this, I was going to kill him then resurrect the bastard so I could do it again. Now he was really starting to anger me. We climbed on up the mountain road but the pursuit did not slow down, if anything, it sped up and another shot rang out.

How many blasted kidnappers *were* there? It didn't matter, as I knew that I could beat them all to a pulp being in possession of such an all-consuming rage. Klaus whipped the horses to blazes and pulled us alongside the abductors' coach where I saw Francesca's screaming face at the window. A hand appeared from the shadows to drag her back, but she bit it with fury and it was quickly yanked away.

"Go on girl!" I raged as one of the hooded villains leapt from the roof of the coach and landed next to us with his sword raised above his head. Astounded by this man's eagerness, I had no time to stop him as his blade slashed down towards Klaus's head but, incredibly, it did not find its mark. Somehow, the heroic driver trapped the sword between his hands and held it inches from his face with blood trickling down his wrists. I watched in awe as he calmly gasped, "Could you... sir?"

He gestured at the reins, which I took from him and he rammed the handle of the sword into his attacker's guts then jumped up and powerfully head-butted him from the footboard. The thug fell away, but managed to drag Klaus with him and the trusty driver scarcely had the time to shout, "Excuse me, sir," "[25.]

---

25. Wolfsegg Castle. Though I cannot find any strong connections linking this ancient castle to the Illuminati, it has had many owners throughout its long and fascinating eight-hundred-year history. Originally built in 1278 by Wolf von Schönleiten, it's steeped in legends of supernatural hauntings and, owing to its prominent position, can be seen from several miles away. It is still there to this day, situated 15km north west of Regensburg near the outskirts of Pettendorf, and can be viewed on the internet.

before disappearing into the night. I glanced behind to see them tumble to a halt, then Klaus take exception to this individual's treatment of him and begin beating the rogue to within an inch of his life - and maybe less. I looked back up the road. Damnation! I was on my own and, as I came to this stark conclusion, the dark towers of a castle appeared over the approaching trees.

"C'mon Seb! Do it before we get there," I told myself, realising that any amount of reinforcements could be waiting up ahead. I hollered at the horses to spur them on again and steadily brought the coaches level. Knowing that I would have to jump for it, for there was no other way, I stood up furiously lashing the reins and waited for the right moment before hurling myself at the other coach. I landed next to the driver, but only made it by an inch with my heels hanging off the footboard and, even from behind his slits, I could tell that he was startled by my verve.

"You weren't expecting that were you, you bastard!" I taunted, but -Damn it!- if he did not return the surprise by producing a huge knife which he started to wield about.

"That's a big one," I fretted and dodged it twice as the coach and horses flew on regardless as we thundered under the castle's portcullis. The driver slashed at me again and caught me on the wrist. Not a fatal wound, but enough to send red-hot pain searing up my arm. I could not take too many more of those and, as we sped into a snowy courtyard, I used my new fighting skills to punch him twice in the face.

From the corner of my eye, I saw the silhouette of a man running next to us who slowed the horses down and we shuddered to a chaotic halt. I dodged another slash as the doors of the coach burst open and Francesca was dragged out by the two waiters. They were obviously too big to be servants and easily wrestled her towards the castle's keep while she screamed over her shoulder, "Help me, Sebastian!"

"In a minute, my sweet!" I yelled, fully sarcastic, for it was obvious that I was having troubles of my own. Though, after another tasty punch, I felt my opponent's nose smash to pieces and he fell onto the icy cobbles with a crunch. I jumped down to pursue Francesca's captors but three more thugs emerged from the shadows and ran over to block my path. The first took a swing at me, which I dodged before kicking him in the crotch, but the other two rushed me and the blows started to rain in. One of these poleaxed me and I crashed backwards into the side of the keep. My head began to swim as the man who I had castrated pulled himself to his feet and, while his friends pinned me to the wall, he came over to finish me off.

"That's enough!" barked a voice and another silhouette appeared. Though I was half unconscious, I could have recognised Weishaupt's arrogant snarl anywhere.

The Doctor came into the light and I fought to break free from his henchmen, but he revelled in a conceited grin and boasted, "Two troublemakers for the price of one. Seems a most agreeable bargain to me."

His cockiness enraged me even further and I struggled in vain to escape, but he smacked his lips in contempt then turned to go.

I shouted after him, "I'm going to kill you one day, Weishaupt!"

"But I wager that day is not today," he crowed.

I went to curse him again but someone thumped me with something hard round the back of my head and everything went black.

Chapter 25

The Pit of Despair

I have woken up in some bad places in my time; classrooms, churches, taverns, prisons, ditches, even in a brothel on my eighteenth birthday -and no, I did not thank you very much- for they were all hideous dogs in that place. But this was worse. Much worse. Much worse than all those places put together and multiplied a thousand times. I slowly came round in total darkness and tried to sift through my ruptured memories.

'This is not my room at the inn?' I surmised, finding my cold hard mattress most disagreeable. Feeling bonds on my wrists and ankles, I wondered 'Where's Francesca?' God knows why, but finding myself tied up reminded me of her. Then I remembered seeing her face pushed against the window of a coach and biting someone's hand and I recalled, 'That's it, she's been kidnapped. I have to rescue her. Oh dear!' Then it all came crashing back in a tidal wave of fear. I was in terrible, terrible trouble.

I prayed to God that I was wrong and checked my bonds -Damn it!- I wasn't. They were chains, big heavy ones and, instead of the ambassador's warm bed in the luxurious inn, I was lying on a cold stone table in a pitch-black dungeon. I listened for any sounds beyond the gloom, but there were none. Not even a solitary drip of water. My fearful frustration quickly got the better of me and I yelled out, "Get me out of here you dogs or I'll smash your blasted heads in!" There was no answer and, already feeling the dismal blackness crushing in, and remembering how happy I was meant to be on this night, I could not help but rage, "Let me go you slitty-eyed bastards or I'll kill the lot of you!"

That very moment, I heard a door slam, the approach of footsteps and the unmistakable jangle of keys. I instantly regretted my tantrum as, whoever was coming, had already beaten the hell out of me and chained me to a table in a dungeon. Suddenly feeling extremely vulnerable, I braced myself as the inevitable key rattled in the door and a handful of hooded sentinels piled into the room carrying burning torches.

They crowded round the table as Weishaupt strode through the doorway and pushed them apart to stand before me. He threw his long fur cloak over his shoulder and chortled in his mocking tone, "Well, well, Herr Drechsler. As I'm sure you can imagine, we're all quaking in our boots to have an *Illuminati hunter* come to visit." His rabble of men sniggered as he went on, "You, boy, have been an annoying thorn in my side for some time, so I'm looking forward to showing you the extent of my displeasure. My men were already following your indiscreet lady friend, but finding you with her is most fortuitous."

"What... are... you going to do to me?"

"Why, I'm going to kill you, Herr Drechsler," he scoffed, "What did you think I was going to do?"

"You'll never get away with this!"

"Oh, but my dear, Herr Drechsler, don't you see? I already have. Surely, even in *your* wildest daydreams, you don't think you can escape from here. Within these walls I can do anything I please. Far better than the university, is it not? I wasn't allowed to torture the students there. Though, in most cases, I'm sure it was the only way that I could have improved their results."

Overcome by a mixture of terror and rage, his scornful boasts were too much and I taunted him as Jan would have, "Well I'm sure you could've *improved your sister's results* if you'd've slapped her when she didn't ride you right you piece of shit!"

"Silence!" he roared.

I did not blame him. I was quite proud of that one; 'Improved your sister's results if you'd've slapped her when she didn't ride you right you piece of shit!' Stick *that* up your arse Weishaupt.

If you're going to kill me then I'm going to humiliate you first and I flew into my next tirade, "I bet you could train your dog to lick your balls if you stuck your fingers up its arse you fuc..."

"That's enough!" he yelled and motioned at one of his guards who rammed a gag into my mouth.

But I was so crazed with fear that I could not stop and carried on in my muffled voice, "Nuh, nuh, hun nuh unh, nuh nu, nugh!"

He clicked his fingers signalling the guard to punch me in my guts, which he did, very hard. That shut me up and I lay there in some agony.

Weishaupt leaned over me, hissing like a venomous serpent, "How could you ever think you could win against us you arrogant fool? If you only knew what you are really up against then you wouldn't have tried at all. No doubt, that imbecile Van Halestrom has convinced you that you can stop something that has been taking place for thousands of years. Ridiculous. You have no idea. How could you, you meaningless idiot? You know nothing of this power. You don't even have the brains to perceive it, let alone understand what it can bring about." He moved closer, breathing menacingly right into my face, "Such is the nature of this force that eventually it will prevail, not only over the lesser, or more important of the populace, but the best of men of all ranks, nations, and religions, until finally giving us absolute control over them all. The pure doctrine of almighty Lucifer is invincible and, in the end, all men will be forced to bow to His eternal light." His face was only inches from mine by now and he finished in a terrifying whisper, "You, Herr Drechsler, are simply the next unfortunate flame who must be extinguished for His glorious light to shine."

"Aarrgh!" I wailed into the rag.

"Take him down!" He ordered his men then turned back to me. "I was going to kill you here, you impertinent little prick, but now I have a better idea. You can watch your lady die *first*."

"Francesca!" I screamed, though it sounded more like "Huhunnun!"

A couple of the guards released my shackles and hauled me off the table then dragged me out of the room and down a maze of dark corridors. Weishaupt led us to a stairwell that we descended deep into the catacombs of the fort. My seething anger quickly turned into pitiful fear and, with every flight of stairs, my spirits fell a little lower until, after the third or fourth, I was in the very pit of despair. Though I tried to have the thoughts of a mythological hero, and not those of a pathetic student, it was no good. This was real. This madman and his lunatic disciples were going to kill me in this freezing castle on, what should've been, the best night of my life and after making me witness the death of my lover, whom I'd never got to love. The shock and terror were overpowering. I knew that I could not handle my *own* death, even if it was quick, but I was certain that seeing Francesca hurt in any way would make me lose my mind. I worried for my parents too and imagined them hearing of my death and my eyes did moisten and I prayed to God to save my soul. Because, this time, there was no way out. I really *was* going to die.

All too soon, we came up to the door which led to the place of my doom. One of the hooded sentinels swung it open and thrust me into a chamber which, unlike the rest of the castle, was brightly lit by many torches burning along the walls. Unfortunately, this allowed me to see, in exquisite detail, the numerous machines of death which littered the room. It was as though every method of killing someone as painfully as possible had been assembled in one place. There was a horrifying rack, a manacled cage, and, in the corner, a fearful oubliette, its sloping sides disappearing into a foreboding hole, no doubt full of the bones of many forgotten prisoners. Worst of all, ominously smouldering next to its lip, stood an iron basket full of red-hot pokers and burning coals.

Everywhere else I looked, knives, drills, pincers, and other terrifying torture tools hung from the walls and, when I glimpsed an iron-maiden in another corner, with its open door covered with spikes and a freakish skull carved on its top, I was almost wetting myself and uncontrollably choking on my gag.

One of the guards bundled me over to a chair set against the far wall, which seemed to be the only piece of furniture that did not have a lethal purpose. Then I realised it had. For there were restraining clamps on the arms and legs to keep the victim in place while they suffered in awful agony. The hooded thug forced me to sit then placed the pins through clasps on my wrists but, at least, not my feet. Although fear was already rampaging through my every sinew, my heart beat even faster when I saw gouges in the arms of the chair, obviously torn by the fingernails of past victims during some unimaginably vicious fate.

Then the next horrid detail. I noticed a large pentagram painted across the floor with Greek letters at its five points. I had already seen enough evil magic over the past year to last a lifetime and knew that this diabolical symbol was used by practitioners of the black arts. Now I fully expected my fate and Francesca's to have some extra demonic twist. And where was she? If she was to suffer too, surely she should be there. Right on cue, the door swung open and what happened next shocked me even further - if that were possible, in this vilest of moments.

She came into the room still wearing her gown and was followed by a grand old soldier in a dark blue full military uniform with a broad red sash over his shoulder and bright white breeches. But I had to look again. Was it her? There was a vacancy in her eyes that I had never seen before. Indeed, it was entirely out of character as her spirit was always shown in her lively features. I watched her distinguished companion obviously a fellow of some renown, but who also possessed the same listless expression. Francesca was not bound either and I couldn't understand why she did not put up a fight. She stood next to Weishaupt without looking at me and was joined by the man in the uniform. Weishaupt chuckled, "It seems she doesn't know you, lover boy. What do you think of her now, eh?"

He motioned at the guard beside me to remove the rag and I gasped a breath of foul air before wheezing, "What have you done to her, you fiend?"

"Oh, Herr Drechsler, it must be love. I can tell by the way you squeal. That will make this much worse. Love always deepens the pain. Seeing a stranger die can be tolerated, even become accustomed to, but, take it from me, there's nothing as bad as seeing a loved one perish." His words slid from his mouth like a dagger being dragged from its sheath, "And she's a fine specimen, Herr Drechsler. You have a good eye for the ladies. Of course, I knew her sister *very well*, in many different ways, before her time finally came." He grabbed Francesca's chin and flashed me a perverted grin. "I will enjoy this a great deal."

Then -Damn it!- if the bastard did not kiss her on the mouth and fondle her breasts. I strained at my clasps so hard that my wrists burned with pain and I bellowed, "If thought were a weapon then your head would be torn apart right now!"

He let go of her chin and gawked at me as though insulted by the remark.

"*If thought were a weapon*? Pah! What little you know. I think it's time that I gave you a lesson in the true power of thought."

With this esotericism, he led Francesca to the centre of the pentagram and whispered something in her ear, before staring into her vacant eyes and sharply clapping his hands.

Incredibly, I saw in that instant, her soul returned to her. For that is how it seemed to be. I could not explain it in any other way. Her spirit was channelled back into her and the girl that I knew returned in front of me with a startled gasp.

She glanced around the room until her eyes met with mine, whereupon she tried to reach out but somehow appeared to be trapped by an invisible force which kept her locked in her place. She winced with effort and cried, "Sebastian!"

I fought uselessly at my bonds and roared, "Francesca!"

Weishaupt shook his head and laughed, "Ah ha ha ha. Young love is such a miracle, is it not?"

What the hell was going on? My mind seethed, 'what is this power that he possesses?'

He circled Francesca as she struggled against the mysterious spell. "As you well know, Herr Drechsler, there are many ways to control people; war, debt, illusion, fear, lies." He leaned in closer to her, sniffing at her neck and musing, "Most people wrongly think that it comes from gold, or force, but real power comes from the mind. After all, knowledge is power. Eh? Therefore, the real wealth on this earth is the minds of the people. For therein lies *true* power. The power of their minds."

"You're sick!" snorted Francesca, but the louse clicked his fingers and, incredibly, her voice disappeared - just like that - causing her great distress. She tried to speak but, though her mouth moved strenuously, alas, she could not make a sound. Poor Francesca broke down at this and her eyes filled with tearful despair.

"Of course, I will make sure to release her tongue when it's time for you to hear her scream." He chuckled heartlessly and laughed in her tear-streaked face, "Heh heh. But still she fights. Have you not heard the term 'resistance is useless,' my dear?" He tutted with disdain and stepped over to the old soldier in the grand uniform.

"Now, I am particularly pleased with this next subject. It has taken many years of diligent work to produce a soul as reliable as his. Like a broken mirror, I have smashed his original persona into a thousand pieces, until eventually creating this empty vessel which you see before you, into which I can place whomever I choose." He faced the expressionless dignitary and asked, "Do you know him, Herr Drechsler? He is a man wielding tremendous power."

I thought that I had seen his face entering the Temple of Eleusis or on some old painting, but Francesca's tormented expression only two feet from his, prevented me from remembering.

"He is General Frederick II, Landgrave of Hasse Kassel. He has been in my employ for some time now. Though he has little knowledge of it. How many men of influence like this do you think we have around the world, who can unquestionably carry out our bidding?" The old duffer didn't look like he could tie his own shoe laces, let alone carry out anyone's bidding, but Weishaupt boastfully carried on, "Observe, boy, the power of the mind when used as a weapon."

He clicked his fingers and, as if pulled by invisible strings, the empty-eyed man briskly walked over to a bench covered with tools. Without looking, he grabbed a barbed spike then marched back to his position where he stood waiting with the vicious implement in his hand.

I started to sweat profusely, fearing the torture was about to begin as Weishaupt said coldly, "I like this part especially."

To my great relief, instead of using it on us, the empty-eyed man raised his other hand and, without batting an eyelid, stabbed the spike straight through his palm. I clawed my fingernails into the arms of the chair as he twisted the tool around, showing no pain whatsoever on his face. Weishaupt muttered to himself and ruffled his forehead, as if somehow intimately controlling the man's movements while the blood dripped on the floor, before taking his eye off the old soldier who removed the spike and stood there as though nothing had happened.

"We will say it was a hunting accident," bragged Weishaupt, "People will believe anything these days. We shall spread the rumours around court and that, my friend, will be that."

Incredible! What could he not do with this blackest of magic? Then, remembering my own part in the unfolding tragedy, my fear rampaged once more, because I knew that it must be our turn next.

Chapter 26

The Chamber of Certain Death

Consumed with infinite spine-snapping terror, clamped to a hellish chair in a chamber of certain death packed with innumerable torture tools, including a haunted living puppet, I watched helplessly as the cursed love of my life writhed in an invisible cage and a vengeful psycopath decided the best way to kill us both. I was a second year history student for Christ's sake. I should have been tucked up in bed studying my books.

Our captor spoke with spiteful malice, "I was going to have our friend the General here abuse your woman first. Have her right in front of you." He gave me a twisted smirk. "That would have been interesting, wouldn't it? Before we really put her through some pain. But, sadly, we don't have time for that."

He nodded over his shoulder and two of the hooded sentinels dragged the iron-maiden from the corner over to the pentagram then left it standing open behind Francesca, who still tearfully struggled against nothing. My heart was banging like a judge's hammer at a witch trial, for I knew that I was witnessing the beginning of the end.

I shook my head, boiling with rage, "You'll pay for this Weishaupt! One way! One day! You'll pay! I feel it in my bones. If not killed for your filthy evilness in this life then when your time comes, God will punish your soul!"

The swine tried to make a joke of it. "I have often noticed that when a man is about to die, he usually expects God to intervene on his behalf. But I'm afraid, poor Drechsler, that won't be happening today. Though, before that moment comes for you, I've devised something to make your journey to meet yours a little more interesting. Are you ready?"

With this, he waved his hand and the pair of sentinels dragged Francesca backwards and shoved her inside the iron maiden.

"No! Francesca!" I gritted my teeth and fought against the clasps on my wrists then kicked out with my feet, hopelessly trying to put up some kind of defiance.

"Now, Herr Drechsler, my hapless student, we shall put you to a little test. This one less academic than the one you so cleverly cheated at last year. This one, a test of physique."

One of the sentinels produced a roll of chain and my mind raced trying to work out what the evil bastard had in store for us.

"Unfortunately, because I am so angry with you, I have decided to let you kill your lady yourself. But first we shall test your strength and, perhaps, the strength of your love for her."

The sentinel placed one end of the chain in my hand whilst the other unwound the rest over to the iron maiden, pulled it taut and hooked a link round the handle then let the door close until it was practically shut. I desperately tried to steady myself as the chain pulled with immense force from my fingers as he found the point where the door hung in the balance. The plan was obvious. The vicious spikes now hovered only inches from Francesca's panting body and she stared wide-eyed at me through the door's tiny window. She shouted silently as the tears rolled down her cheeks and I strained with effort to hold the chain which was already tearing itself from my hand. I wondered how long I would have before losing my grip. Maybe a minute. Maybe less.

The torment and anguish of it all was sending me mad. I wondered if I would lose my mind and not be able to suffer, but my senses only heightened as the hellish torture continued.

'Please God save me from this and I shall be forever in your service,' I beseeched as Weishaupt and his hooded devils stood on either side of the maiden, laughing and whooping and revelling at our calamity, something that they had obviously done before.

"You seem to love her a great deal, Herr Drechsler," chortled Weishaupt and carried on with revolting pleasure, "But like all things, the chain of love has its breaking point. *Awh, dear, dear. Are you nearly there, pretty boy?*"

As he said this, the chain slipped from my fingers, letting the door fall a couple of inches but somehow I managed to catch the next link then immediately felt it dragging from my grasp. I flung my head back, summoning every ounce of strength that I had left as Weishaupt cruely scoffed, "Oh. Nearly."

This was it. I was going to lose my grip. Weishaupt and three of the sentinels crowded round, with two of them on each side of the iron maiden, all concentrating on the spectacle's wicked climax, while the fourth, who had fixed me to my chair, began suspiciously fidgeting under his robes. He saw me watching and I was stunned when he put his finger to his lips outside his hood.

'What was this?' I wondered with my mind a blaze of pain and regret and fear of death. I focused back on the chain as he circled around the others.

Weishaupt goaded me, "As you can see there's a window in the door so you can watch your lover's soul leave this world forever. Are you ready to see her go, lover boy?"

"No!" I roared, as my very last remnants of strength fell away.

The chain quivered in front of me as the evil bastards laughed with glee but, from under his robes, the odd sentinel standing behind them pulled out a silver knife. Good God! It was Van Halestrom's. He raised a solitary finger and moved up to the nearest sentinel. What did this mean? One second? One minute? One hour? One blasted day? Could he not see how close I was to losing the chain? 'Do it now!' I screamed inside, but he began fumbling underneath his costume once more.

"C'mon you fool!" I shouted, knowing that no one would know what I meant. But - Confound it! - the clever old buzzard, for I knew that it was him, still continued to rummage about. Now I recognised his familiar form underneath the robes. Of course! The finger to the lips, leaving the foot clasps undone - obviously hoping for a chance to come. I did not care what miracle he had performed to get there, I only cared that he would stop this insanity before it was too late. I groaned with the strain and felt the link about to wrench from my hand. It was no good. I knew that I was going let go. Van Halestrom pulled out a small cutlass with his other hand and triumphantly held it up behind them all, as though impressed with his work.

"Just do it!" I cried in apoplexy as, at last, the link slipped from my grip and the door dropped. "No! Francesca!" I screamed, but Van Halestrom threw the knife which, by utter magic, wedged in the door's hinge and stopped it from slamming shut.

Incredible! My eyes nearly popped out at this but there was not even time to register it. The Professor skewered the nearest sentinel with the cutlass and pulled it out so fast that he was able to stab the next in the back before he had time to react. Weishaupt and the remaining sentinel finally realised what was happening but, before they could stop him, Van Halestrom bolted over to my chair and pulled out one of the pins from the clasps.

"Yes!" I yelled, removing the other and jumping up. The Professor threw me the cutlass and I turned to meet the sentinel who had armed himself with a mace.

"Prepare to die!" I roared, engulfed by an all-powerful rage. I had enough fury to kill a squadron of pirates at that moment and the swine knew it. He wisely took a step back, but it did him no good and I unleashed a storm of frenzied blows which clashed against his mace and drove him towards the wall. I feigned one way then swiped the other and took the bastard's head clean off with one powerful slash. It fell to the floor still in its hood with blood spraying from its neck and serve the bastard right.

I turned to see that Weishaput had picked up a glowing poker from the basket, using his cloak to protect his hand. He pointed it at the Professor and provocatively beckoned with his finger. "You meddling fool, Van Halestrom! You have troubled me for the last time. Now prepare to meet thy doom!"

"If it's my doom that I must meet, then I go there with a fight!" called the Professor and grabbed a spear leaning against the wall with both hands then charged at the Doctor. Weishaupt dodged the lunge and, when the Professor went to parry, he mercilessly whipped down the glowing rod and broke the spear in two.

"God's teeth!" cried the Professor, taking two steps back.

Weishaupt grinned and taunted him, "Ha ha. *Now* let's see you fight!" then clicked his fingers. The empty-faced General dropped his spike and marched back to the bench where he grabbed an axe then came towards me, chopping it up and down like a horrifying figurine from the devil's own clock.

"You can do it, lad!" called Van Halestrom.

"Don't encourage him fool! You know you're doomed to fail. Or have you not told him of man's true destiny?" The General came at me, chopping so hard and fast that he almost knocked the cutlass out of my hand and Weishaupt raged, "Ha ha. Resistance is useless!"

In this moment of despair, I was astonished to hear, "The future's not written yet you piece of shit!"

Holy Mother of God! Francesca had escaped the casket and her spell and she yanked Weishaupt back by his cloak. He fell on his arse clutching at its fastening round his neck then dropped the poker and knocked the basket of coals all over him.

"Yeehaa!" I cried, narrowly avoiding another chop from the General which went crashing into a rack of spears behind me. While he struggled to free it, I saw that the burning coals had set fire to Weishaupt's cloak and, though he patted down the flames, he was too slow and the blaze quickly took hold. The Professor bravely picked up one of the sizzling pokers and, with smoke literally pouring from his hand, thrust it at Weishaupt's face. The fiend shrieked a horrid squeal of death and toppled backwards over the obliette's lip then plunged down the hole, engulfed by a pluming black cloud of firery smoke.

"That'll shut him up!" called Van Halestrom, peering over the edge and throwing the poker after him.

It was my turn to cry out next, "Now come here and help me!" The General had freed his axe and swung it inches from my face. I slashed him in his left arm, almost cutting it off, but he kept remorselessly advancing and chopping like a man possessed. Adding to this onslaught of action, there was a stampede of footsteps behind the door, but Francesca jumped over the dead bodies and slammed the bar into place seconds before the guards piled into it with a crash of weaponry.

"What shall we do now?" she cried.

"We shall help Sebastian!" I yelled, frantically dodging another slice.

The Professor grabbed a sword and came over, ordering us, "If we can kill the others we can kill this one too!" As he said this there was a colossal thump on the door which sounded like a battering ram.

"We don't have much time!" cried Francesca.

"Right, time to leave," declared Van Halestrom, totally changing his blasted mind.

"Leave?" I shouted, simultaneously parrying a chop of the General's axe. "I don't know if you've noticed, but there is only one door out of here and the castle's garrison is currently behind it trying to get in!"

I flashed another cut at the General, taking half his ear off and splattering blood across his face, but still it didn't even slow him down.

"Nothing can stop this one!" I gasped.

But the Professor was already back at the other end of the chamber and, amazingly, lifted up an iron grill exposing a hole in the floor.

"You first, Francesca!" he called as another massive crash nearly rammed the door off its hinges and she ran over to him.

"Sebastian!" she yelled and disappeared down the hole.

I managed to force the general back against the wall with a flurry of cuts, one of them injuring his shoulder so badly that it would have killed a normal man, and he finally dropped the axe. I grabbed a burning torch from a bracket over his head then stuffed it into his dead eyes, screaming, "Die you bastard!" and he slid down the wall with half of his blood-covered face on fire. I threw the cutlass, and the torch at him for good measure then dashed between the bodies strewn across the floor and over to the Professor.

"Down you go, lad!" he ordered and, bursting with relief, I jumped into the hole.

Chapter 27

No Light at the End of the Tunnel

I splashed down in a stinking puddle on all fours and, once again, in total darkness. Although this was an improvement as, wherever I was, it wasn't full of people trying to kill me. Before I could move, the Professor landed on top of me and painfully pinned me to the ground.

"Oww!"

"Oh, sorry, Sebastian," he apologised and called into the dark, "Francesca, are you there?"

"Where else would I be, Professor?"

"You have a point," he conceded, clambering off me and encouraging us, "Right, off we go."

I heard Francesca scramble down what, I began to make out, was a very narrow tunnel, perhaps four feet wide. Van Halestrom sparked his firebox into life and followed after her, leaving me bringing up the rear crawling as fast as I could.

After a moment, I begged, "Where are we going now?"

"Out!" called Van Halestrom.

"Good!" I panted and, with my mind beginning to clear as the shock of freedom and potential safety started to sink in, I could not help but demand, "In God's name, sir, would you please tell me where in hell are we now?"

"I believe we are in the castle's sewer, Sebastian."

"Sewer?" Astonished at the existence of such a fortuitous, if foul smelling escape route, I beseeched him, "How long is it?" For there was no light at the end of the tunnel.

"I estimate, with the lie of the land and our current tradjectory... humm... let me see... about twenty minutes."

"Well good news, for once, sir, as that will allow me to ask some damnably important questions."

"Fire away, lad," he replied, with all the calmness of a man picking strawberries in the meadow.

I collected my rampaging thoughts and picked the first, "Why did you not tell me Weishaupt possessed such evil powers?"

"It is not black magic he has mastered, Sebastian, but Doctor Mesmer's hypnotism. I have to admit, when I first saw other Illuminati agents behaving in the same way, I presumed that they had lost their minds due to the heat of battle. It is an awesome power, lad, but still just a trick of the mind."

"Just a trick of the mind? Damn it!" I bit my tongue and tried to control myself as my thoughts turned to the next point. "What in God's name were you doing at the castle?"

"Ah yes, stroke of luck that really. Weishaupt was refused an audience with The Elector Duke CharlesTheodore this morning, guaranteeing his expulsion from Bavaria, and so, this afternoon, when he fled Ingolstadt, I followed him here. Serendipitous wouldn't you say?" [26.]

"Serendipitous!" I yelled, but before I could tell him to exchange this word for 'blasted miracle,' there was a lurching crunch behind us followed by a spine-chilling scraping noise. My blood froze solid in my veins, for I knew that it was the grotesque General who somehow did not want to die.

"How the hell is he still alive?" I wailed, glancing behind me. "I've killed him twice already."

---

26. Charles Theodore & The Banishment of The Illuminati 1785. On March 2nd 1785 the second edict was passed specifically banning membership of the Illuminati and making it an imprisonable offence to be part of the order. Initially, Weishaupt fled to the principality of Regensburg, but finally settled in Gotha under the protection of Duke Ernest II of Saxe-Gotha-Altenburg. He is rumoured to have hidden in many places whilst escaping the authorities including, amongst others, a chimney. Although S. Drechsler does not give a precise date for this evening, we could have expected Weishaupt to have thought the decree inevitable and therefore may well have left his homeland some weeks before, which would tie in exactly with these recollections.

"Oh dear," murmured the Professor. "Better get a move on."

Most unhappy to be the last in the shaft, but having nothing else to do but carry on my interrogation, I continued ranting, "Another thing, Professor, could you please tell me what in Hell's name took you so long to get your blasted cutlass out from under your confounded robe?"

He chuckled, "Oh yes, the stupid thing got stuck in my belt."

Although momentarily wanting to murder him for his breath-taking off-handedness, I muttered, "Thank you," for the shot that saved us all. Still, there was more that I needed to know and, as I splashed along, I gasped, "So, where the Devil did you get the robes from?"

"Oh yes. I found them on a dead sentinel lying in the road leading to the castle."

"Well, it was me or Klaus who put him there," I proudly shouted. Then, suddenly remembering the most important point of all, I cleared my throat before asking, "One more thing, Professor, this 'End of Times' prophecy that we are all doomed?"

"Ah, that old chestnut, what about it?"

"Well, damn it man! Would it not have been a good idea to tell me about it *too*?"

"Look, Sebastian, some people will always be hell-bent on fulfilling biblical prophecies. Being Luciferians, the Illuminati are bound to mold their plans to mirror what is written in the Book of Revelation, where Satan's armies conquer the world. But the rumour it was inevitable was started by that idiot Comte De Viriue when he realised the Illuminati had aligned themselves with the biblical prediction of the future. This trick of making the people fall for prophecies is known as a 'cosmic trigger.' Of course, the Order will spread this insidious idea, so that man thinks that it's his destiny to finally succumb to evil, with all that '*six six six*' mumbo jumbo and '*no man shall be able to buy or sell without the mark of the beas*t' rot. But this absurd dogma has always been the inherent problem with organised religion..."

He was straying from the point and I reminded him by butting in, "Professor, is the prophecy true or not?"

"Well, it's *true* that it exists, but so do many other prophecies. Think of it this way. The fact that we're here at all, and choose to fight, is proof that God, whatever God is, has not forsaken us. Moreover, we are made self-evident by our freewill, which, in turn, means logically there is every chance that we will win in the end."

As you may imagine, this was a difficult philosophical conversation to have when crawling down a pitch black, shit-filled pipe with an unstoppable zombie scraping an axe along behind you. But we were still debating it ten minutes later when we emerged from the tunnel into the bottom of a steep wooded valley dotted with patches of snow and brightly lit by moonlight.

"But, if it is possible that we might prevail in the end then why did you tell Francesca the prophecy is inescapable?"

"It's only a prophecy, Sebastian. It's not carved in stone or anything. Come to think of it, it probably is. Look, perhaps you should find out for yourself and not believe everything I say."

"Would it not be wise then, Professor, for you to indicate when we should, *or shouldn't*, believe what you say?"

An awkward silence passed while he thoughtfully stroked his beard, before Francesca implored, "Can we?" and threw an anxious glance at the dark mouth of the tunnel. We nodded at one another and hurried off between the trees. *[27.]

---

27. The Illuminati & The Compte De Viriue. This French aristocrat was made famous by his statements regarding the Illuminati after attending the order's grand congress in Wilhelmsbad in 1782. He said, "*The conspiracy that is being woven is so well thought out that it will be, so to speak, impossible for the Monarchy and the Church to escape from it.*" He could thereafter only speak of Freemasonry with 'horror.' The 'cosmic trigger' has been termed a 'thought tunnel' by Robert A. Wilson in '*Illuminatus*' (1977). Also known, in certain traditions, as 'The Chapel Perilous,' it broadly refers to an induced public state of mind.

It was true that the Professor was my guardian angel, coming to my aid in times of need, but should an angel put me in these situations in the first place? "Audacity, audacity," he had boldly declared, "You'll be fine pretending to be the Count." But that had blown up in our faces like Francesca's jewellery box. Running down the hill through the snow-covered trees, I remember thinking that, though he was not perfect, life had certainly become a lot more interesting since making his acquaintance. At that moment, I actually thought that we might survive the petrifying night and live to tell the tale. But it was not over yet. Not by a long chalk.

We heard the roar of rushing water and soon came to a powerful river but, daunted by its high banks and fierce current, hurried on down the hill searching for somewhere else to cross. A little further on, we discovered a fallen tree spanning the gorge, so Francesca got on first followed by Van Halestrom and then me and the three of us shimmied along. 'Snap!' I heard something crashing through the undergrowth behind me and flung my head around to see the General's white blood-stained breeches running towards us through the trees.

"We should be quick!" I yelled, shimmying as fast as I could.

In one awful moment, the gruesome old soldier reappeared at the riverbank and clambered onto the tree, dragging himself along with his axe. Half his face and left arm were hideously mutilated and I could not believe that he was still alive, let alone able to keep up with us. Now there were four of us on the rotten old trunk, and one of them was belting it with an axe. Unsurprisingly, it began to creak beneath us and, as the four of us edged to the middle, it could bear the weight no longer. It creaked once more before, in one heart-stopping moment, snapping in half and plummeting towards the river.

Sweet Mother of God! It had been a bad night already, but it was about to get a lot worse and the pieces of log hit the ice-cold water with a tremendous splash.

Though we all managed to hang on, to my maddening despair, the ghoulish general managed to cling to my half with extraordinary resolve and we were quickly gathered by the current.

"Sebastian!" cried Francesca, but her voice was hardly audible above the roaring water. The log she and the Professor were sharing drifted towards the bank and they grabbed the branch of a tree to pull themselves ashore. But mine, being in the middle of the river, surged on downstream. As they faded into the dark, I heard Van Halestrom call out, "Audacity, audacity, Sebastian! Don't worry, we will find you!" before I lost them from sight.

"Francesca!" I yelled back, but my voice was drowned out by the deluge. The log tossed so violently that I had to brace myself with both hand, but, at the other end, the General whacked his axe into it and relentlessly pulled himself closer - still on his mission to kill. No! How was he capable of this? I babbled a flurry of curses as we passed through some rapids, hectically half submerging then bobbing up again but, though the log was thrashing about like a wild horse, the ghostly soldier was still able to drag himself another foot towards me. God's blood! If there were ten men like this they would be invincible.

Onward the log sloshed, writhing in the turbulent waves and all the time picking up speed. We slammed into a rock which I tried to grab but the slippery stone was too far away for me to grip properly. The noise increased to a deafening roar until the terrible moment that I saw - the waterfall - and I yelled, "I don't believe it!" with such force that it blocked out the sound of the water crashing around us. I could tell there was a huge drop beyond the lip as I could see the top of a distant mountain range looming up, but also because of the ever-increasing roar of water pounding over the edge - the edge that I was remorselessly being swept toward! Now I panicked seriously - again - and jabbered, "Please God, I know I've asked you once already to save me and I haven't yet had time to keep my promise but, if you're still listening, please save me again. Right now!"

I screamed as the General inched closer, only seconds away from being in striking range. I was already too near my end to move any further away. Why did God keep plucking me from danger only to throw me back into another endless maelstrom of peril? Could he not make up his blasted mind?

Then a single fragment of hope. One last glistening rock came speeding towards me on the water's blackened surface and I leaned off the trunk as far as I dared, knowing that this would be my last chance. It was impossible to swim in the surging current. Any man would have drowned or been swept over the edge. I had to make this work or die. The log dipped and rose and I reached out, but screamed in terror when, at last, the General came close enough to get me and pulled his axe up ready to kill.

Chapter 28

The Hound of Hell

The gruesome General stared emotionlessly at me with his one remaining eye and swept up his axe as the water crashed all around us. I lunged at the rock and clung to it in desperation as his end of the log swung over the edge of the waterfall. I'm sure that it was the weight of his axe that tipped it in my favour because the trunk hung for a split second before falling over the side and the zombie soldier, still dressed in his full uniform and with his infernal axe raised above his head, finally disappeared.

"Thank Jesus Christ for that!" I gasped, staring where he had been. "I was begining to think he would never leave."

I clutched the rock for a moment before pulling myself up to get away from the water splashing on my legs. I was only a couple of yards from the pounding waterfall's edge and I cautiously stood up to look at the view. It was so stunning that it took my breath away - even further. Such beauty in such a mad, mad world. The snow-covered Bavarian mountains all around with their jagged ridges lit by a sky full of stars and a huge glowing moon. Yes, it was indeed a beautiful night. That's when I realised, 'I must get warm or I will freeze to death.' To my good fortune, the stones to my right were close enough together for me to leap, very carefully, from one to the next to reach the riverbank. But I took my time doing this for, had I gone in, I would have died for sure.

Once I had clambered onto the bank, I pelted off through the trees like a hare, more than aware that the best way to get warm was to keep moving fast. I was not totally soaked, in fact my upper half was surprisingly dry, so maybe I would survive after all. That was when I heard shouting and saw the glow of many lanterns coming down the hill. A search party. Damn it!

I wasn't out of this yet. Now I could not go back upstream to search for the others. I prayed that they were safe and bolted back down the hill. Tearing through the snowy undergrowth, my heart jumped again on hearing the awful sound of barking dogs and I pushed on even harder. For I knew that they had released the hounds.

I flew down the hill, barging between the trees and bushes, even once or twice taking a tumble but running on again without stopping. The dogs were faster than their masters and, such was my progress, that after a while the lanterns and the shouts began to fade. But above my panting I could hear, and sometimes very well, the growling of a dog.

For maybe fifty paces behind me, I could make out the movements and incessant snarling of what, I estimated to be, an extremely large creature. It had obviously picked up my scent and was now homing in for the kill. I flung myself on ever faster making my lungs burned from the effort. I took a massive leap and landed on some shale then slid down the hill to some rocks at the base of the waterfall, descending thirty feet in a matter of seconds. I did not stop but vaulted another huge boulder at least a dozen feet high and sprinted off along the riverbank, thinking, 'Let's see you do that as fast you stupid animal' and, of course, that's when I tripped and took a fall.

It was the sort of tumble that a distressed damsel makes in a poor play when the writer cannot imagine a better way for her pursuer to catch her, and I would have kicked myself had I not fallen flat on my face. I looked up in some pain, but had to look again when I saw the mad General only a few paces away and marching towards me still holding his wretched axe above his head. Somehow he had survived his deadly fall and was going to get me after all. "Please! No!" was all I could wail and pathetically put my hands up in front of my face.

I heard the snarl of the dog first then gasped as the huge beast flew from the shadows and clamped its jaws round the General's throat. The two of them crashed in a sprawling heap behind a boulder as the animal tore away at its prey. I didn't stay to see what happened next but sprang up and bolted off in pure disbelief at the miraculous attack that had saved my life for sure.

"Christ that dog is big!" I yelped, as I dashed into the night. But I had only got twenty yards when I heard a stunted whimper. Had the General killed the thing? I could not believe it! Sweet Jesus! Could nothing stop this one-man army? The dog was as big as a blasted bear for God's sake. However, after running a little further, I was sure that I could hear the creature behind me again. Or was it another? There was definitely something chasing me, though, whatever it was, it was not catching up. Eventually, I guessed that it must be the same animal but, now wounded by the General's axe, it had been slowed. Did this mean that the giant beast had actually got the better of the old soldier? I prayed to God that it had and that mad General Frederick II, Landgrave of Hasse Kassel had, at last, been killed. It was hardly surprising considering the barrage of deadly injuries that he had received.

Now at least, it was only a wounded hound pursuing me but, by the sounds of the growling, it seemed more determined than ever to catch me. But I was determined too. The land at the base of the valley opened out into a flat narrow plain with near vertical flanks and, due to my terror, I was going at a fair pelt. I was a healthy nineteen year-old in those days, and fit. Really fit. After a few minutes, I found my running pace and looked up into the skies far above. I must have lain unconscious in the castle for hours, because I could already see the first glow of sunrise over the mountains to the east. I carried on going, for now I was getting warm. "Come on dog. Let's see who can win this now," I grunted and pushed on into the night.

And so the chase went on. A few times, I thought that I had lost the beast, but it seemed able to keep up with me whilst on level ground, so, as soon as the terrain allowed it, I started to climb. Making good use of my new-found mountaineering skills, I ascended a ravine in the side of the valley but, when I looked behind, the huge black dog was already halfway up and hungrily staring back at me.

"They certainly feed that dog well," I puffed, "Or maybe not well enough." When I reached the top, I kept up my pace and belted along and, more determined now than ever to lose the hound, sprinted as fast as I could for at least a mile until I was confident that it had given up. However, an hour later, I saw the creature yet again. Though it was a whole rise away, perhaps half a mile, it was still doggedly keeping up the pursuit. At that moment, I even considered confronting the thing, but thought better of it, fearing its powerful jaws and extraordinary energy.

"Every time you let me think I've got away Lord, I find it to be an illusion." I cursed the never-ending chase. It was as though a test had been sent down to me by some misanthropic Greek god. Well, if it was a test, then, like Hercules, I was determined to survive it and sped up my pace once again. By this time Francesca and I should have pleasured each other extensively, and I lamented the sweet smelling warm sheets at the inn and the soft skin of my lady who was now so far away.

And where was I? So far, the lie of the land had forced me to travel in the opposite direction to Pettendorf but, after another mile or so, for the first time, there were two paths which I could take. I could go west, back down into the valley, or turn east and carry on up the snowy ridge, where I could see some steep bluffs that would favour my abilities over the dog's. I glanced over my shoulder. Though the brute was nowhere to be seen I sensed that, wherever it was, it would still be stubbornly chasing after me.

I pushed on up the ridge, where I found a sheer escarpment of rock which I spent several minutes climbing, certain that the animal would not be able to get a purchase on the tiny finger holds. When I reached the top, I looked down and, sure enough, the persistent beast arrived below. It glared up at me, barking viciously and limping round in circles, obviously unable to get up the small cliff. I could see that its front leg was badly wounded. So why didn't the blasted thing just go home? I wondered if Weishaupt's soul had entered the creature instead of going to Hell, or that maybe he had put it in a trance like the mad General.

Once at the top of the escarpment, I looked back over the lip and stuck a finger up at the animal before making myself scarce. Though I was sure that was the last I would see of it, I still kept up a trot, just in case. It had been such a horrendous night that every yard away from the dog and the horrid castle made me feel a little better.

Hours later, with the low winter sun at its highest point, I came to a stop in the snow at the top of a gentle rise and took a breath of fresh mountain air. I relaxed then, about the chase anyway, convinced that the dog and everyone else had given up. At least I was dry, but now the most important thing to do was to find shelter, because I was getting tired. The countryside was a white wilderness in every direction and I still had no idea of where I was going. I checked that my bearings were right by the sun, to stay on the course which I had charted, then set off again tugging my tattered coat round me to keep warm.

I gave a little whistle as I came down the rise to keep my spirits up, but they toppled like a felled tree when I saw the dog's black head appear over the crest ahead. Somehow it was back, six hours since I had last seen it, dragging its front leg but fiercely growling. The terrifying creature stared at me with death in its eyes from only thirty yards away and moved in for the kill.

I tried to run off but the snow was so deep that it was impossible to get away. There was no cover around and no tree to run up like a frightened cat. Shit! Shit! Shit! What was I to do?

When the animal got within ten yards, I turned round with my hands out as it lowered itself to spring. It leapt at me and I desperately tried to grab hold of its mouth. "Damn you!" I yelled but lost my grip as its massive head thrashed about trying to catch me in its jaws. It clawed my face and nearly got the better of me, but I smacked it on its nose and it pulled away. My God - it was big! Nearly as big as me. Before I could get my breath back, it leapt at me again but his time I caught its face and, using all my might to hold its teeth apart, I somehow managed to wrestle the thing to the ground. It really was the size of a small bear, but its front leg was virtually useless and it was also bleeding heavily from its neck. I am sure that it was these injuries which allowed me to get the upper hand and keep its jaws at bay and that, had it not been wounded, it would have easily won.

This was a fight till the death and I knew it. It was either me or it. One of us was going to die. I had heard that the only way to kill a dog with your bare hands was by ripping its mouth apart and, although the thought disgusted me, I had to make it stop. It put up such a fight trying to push me off with its back legs, and find the power in its teeth, that I feared it would never give up. But, after ten truly horrific minutes, I eventually overcame its strength and, with a terrible whimper and an almighty crack, I split its jaw bones apart and the dog from Hell was finally dead.

I burst out crying with relief and fatigue and pain and sympathy for the poor beast. I no longer believed that it was possessed. It was simply determined to do what came naturally. Unlike a man obeying cruel orders, the dog somehow had more dignity. It had no idea of morality. I was simply its prey. There was no right or wrong to its savagery. It was just its way.

I pushed its huge carcass off me and got up then wiped my face on my sleeve. The animal had bitten me after all. I had not realised in the fight, but I was bleeding badly from my face and saw fresh droplets of blood staining the snow. I turned around and moved off again keeping to my course. Now I was exhausted, freezing, *and* injured. I knew that I had to find some people, or a road soon, or I would be in real trouble.

Three hours later, with the sun going down, I started to panic anew as I had still not seen anyone, or a house, or a road, or even tracks all day. There were no signs of life anywhere. By then, I must have travelled twenty miles over extremely rough terrain, I was lost, tired, scared, getting colder by the minute, and too exhausted to move about quickly to keep warm. I stopped for a moment to try to get my bearings and shivered in the biting wind.

My mind was awash with self-pity and regret. I couldn't be killed now. Not by the cold. Not after fighting off such odds and coming through. I stumbled on, feeling angry with myself. If I did die, it would be my own fault for getting lost. I dreamt of Francesca and the Professor's warm study at the university and the comforts of my family's house and my mother's kitchen with the sweet smells coming from her oven. My mind started to wander as I staggered along gazing into the clouds above me. The weather was worsening by the second and a blizzard was starting to gather. I knew that I must find shelter quick or perish.

An hour later, with only a few minutes of life-preserving twilight left, I blundered through a swirl of snowflakes which flew so fast they were like nails striking my skin. I stumbled on like a blind man with my arm out in front of me as the last of my strength ebbed away, thinking to myself, 'It's all over Seb. You're going to die. Admit it.' I had exerted myself so heavily over the past day that I had nothing left and I eventually went down on my knees in the snow, unable to go any further.

I began to pray, "At least I tried Lord. But, in the end, I have failed to stay alive and keep my promise to you. So prepare to receive me into your arms." With the storm raging about me, I went to curl up and die right there, because I knew there was simply no point in carrying on.

For some reason, I lifted my head once more and stared into the gathering dark. I don't know why. It was simply instinct but, as I squinted through the blustering flakes, for a second, I thought that I saw a faint light twinkle in the distant gloom. Then, no sooner had I looked, than it disappeared. Blaming the mirage on my imagination, and my deluded state of mind, I cursed the heavens and the blizzard swirling around me and went to find my icy grave. But, as I turned away, my heart leapt when I was sure that I saw the light again and I knew that it was real. Sensing that it must be a house, I focused on the distant pinprick of hope and stood up. Joy of joys! I was to be saved. I pulled myself together for the final part of my awesome journey and staggered off into the gale, gasping, "You're going to make it Seb! You're going to blasted-well make it!"

I sped up, feeling a new found vigour flowing through my aching limbs, inspired by the prospect of warmth and safety. For a moment, I worried that the house might be full of thugs or, even worse, monsters like the ones that I had already fought. But I was so cold that I did not even care. All I wanted was to be warm and I would not have given a fig if the Devil was there rubbing his feet by the fire. When I came up to the tiny cottage, I was certain that it was safe because I saw a line of horseshoes on the door to ward off evil spirits, and the Devil doesn't usually hang good luck charms on his house.

Seconds later, I was pounding on the door which was opened by a family eager to help a needy traveller and give him shelter from the storm. They took me in and I was saved as the warmth of their fire flowed into my body..

I was given broth and a blanket and I knew that the chase was really over, and that the terrible ordeal had, at last, come to an end. After all the horror that had befallen me on my astonishing saga, and all the heinous evil that I had seen, it was the humblest of things which had been my saviour. A fire, a roof, some food, and care from those decent people. I realised at that moment that, however much death and terrible horror exists in the world, there is always some love somewhere and, sometimes, thankfully, in the places where you least expect to find it. And thank God for that. *[28].

---

28. General Frederick II, Landgrave of Hesse Kassel. This character, who made his fortune renting Hessian troops to the British Army during the American Revolutionary War, had definite connections with the Illuminati and must be who S. Drechsler is describing. Though his death is recorded as being on 31st October (All Hallow's Eve) 1785, some seven months later meaning that, if the author's account is to be believed, General Frederick would have had to cling on to his life for some time, with an amazing set of injuries, before finally dying. Although, tellingly, S. Drechsler never actually sees him die, so this may explain this intriguing anomaly in his story.

Chapter 29

Odysseus Returns

My odyssey was not fully over and, perhaps, I was beginning to understand that nothing ever was. We were snowed in for two days by the blizzard that would have certainly killed me had I not found refuge when I did. The master of the house told me that I was miles from anywhere else where I could have found shelter and had been very lucky to find them the way that I had come. He promised to take me to Regensburg as soon as the snow had cleared, where I could make arrangements for my journey home. I lied, of course, about the circumstances which had brought me to their door. I am sure that they had no wish to hear the real version of events. So I kept my mouth shut about my adventures, not wanting to risk being thrown out for scaring the children. Fortunately, my fine clothes, although damaged beyond repair, convinced them that I was a man of distinction. So, with my tired disguise still working, I was treated with the utmost respect and courtesy while we waited for the snow to stop falling.

Two days later, the master of the house brought me into Regensburg onboard his old cart. I thanked him kindly for his family's hospitality and paid him for his help, then booked myself onto a stagecoach with the money that Bacon had given me for tips. Twelve hours after that, I was finally back in Ingolstadt and walking through the door of my humble lodgings.

"My sweet Lord! It's good to be home," I cheered. My little place seemed so wonderful right then and I finally felt completely safe. Instinct told me that my friends had also escaped and I prayed that, with the whole business at an end, we could relax about the future with our work, at last, completed. So, I hurriedly changed back into my normal clothes and, after finding the box of pearls under my bed, which had been very much on my mind,

I ran all the way to the university to find Van Halestrom and hopefully Francesca to tell them that I was alive and of my incredible escapade.

As I had expected, the clerk at the door told me that the Professor was there and I was delighted to find him in his study. He too was thrilled to see me safe and sound and we exchanged our amazing accounts of escape. But on hearing his final piece of news, I shouted out in misery, "What do you mean she's gone again?" For it was true. The blasted woman had gone again. This time to Paris of all places.

"Paris!" I cried, as if to confirm it, considering that this lady and I were like a pair of opposing magnets, constantly repelling each other whenever brought together.

"But *why* in Heaven's name?"

The Professor opened a drawer of his desk and took out his pipe. "There is much upheaval in the land of France, my lad. Threats of bloody revolution sweep the streets. Brave Francesca travels there as we believe the Illuminati wish to control this force, which may be natural or maybe not. Though, I believe it is the latter and created in order to bring about their seditious plans - To bring about the fall of an entire nation by stealth." [29.]

I shook my head. "Is this possible?"

---

29. The Illuminati & The French Revolution. Many historians have long contested that the Bavarian Illuminati were involved in the fermentation of the revolutionary forces that led to the overthrow of decadent King Louis XVI's '*regime ancien*' which ruled France until 1789. Notable works such as; '*Secret Societies; Illuminati, Freemasons and the French Revolution*' (2007) by Una Birch and John Robison's '*Proof of a Conspiracy*' (1798), document detailed plans of how the Bavarian secret society, along with many influential French Freemasons, conspired to bring about a popular nationwide uprising. A list which included, amongst others; the Duke of Orleans (Freemason), the Marquis de Lafayette (Freemason) and the Jacobin Club, a radical nucleus of the revolt formed by other prominent Freemasons.

"Oh yes, my lad, believe it." He puckered on his pipe and sparked his firebox into life. "A few men sitting in a room hundreds of miles away can most certainly induce such massive change. Francesca has gone to find out who these men are and will return when she has done so and not before." He blew out a ring of smoke and settled back into his chair. "Just be patient, Sebastian. The best things come to those who wait."

Having hoped so desperately to find her there, after coming through so much, and so far, and with nothing else on my mind but to make the unpredictable woman mine, I quipped, "Patient, sir? I have been patient for a blasted year," and pushed myself from my chair impetuously going to find her.

"Calm yourself, lad. If it is truly love then I'm sure it will survive the test of time." He chuckled to himself and blew out another looping ring of smoke.

His patronising attitude was insufferable and I snapped, "But what do you know of *love*, sir? I see no woman in your life."

As soon as I said these churlish words, I realised that I had crossed a line. He looked me right in the eye and suggested, "Perhaps it would be best if you sat down, Sebastian. I feel there is something that I must share with you."

I eased myself back into my seat as the Professor rose from his and faced out of the window. After a moment to collect his thoughts, he spoke softly over his shoulder, "I can understand your longings for Francesca, Sebastian, because, like you, I was once very much in love myself. I have not told you of this before as I felt it was unnecessary, but now I feel that I must explain."

He paused for a moment staring into the distance then began, "I was married a long time ago to a wonderful woman called Theresa. Much like you, my feelings for her were such that I did not care about the ramifications that our union would have upon our lives, and the lives of others."

"At that time, I was a member of an organisation which barred its membership from matrimony and, although I tried to keep our union a secret, eventually it was discovered and I was forced to leave. This may not seem important, but it had huge consequences for those around me, especially poor Bacon. He was the one who had mentored me during my indoctrination into the order and, because of my indiscretion, he was also made to leave. I believe he has already told you of the system to which we adhere. This was a legacy of this order to which we once belonged. It was the noble order of the Rosicrusians. This esteemed institution originated to oppose the dogma of organised religion and to support ideas of science, empiricism and the true understanding of nature. Presiding over the society were eight members who took oaths to heal the sick without payment, to maintain a secret membership, to find a replacement for themselves before they died and to remain sworn bachelors. When I was found to have broken this last oath, unfortunately both mine and Bacon's involvement was at an end. Though we had both realised that, in the future, it would not be the church, but the Illuminati that posed a threat to civilisation, it was still humbling to be excluded from the society in which we had invested so much of our lives and it came as a terrible blow." *[30]

---

30. The Order of The Rosicrusians. The Rosicrucian order was a secret society founded in late medieval Germany by Christian Rosenkreuz. The sect's manifesto was heavily influenced by alchemist, astrologer and occultist John Dee, Queen Elizabeth I of England's head of security, and Dee's pupil, Francis Bacon. As S. Drechsler describes the mandate of the order was one of scientific empiricism over religious dogma, especially that of the Roman Catholic Church, which may explain Van Halestrom's philosophical approach, though the Brotherhood certainly did not shy away from mysterious theology themselves. The history of the Rosicrusians and the Illuminati is interestingly intertwined, some historians even comparing them in purpose and manifesto. Though, if S. Drechsler's comments are to be believed, this seems less likely.

'More secrets,' I thought, but he had still not told me everything so I probed, "But then, what happened to your wife, sir?"

He sighed before turning back to me. "That is the worst part of all, Sebastian. Theresa paid the ultimate price for my membership. She is dead."

"Good Lord. I'm so... sorry, sir. How..?"

"I killed her."

"Holy Mother..."

"When the Illuminati infiltrated the Rosicrusians they found out that we knew of their plans and we became marked men. Thus those around us also became targets. The Illuminati kidnapped Theresa's parents and threatened to kill them if she did not kill me. She had no choice in the end. Of course, I did not know it was her when she came for me, but thought that the robed figure was one of their agents and, sadly, I took her life."

I could not believe this earth-shattering news. It was as though a millstone had been hung around my neck. What could I say? What could I do? At least now I fully understood his obsessive will for the Illuminati's destruction. I struggled to think of a way that I could console the man, but it was impossible. In the end, I considered revenge and ventured, "But, sir, why did you not do away with Weishaupt yourself? You have had so many opportunities."

"This happened before Weishaupt was enlisted into the Order. He was merely a Jesuit scholar back then. It is those that are behind him whom I seek to destroy, and Herr Weishaupt was useful in leading us to them."

A rare silence fell between us and, after a while, I pushed the box of pearls onto the desk. I did not know how to comfort him and was deeply ashamed about the way that I had brought up the harrowing subject. With this catastrophe weighing heavily on my mind, and obviously his own, I decided to take my leave.

"I should go, Professor. I am sure there is much that requires your attention."

Humbled, I got up and made my way to the door. As I opened it he asked, "I trust you took one of the pearls for your old age, Sebastian?"

I hung my head. "Yes, Professor."

"Then, I fear I have more bad news for you. It seems that you have been labouring under another misconception. I'm afraid the pearls are fakes. Weishaupt has used a similar trick before. He was always the illusionist. Until the bitter end."

He was so confident that he did not even turn around to check. I was devastated to hear this. My mind returned to the pearl hidden back at my house. It would have been worth a fortune. Now, along with my dreams of a pension, it had been taken away in the blink of an eye.

"Though it will not be equal to the amount you have lost, Sebastian, I will of course pay you for your recent work. I shall instruct my clerk to make up the sum and have it delivered to you."

"Thank you, sir," I answered quietly.

He remained staring out of the window and I left, gently closing the door behind me. Walking back to my lodgings, I was suddenly possessed with an overwhelming sense of grief. Good Lord. I had been so happy moments before, glad to be alive and overjoyed that those close to me were also safe from danger. But the Professor's revelations had changed everything. Not only was I crestfallen about the pearl, but his terrible story made me worry anew.

My way took me past Jan's old rooms. It was a path that I had been reluctant to take only a few months before, as I feared accidentally bumping into him. Now the pain of his loss was made raw again by the awful tale that I had heard.

I had already lost my oldest friend. How many others in my life might die if I carried on my battle with the Illuminati? Van Halestrom had lost his wife, Francesca her sister. Who might be taken away next? My parents? Francesca? Let alone me. It seemed that my new self was merely the old one, but with a hundred terrible ordeals polluting my memories. Whatever it was that I had discovered in my new life, it had not given me the courage to beg my best friend to change his ways. The money that I had earned had made me feel as though I was a gentleman with the things it allowed me to buy; the fine clothes, the saddle and bridle for Petrova, but was it really worth it if I was dead along with everybody else?

There was another uncomfortable aspect that occurred to me. Was I being used by Van Halestrom as an instrument of revenge? This may seem cynical, but I worried that, in his eagerness to smash the Order that had wounded him so terribly, he would overlook the safety of others. I could not be sure. At that moment, all I wanted was to find Francesca and convince her to move away with me to somewhere in the country miles away from anywhere. A place where we could be together and be safe from the seething forces of darkness that conspired against us. I also thought then, for the first time since beginning work for the Professor, if I really wanted to carry on in his employ. Even picking up a letter for the man could have potentially lethal consequences, and doing anything more than that was surely always going to be a matter of life or death.

I let out a forlorn sigh as I let myself back into my lodgings. Van Halestrom had told me to be patient. 'The best things come to those who wait,' he had said and, as I considered this, I realised that there was no other option. All I could do was wait. All I could do was wait, and hope.

Chapter 30

The Waiting Game

So I waited, and waited, and waited some more and, even as spring burst into life all around me, I waited, but still she did not return. It was three whole months later in May, when, at last, I received a letter sent by her from France. Though it had been a long time, her tender words instantly brought my fondness flooding back in waves. She thanked me for saving her in the dungeon and told me how she would come to me instantly if she were not so far away.

This was a great relief to me as, during the past few months, I had begun a friendship with a pretty young woman from town, of whom I had grown fond. Though I had not attempted to consummate this relationship, having not given up the hope of seeing beautiful Francesca again, I had found that this lady's company eased my mind and I was proud to court such a beauty.

I worried that, in the end, I was only a man and I could not wait forever. Simultaneously, I realised that Francesca was only a woman. A woman with so much on her plate, so to speak, and that I could not expect her to be faithful forever too. However hard it was for me, I tried to put these pangs of doubt to one side.

You must understand that, though I truly believed I loved Francesca, it had been three long months since I had seen her last, and that had been for less than ten minutes at the inn where she had called me a foolish boy. It had been another four months before that when we had shared a single kiss at the Professor's castle. I was not a priest. I was a normal young man. So don't go thinking good old Seb was disloyal to his romantic feelings and go calling me a heartless cad or worse, thank you very much. I was merely a human being, that's all, and a lonely one at that.

There was still much gossip around the campus about Weishaupt's disappearance and the banishment of the Illuminati. The Professor informed me that arrests of the membership had started and, though my meetings with him continued, there was noticeably less urgency in his plans. Although he maintained there was 'much to do' and that 'the fight wasn't over by a long chalk,' I found this hard to understand. Surely, if Weishaupt was dead, sent back to the rancid hell from whence he came, and the Order had been banished, what were we fighting against? But the Professor assured me that 'the forces of evil still lingered in many places' and, though I was growing evermore reluctant to envisage myself part of the army that would defeat them, I remembered the cast of despicable villains already supplied to the fray and it was not so hard to believe. But then, nothing happened for a month and, by the beginning of June, I began to think that nothing would. Van Halestrom went away on business and the days turned into weeks.

Meanwhile, my strangely fractured social life still refused to die and, as such, I had been honoured, if a little surprised, to receive an invitation to a society wedding. I say friend, though, in reality, he was more of an acquaintance: aristocratic Otto Goring from the university shooting club. His cousin, a Prussian nobleman, was marrying an English aristocrat's daughter. The ceremony was to take place in Vienna, a city to which I had never been but had always wanted to see. It was later that month and, although I received the invitation by post and did not know the bride or groom, and would not see Otto until the wedding itself, as he had already finished his studies, I decided that I would go.

In the envelope along with the invitation, I was overjoyed to find a banker's draft for one hundred thalers. Otto informed me this was to pay for my journey and to buy some new clothes '*befitting a ceremony of such noble distinction.*'

The amount of money was much greater than the sum required, even if I had gone to the Emperor's tailor. This was more than convenient as I had not worked for the Professor for a while, and of course I had lost my pearl, so I was once more finding myself severely out of pocket. Whilst considering Otto must have been slightly eccentric to be giving away his money like this, in my vanity, I decided that, although we were not the closest of friends, he had done well to select me for his honourable companion at such a refined gathering and so I went out and bought a fine new outfit.

In the days leading up to the wedding, I began to look forward to the prospect of the lavish ceremony and the fine food and drink with which we were to be indulged. I was also secretly interested to see for myself the enviable lives of the aristocracy and hoped that, if I was lucky, I may be able to seduce one of the elegant bridesmaids that would, no doubt, be there in abundance.

I had recently parted from my new young lady friend from town, as no love had been forthcoming on my behalf. Probably because I was pining for you-know-who. But, after receiving no other communications from my distant Francesca, I wanted to try, once again, to forget her. And so, for the want of some free food, a little casual romance, and the chance to sample the grand life of a gentleman, I had sealed my fate, as the next part of my tale was now determined. For, as you have probably guessed, being no village idiot yourself, my tale was far from over. And you would be more than right to think such a thing. It was far, far from over.

Chapter 31

The Wedding

The two hundred and twenty mile journey to Vienna on board a packed stagecoach was exhausting but, due to strict Austrian efficiency, achieved in less than thirty six hours. Unfortunately, due to the hard Prussian seats, my backside was as sore as a blind cobbler's thumb by the time we finally reached our destination, The Imperial Hotel De Place in the heart of the old city and my spirits lifted upon seeing its gracious towers as we rattled, rather painfully, up its cobbled driveway.

I enjoyed a more comfortable evening in the serenity of the hotel and rose early the next morning to make the most of the day. The service itself was at ten, which left a couple of hours to idle about and have breakfast before meeting Otto outside the church to show off my splendid new clothes.

An hour or so later, I strolled past the plush suites on the hotel's ground floor contently patting my belly and adjusting my glorious cuffs when, to my surprise, a door opened in front of me and the figure of a priest came out and pulled me into his room. I say that he was a priest, because he was wearing a long black cassock and an enormous silver crucifix which dangled down to his waist but, if I hadn't of known better, I could have sworn that it was Professor Van Halestrom. Not that that would have been possible, as it would have been sheer madness. Then it all started to happen again.

"Hello there, lad. Good to see you," welcomed Van Halestrom, shaking my hand, but I was too shocked to shake his back.

"What are you doing here?" I asked soberly as he brushed down his cassock.

"I'm to carry out the service at the wedding."

I had not seen him for several weeks and was out of practice with the way that my mind started to fly about whenever in his company.

"What do you mean? You are not a priest."

"Exactly," he said, spinning on his heel and viewing himself in the mirror of a bureau set against the wall, "That is the plan."

"But you will be recognised. There will be people here from the university."

"We don't think that will be the case."

"We?"

Klaus appeared from the door of the bedchamber carrying a tray and gave me a wink. "Hello, sir."

"What are you doing here?" I hissed, trying to conceal my growing consternation and noticing on his tray, next to a large black kamilavkas hat, a huge false beard.

"Part of the operation, sir."

The Professor sat in a chair in front of the bureau puckering up while Klaus used a pair of tweezers to pass him the ridiculous facial hair which Van Halestrom stuck on his chin.

"You can't wear that," I fretted. "Priests don't have beards."

"This is Austria, Herr Drechsler. Everyone has a beard. Even the babies are born with them."

He turned to me with the preposterous thing hanging off the sides of his face, Klaus placed the hat upon his head, and the Professor put on some blue tinted glasses to complete the disguise. Although I knew it was him, I had to admit that he looked completely different and he began to speak in a hammy Russian accent, "Hello, I am Bishop Uzbek Natzirkov of the Eastern Orthodox Church and, as a proud Russian, thoroughly expected to have a fine display of facial hair. *Da?*"

I shook my head as he removed his spectacles and groomed himself in the mirror. "Why is this deception to be performed?"

"This is an Illuminati wedding, Sebastian. A sham marriage. A political arrangement to unite two eminent European families, Schweizer and Oglethorpe, both of huge influence, privilege and great wealth, coming together in the interests of dynastic tyranny, not love, and we, through a certain degree of serendipity, find ourselves in a position to scupper the deal. If the priest is found to have been an impostor, the union will be annulled and, thus, we will have ruined their plans."

He flicked his eyebrows, which were the only thing on his face that were not fake, apart from his eyes, which were deadly serious.

"So, let me understand. You're going to perform the ceremony, but then pronounce it null and void. Won't they simply remarry?"

"It's all about timing, my lad. This is the plan. I marry them, they believe they are so, then, as we have discovered, the unfaithful groom intends to reveal his countless infidelities to the bride in spite of her, and she will become trapped in this unhappy union. The Lady Philippine is not as joyous as her groom about the marriage brokered by their clans, but is prepared to submit to wedlock to appease the families because she does not yet know the extent of his debauchery. After his affairs are made clear, I will write a letter to the church explaining that I was a fraud and that my claim to this is sealed in the envelope containing the marriage certificate. Once the ceremony is proved to be a hoax, an avenue of freedom will become available to the bride, she will then be able to have the marriage declared null and void and the deal will be broken. This will, in turn, destabilise the conglomeration of their political power and put the Illuminati's plans back several years."

I glanced at Klaus then back at Van Halestrom and ventured, "Such complexity. Enough to make the mind boggle."

"Ah, but your job is clear."

"My job? What is that? I am merely a guest."

"And as a guest you will kill the father of the bride."

"What!" I blared, "Kill the father of the... what..?"

Infuriatingly, he repeated himself, as was his way, "Kill the father of the …"

" Kill! Kill! Yes, I heard you - All the Saints- I heard you!"

Klaus cautioned me, "Best not to shout the word '*kill*,' sir. They may not look it, but the walls here are paper-thin."

He was right. I had shouted it loud enough to be heard on the other side of the city. But it was because of the shock you understand. What could be worse? Kill the bride herself? Damn it. What was this darkness that had come into my cursed life again?

"He is an English gentleman, Brigadier James Oglethorpe, member of parliament, banker, occultist and one of the Kabbalist priests you saw at the Temple of Eleusis. He has achieved much authority in the Illuminati since Adam Weishaupt's departure and is one of the Order's top agents in the Americas. As the founder of the state of Georgia, he provides them with a foothold from which they inject their evil into the new colonies.

"So... why must *I* kill him?"

"I am the priest, I cannot."

"But you are not a priest."

"And you are not a proper guest. We elicited that invitation ourselves."

Klaus nodded to confirm this deception and, apart from everything else, I was disgruntled not to be a genuine guest.

"So you tricked me into coming here to complete this task?"

The Professor conceded - after a fashion - "Well, I suppose, in a way... yes. We sent you the invitation because we believed you might not come had you known what we wished you to do."

Before I could complain, Klaus handed me an impressive breach-loading pistol and half a dozen cartridges.

Van Halestrom carried on, "That's it, remember, in the head."

"What..?"

"Yes, after the speeches, you will find Oglethorpe in the drawing room of the hotel. He will be waiting for a courier to collect his letter informing his Illuminati masters that the wedding has taken place as planned. Then, when the deed is done, you will leave in the dumbwaiter situated at the back of the room and find Klaus in the basement to provide you with your alibi. When the murder is discovered, the party will be broken up, whereupon you will make your getaway."

"But…"

So, that was apparently that. Or so the old bird thought. I sneaked through the reception hall trying not to draw attention to my suspiciously bulging jacket and glanced over my shoulder thinking to myself, 'He must be truly mad if he thinks I'm going to carry out this barbaric act. What on God's sweet earth does he think I'm capable of?'

I left the gates of the hotel and hurried round the corner to find a café and have myself a drink. Two large glasses of beer were necessary before I began to calm down. Of all the lunatic suicidal violence - to kill a man at his daughter's wedding. Could anything be so cruel? There must be a word for this act. To inflict such terror on those around you. Terrify. Terrorise... 'Terror*ist*.' Yes, if a man made it his life's work then that would be his name.

I could not go through with it. It was as simple as that. It was sheer madness. Weishaupt was dead. The Illuminati, as far as I was concerned, or could tell, or care, were dead too. Killing this man, who posed no obvious threat to me, apart from telling me off for seducing a bridesmaid, was utterly pointless. I finished my beer and checked the time by the church clock in the square.

I was going to be late if I didn't get a move on, so I hurried off across the city and got there with minutes to spare.

A crowd was gathered in front of the imposing medieval church - a beautiful example of Gothic masonry, its flying buttresses so outstanding that I did not see what was coming next, and it was a sight that changed my life. For, when I reached the steps, I had to look once, then twice, then again, until glaring in disbelief, because there, in the line of dignitaries, shaking hands with the guests, I saw him, the human devil himself, Adam Weishaupt.

Poleaxed by fear, I edged round the back of the line, desperately trying to hide my face and chattering to myself, "But he's dead. He's dead. He's damn-well dead. I saw him die twice, at least, set on fire in the ghastly dungeon then shoved down the dreadful pit. Surely that should have been enough?"

Would God have to take him apart piece by piece, getting down to the tiny individual fragments smaller than grains of sand before obliterating every single one of them until he was gone? I looked again to make sure. It was definitely Weishaupt alright and no mistake. There was never another like him. I sneaked behind a cluster of bridesmaids at the foot of the steps and chewed at my fingernails. What should I do? Shoot him with the gun? What would be the point if he could keep coming back again and again? I remembered what the Professor had said about 'the lingering forces of evil' and the awful feeling of wickedness returned. I ducked my head and ran up the steps to seek the sanctuary of the church.

I crossed myself going through the doors and slid along a pew into the shadows at the back behind some old ladies. Weishaupt soon came in with the heads of the families and they took up their positions at the front below the altar. Why did he not burst into flames inside this sacred house? Could God not destroy him? Or was the prophecy true, and He had forsaken us to our fate?

The remainder of the guests came in, the organ started to play and, without further ado, the ceremony began. The bride entered, escorted by my elderly target, James Oglethorpe. I wondered if he was indestructible too. I doubted it. The old fart looked like a spider could knock him over. Though I knew that I could not complete the murder anyway, so what did it matter if he was gunpowder-proof?

The bridal procession made its way to the front and joined the husband-to-be. Although there were two clergymen present, Van Halestrom was nowhere to be seen and I wondered if things were not going exactly according to plan. As I suspected, when he did appear, even under his disguise, I could tell that he was flustered. Yet his timing was perfect, for the moment he walked out and took his place behind the altar, the music ended and the congregation sat down as one.

He collected himself and began in his overzealous Russian accent, "Dearly beloved, we are gathered here today in the sight of our Lord God Almighty to join these two souls together in joyous union."

He paused for breath, gazing out at the gathered multitude but, as he did, his eyes fell on Weishaupt in the front row and the sight stopped him in his tracks.

"It is… It is… It is… " he spoke as if his tongue were nailed to a spinning top and I realised that he was going through the same shock that I had suffered upon seeing our nemesis returned from the dead. In my own state of mental imbalance, I had not considered how it would affect his performance. He stumbled once more and uncharacteristically crossed his chest.

"Come on Van Halestrom," I muttered, fearful that he was going to ruin the service in thoroughly embarrassing fashion in front of two hundred guests and dignitaries. It may sound strange, but so sensitive was I to such scenes of a publicly humiliating nature, that I considered our exposure, and all its consequences, incarceration, violence, and even death, a mere inconvenience in comparison. My toes curled tight in my squeaky new shoes as a lonely cough rang out.

"Please God," I murmured, from the very edge of my pew, "Let him do it." Then. to mine, and everyone else's relief, he pulled himself together - 'Just.'

Glancing back and forth between Weishaupt and the congregation, and with his hammy Russian accent coming and going, he stumbled, "...Marriage... is the most important of human bonds…"

I listened to his every word praying for its safe and punctual delivery, desperate for it to be made without error, until, thankfully, he reached the end, "Should anyone present know of any reason why this couple should not be joined in holy matrimony then speak now or forever hold thy peace."

Well if everyone had had their say we would have been there forever I reckoned, with all the affairs, infidelities, plots, pox and other sordid immoralities going on behind the scenes, there would have been a line of prospective confessors running out of the church and halfway round the city ready to disclose any number of reasons why this 'joyous union' should not take place.

Although, as always, none were forthcoming, so Van Halestrom carried on. The pair exchanged vows and, after dropping the ring twice, the Professor eventually ground the ceremony to a conclusion, but only maintaining his deceit by the very skin of his teeth.

There had been gasps of surprise when he had mistakenly asked the groom if *he* would, "Take this *man* to be your lawful wedded *husband*." Although he had laughed it off and corrected himself, repeating the question the right way round, there were a few angry murmurs from the guests around me.

One old fossil in a military uniform sitting in the row ahead, blustered, "This priest is a fool. He should be sent back to the steppes aboard the donkey on which he came."

At last, the Professor's improbable Russian accent boomed out, "So with the power vested in me by the Great Orthodox Church, I hereby declare these two children of our Lord bound together in eternal union."

With this, the ceremony finished, the congregation stood, the organ played and that part of the awful day ended. The crowd spilled outside and milled around on the steps. I spotted the Professor greeting some of the guests so I made my way over.

"That would be an ecumenical matter, my child," huffed Van Halestrom and I winced as a man, at least ten years his senior, walked away with a confused look on his face.

"I think that went well," whispered the Professor from under his bushy moustache and pretended to bless me.

"That is a use of the word *well* of which I have been previously unaware," I complained under my breath, "It was excruciating."

"But, as far as they are concerned, legally binding."

He checked that his beard was not drooping and I recalled our more pressing matter, "Weishaupt. Did you see him?" I peeped over my shoulder at our arch-enemy, who was in discussion with a group of men at the bottom of the steps.

"Of course I saw him. Did you not see me see him?" he assured me and ruminated, "He must have been saved by the water in the dungeon's oubliette which doused the flames."

Was this possible? I stuttered, "But... but what are we to do?"

"Carry on, my lad. You know what you must do. With Oglethorpe gone, and the dissolution of the marriage, and therefore the merger, the Illuminati's plans will be left in tatters, saving many thousands of lives in the future and stifling their rancid movement. Remember, lad? The lesson? Moral calculus.

I have sealed the marriage certificate, along with my letter, in an envelope and secreted them in the church. That part of the mission is complete, now we must finish the rest." He looked behind me and smiled. "And now, how can we fail with such wonderful help at hand?"

I turned round and was stunned to see, Lady Francesca, of all people, a bridesmaid. She was standing amongst a gaggle of women waiting for the bride to throw her bouquet but, much to my frustration, watched with complete disinterest and rolled her eyes as a tall woman with horsey features caught the bunch of flowers and excitedly showed them to her jealous friends.

"Francesca? Here?"

"Oh did I not tell you she was coming?"

"No you did not tell me she was coming," I quietly wrangled, secretly remembering that I had planned to seduce a bridesmaid.

He put a hand on my shoulder. "Klaus will take you to the hotel in our carriage whilst I cause a diversion to keep Weishaupt here until the speeches are over." He looked me in the eye. "Remember, Sebastian - in the head." He pointed at his own before finishing, "I will see you later, my friend. Good luck."

"In the head! In the head! Yes," I peevishly whispered as he squeezed my arm and shuffled over to Klaus. Turning my attention to Francesca, my heart leapt as she sailed up the steps and regarded me with a tender smile.

"You're here," was all I could limply sigh before remembering our perilous situation and dragging her behind a couple of nuns.

"I see that your mind's as sharp as ever," she teased, looking round and obviously nonplused by my seriousness. She was wearing a beautiful gown of white satin and lace that would have made the goddess Aphrodite look like a tired old prostitute who worked at the docks, but my pleasure was curtailed by our most urgent problem.

"Have you seen?" I threw a glance down the steps.

She followed my eyes and gasped, "Weishaupt!" then covered her face with her shawl and hissed, "He's alive?"

"I see your mind's as sharp as ever," I jibed, but she was too shocked to pay attention.

"Then we cannot afford to fail. You know what you must do?"

"Yes, yes, I know what I must do. All but the Pope himself keep reminding me. I must approach the man who has me as a guest at his daughter's wedding and shoot him ..."

"In the head, remember?"

"Yes, yes. In the head, in the head. I would like to point out that that is the hardest part to forget."

"Good. God speed." She did her best to smile and squeezed my hand. "Now I must retire with the other bridesmaids back to the hotel."

She kissed me on the cheek before replacing her shawl and gliding back down the steps to find her carriage. Watching her pull away, I was overcome by a torrent of morbid stress and confusion but, when Weishaupt glanced over in my direction, my bowels turned inside out. So, hiding my own face, I sidled away to find Klaus's carriage and found him sitting behind the reins. He went to speak but I interrupted, "If you also attempt to remind me of what '*I have to do*,' I'll shoot you in the blasted head myself." He nodded in his own understated way and I boarded the carriage before we set off back to the hotel.

Rattling through the streets, I was gripped by an ever-intensifying sense of delirium. Weishaupt's return from his watery grave was hard enough to comprehend, but my impending act of murder now raised my pulse to a frenzied blur. Assassination was something that I had never even contemplated. Yes, I had killed, and rightly so, for those I had slain would have done the same to me or my friends. But this man was not trying to kill me.

In fact, as far as I could tell, he was not trying to do me any harm at all. How could I take his life in cold blood?

My anxiety only deepened upon reaching the hotel and, by the time I entered the banqueting hall, I could already feel the hot prickle of sweat clinging my new frilly shirt to my back. The reception was already well underway and full to the brim with the most pretentiously dressed individuals that I had ever seen.

Keeping my head low, I navigated my way through the crowded room to find my table and it struck me that there was some fine music coming from somewhere. I spotted a rather frail looking gentleman with an unruly wig playing a harpsichord in the corner and recalled that the talented composer Mozart had been hired to play at the wedding. His music was the only pleasant thing in the room, as the rest of the place was a forest of obnoxiously high wigs, plonked upon pompous snobs with vain, self-important expressions and supercilious smiles.

It was true that I enjoyed the finer things in life, but this overly-powdered lot were well beyond the pale. Though I had thought my new clothes a trifle immodest before, they now seemed plain in comparison and I felt thoroughly under-dressed. Looking around, I recognised no one at all. Fortunately, Weishaupt was nowhere to be seen, but my heart sank when I scanned the room and could not spot Francesca anywhere. Upon joining the party at my table, I did not like the look of the characters who were seated. I had barely pulled up a chair before my suspicions were confirmed when one of the dusty dandies, sporting a gay vanity spot on his cheek, idly proclaimed, "Mozart bores me these days. I fear he is too complicated. His music has far too many notes." I had heard the same stupid criticism from an idiot student back in Ingolstadt who had probably heard it from another idiot who did not understand what he said. Mozart was clearly a genius. Any man - who was not a fool - could hear it, especially when he played but thirty feet away.

Angry anyway due to my dreadful predicament, on hearing this ridiculous remark I could not help but spit, "He's over there right now. Why don't you go and tell him which notes to remove so you could enjoy it more?" *31.*

Suffice to say, the next ten 'minuets' went by uncomfortably. I hunched in my seat, petrified that Weishaupt would reappear and expose me, while the snobs round the table took it in turns to show me their contempt. And they were snobs of the worst sort. All of them had at least one servant in attendance, whom they abused and humiliated with great pleasure. Van Halestrom's lessons had transformed my opinions on matters such as these, and now this behaviour sickened me to the core. After the speeches had finished, I left the table to relieve myself of both my company and the contents of my bladder, considering them to be pretty much the same.

I found the hallway and crept to the water closet in a state of fevered apprehension as the moment of my heinous task fast approached. I slumped inside a cubicle on a fine porcelain toilet with my head in my hands in a flush of palpitations. The fact that I was on one of the finest lavatories in all of Europe, did not ease my raging mind, or my shuddering bowels. I was a student for God's sake. Not a trained assassin. I shut my eyes and tried to stop myself from shaking. What would my poor parents think?

---

31. Mozart & The Illuminati. There is no doubt that Mozart was in Vienna at this time. The famous composer was also a friend of Adam Weishaupt and a member of a Masonic Lodge *Zur Wohltatigkeit* (Beneficence). His most famous opera ***The Magic Flute*** features an array of Masonic rituals and symbolism and his presence at the wedding shows the influence the Illuminati had on the cultural life of the day, as he would have been at his peak then and very much in demand. Much speculation exists suggesting that he was actually killed by the society for revealing their secrets in his work, and some that his death was brought about by his rival Antonio Salieri. Though, this topic is such a contested one that it would require a book of its own.

Maybe I could tell them one day and they would understand? I only had to consider this for a second to realise the impossibility of it and, in a fit of desperation, I explored any other way out. That was it! I would gather my friends and we would shoot Oglethorpe with a cannon from half a mile away. Yes! That was the way to do it. Long distance was the best range from which to kill a foe in cold blood. None of this close-up stuff.

Then, as you sometimes do when sitting on a water closet, I overheard something which was of great interest to me. Outside two men were talking and the first, an old Englishman, boasted, "As you know I have much profitable business in the colonies, representing a financial interest lending money to the Americans for their war against the British. And therein lies the trick, old chap. You see, my associates and I are also funding the British, but neither to the extent that one side can become victorious. Then, as the length of the conflict and the interest on the debt can be controlled, the adversaries become as shackled as the slaves on one of my plantations and will never be free. Haw, haw."

The voice of the other man, an Italian, chipped in, "I hear there have been terrible casualties in the war, Brigadier Oglethorpe."

"That is of no consequence to me, my dear Salieri. After all, I'm a banker, not a doctor. Haw, haw. Maybe one of you composer fellows should write an opera about me? ♪ I'm ♫ a banker ♪, not a doctor ♫. Dah de ♪ dah, dah ♫. Dah de ♪ dah, dah ♫. Haw, haw. I'm ♫ a banker ♪, not a doctor ♫ haw haw haw."

They both laughed and washed their hands before leaving and I peeped out of the closet to see James Oglethorpe and his acquaintance, who I guessed must be Antonio Salieri, Mozart's rival, the man rumoured to have eventually brought about the great composer's downfall, and also said to have done away with him too.

I slipped out of the cubicle and faced myself in the mirror.

The young exotic black servant in waiting looked up at me from under his turban with a doleful expression. I considered the thousands of men dying in the war that had been spoken of so callously and recalled the wickedness that I had already seen in my battles with the Illuminati; the scheming, the killings, the sacrifices, the horror, and thought of the same devilishness taking hold in another country far, far away. I patted the pistol bulging inside my jacket and looked at my reflection one last time. 'Well Sebastian, this is it old boy. This is when we find out whether you're a man or a mouse.' My decision was made right then.

It was *mouse*, and I scurried off like a little frightened one being chased by a big hungry cat, out from the privy, into the hallway, past the doors of the banqueting suite and away through the hotel. I could not do it. I was no killer. I was an ill-disciplined student who was going to go home right away to read his books. Someone else could do it; Van Halestrom, or Francesca, or Klaus, or Bacon, or the courts, or anyone else, but not me. My father would spank me for years, disinherit me, sell me into slavery then buy me back so he could do it again, and I wouldn't have blamed him. Not one bit. What had I been thinking? Some killer me. Francesca, Jan, Weishaupt, all of them were right, I was just a boy. A boy who was way, way out of his depth.

I hurried along the corridor towards the entrance but cursed my luck when Van Halestrom reappeared from his room with his back to me and still wearing his audacious disguise. Even without seeing his face, I could tell that he was vexed and obviously looking for me to remind me of what I '*had to do.*' So I dived through a door at my side and hastily crept through a room then out into another corridor and, when I heard loud voices coming from somewhere behind me, in an extraordinary twist of fate, went through yet another door and froze as stiff as a gravestone as I did.

For ten paces in front of me was Brigadier Oglethorpe with a cane in his hand hovering over a whimpering servant boy and, without looking up, he bawled, "When I want you to clean the piss off my boots, boy, then that is what you shall do!"

I was appalled when he whipped the youth in the face, spilling blood from his mouth and driving the blubbering child to the floor. I took a step closer, but the old soldier shot me a glare and wheezed, "What the blazes do you want man? Can't you see I'm conditioning my servant?"

I bit my lip and turned to go, murmuring to myself, "Just walk away Seb."

But I could not help but glance back when the boy shrieked out in pain as Oglethorpe rained down a storm of vicious blows. Again and again he whipped down the cane, his mean old voice panting with exertion, "If-I-want-you-to-clean-the-piss-off-my-boots-boy-then-that-is-what-you-shall-do!"

I stood in the doorway clenching my fists with the boy's harrowing screams ringing in my ears, "Please, sir, no more! Please... please! Uh..! No! No... more!"

At that moment, I was so consumed by an inseparable mixture of fear and rage that I could no longer tell them apart. In a haze of bewilderment and fury, I pulled out the pistol from my jacket and turned around then took a handful of steps towards the Brigadier, holding out the gun in my trembling hand and awkwardly cocking the hammer.

He saw me coming and contemptuously snarled, "Ha! You don't have the guts boy," and struck the servant even harder, grunting with the effort, "Haw! ...*Haw*! When I've finished teaching this one a lesson, I'll teach you some manners too. Like one of the niggers back on my plantation."

He brought down his cane with such sickening force that I thought he would kill the youth then raised it to strike again.

With my hand sweating on the handle and my heart pounding in my chest, God have mercy on my soul, I took another step closer, pointed the barrel at his head and pulled the trigger.

'Click!'

Saints alive! The gun was empty! Empty! In my delirium, I had forgotten to load it. The Brigadier stared at me wide-eyed, clearly shocked that I had tried to kill him, and also that he was still alive. After a handful of confusing seconds his eyes narrowed before he threw down his cane and dashed to a table then pulled a flintlock from a drawer. I watched him in a frantic daze while he primed the weapon with trained, military precision. What should I do? I did not want to have to beat him to death in the drawing room. If I had to kill him, I wanted to shoot him. And apparently I did, as he was already ramming his powder home.

I fumbled open my pistol and began digging in my pocket for a cartridge. For an older man, Oglethorpe's hands moved at an astonishing rate and I could see that he was about to finish.

"Come on Sebastian," I muttered, cursing my sweaty fingers and bungling a cartridge into the breach. His gun clicked first and I raised mine to find myself staring down his barrel as we both fired at each other's shocked faces.

'Bang!' He missed. I didn't, and a dark blast of blood spat over the portrait behind him as he fell to the floor. Amidst the gunsmoke I gasped, "That could not have been closer," and turned to see a large smoking hole in the wall behind me.

My very next and overriding thought was, 'Flee!' Stealing a glance at Oglethorpe's lifeless body, and seeing that the servant boy was at least still alive, I ran over to the dumbwaiter and threw open the hatch but, to my unforgettable horror, it was empty. Empty! Like the blasted pistol. Shit! I spun round exploding with panic and watched the incriminating trail of smoke slowly rise from behind Oglethorpe's desk.

"Why did I do that? Why did I do that?" I panted, "What on earth have I done?" My eyes shot from side to side as my mind raced, 'But it was self-defence. I was trying to save the boy and myself. Everyone would understand, wouldn't they?' I frantically recalculated, 'Of course they wouldn't you fool!'

This was the end for me and I knew it. I was trying to remember if they had the death penalty in Austria, when I saw the rope hanging in the shaft. Two seconds later, I was sliding down it with the gun stuffed in my jacket and my hands almost catching fire with the friction. I landed with an almighty crash in the basement and lay there shaking with pain and fear of death.

The hatch quietly opened and Klaus murmured, "Well done, sir." He offered his hand and urged, "Walk with me."

I got out rubbing my arse with my burning hands and relentlessly complaining under my breath about the abject failure of his part of the plan; i.e. To have the blasted dumbwaiter ready so that I did not have to half kill myself making good my escape. He explained that it had jammed when the waiter took it down and swore that it was the only eventuality that he could not control, but that he had been confident that I could use the rope. We hurried upstairs and into the courtyard where he handed me a cheroot as all hell broke loose around us.

The shots had, of course, caused a serious commotion at this, the most respectable wedding of the year and, in no time at all, the place was heaving with hotel staff and members of both families plus their servants, all running about in the confusion. My alibi was secure now that I was seen with Klaus strolling through the courtyard. Also, I was sure the servant boy had not seen my face and that the poor youth would probably not be conscious for a week.

Incredibly, it seemed that I had got away with killing the vicious old bastard, but my hand still shook while I smoked the cheroot.

I have never been a man of tobacco, believing it to be poison but, at that moment, I pulled the smoke right in. Coughing loudly, I tried to look as casual as I could as we strolled round to the front of the hotel where all hell was, indeed, breaking loose - literally. Because that was when I saw Weishaupt leaving in his coach, escorted by two mounted dragoons. As they flew out through the gates, I nervously smirked to myself, "Get your friends at court to say *that* was a hunting accident you evil gloating smartarse."

Klaus murmured next to me, "I should tell the Professor," and strode away into the throng pouring out into the driveway. The women in their gowns crying and screaming, the men pompously advising each other what to do now that the deed was done, and some of the abused servants, from time to time, sharing secretive grins. And in the middle, the poor bride, crying and wailing more than anyone else. Her day, if not of love, but much earnest preparation and care, was ruined. How could it be worse? It was Francesca who showed her exactly how, leaving her in no doubt that being married to a greasy, cheating, pox-ridden liar, and having a dead scheming Illuminati father, were not the only indignities that she would have to suffer on this most important day of her life, *My Lady* roared into the courtyard standing strident on the footboard of the bridal coach, cracking the reins and yelling, "Get on, Sebastian, that son of a bitch Weishaupt has the marriage certificate!"

I have suffered some ungracious moments in my life, but jumping aboard a stolen bridal coach, driven by an obvious imposter, at a wedding where I had assassinated the father of the bride, within earshot of said bride and her family and friends, was perhaps one of the worst. Maybe if no one had been watching like that, but in full view of everyone outside the hotel, and the bride of course, for whom this really was the last straw, marked, for me, a new social low.

"Sorry." I called, attempting a pathetic and thoroughly useless apology. Unsurprisingly, it didn't help and she fainted into the arms of her bridesmaids with the shock and despair of it all. With this last cataclysm complete, and the traumatised crowd staring agog, we sped out of the hotel's gates and, along with my first foray into high society, the wedding from Hell was over. Although, come to think of it, because of Van Halestrom's deception, perhaps it never really happened at all. *32.

---

32. Brigadier James Oglethorpe & The Illuminati. I can find no reliable information suggesting that this venerable English politician and Freemason was an important Illuminati agent, though, interestingly, he was responsible for founding the '13th' state of Georgia in the U.S.A. on the '33rd' parallel. It is also intriguing to note that James Oglethorpe is recorded to have died on the 30th June 1785 in London, which would have allowed exactly the right amount of time for his body to be returned to England. Perhaps, unsurprisingly, no details of this wedding exist although, if Drechsler's version of events is to be believed, this could have been for any number of extraordinary reasons.

Chapter 32

Secrets of the Ancients

"Well that's the last wedding of theirs that I'll get invited to," I muttered to myself as the bridal coach tore along and Francesca bellowed at the galloping horses, "Get a move on you buggers, or I'll take you to the glue factory myself! Come on there! Yah!" She shot me a stare and yelled, "Did you do it?"

"Do what?" I was still in a daze and had to search her eyes before understanding, "Yes! Yes! In the head! In the blasted head!"

She grinned and gazed up the road lashing the reins and bellowing even louder, "C'mon you buggers! Yah! C'mon!"

Vienna is a beautiful city and I had been looking forward to see the many charming buildings that lined its pleasant streets, but now those buildings flashed by so fast that I could not have seen them even if we had hit one, which we nearly did on several occasions. I grasped the side of the seat as we slid luridly around a corner and shouted, "What are we going to do now?"

"You jumped onboard, Wunderkind, so I assumed you knew! We need the wedding certificate and Weishaupt is on his own apart from his driver and the two horsemen!"

I knew how much trouble *one* of his friends could be, and worried that I might need a new pair of breeches if I was going to go a few more rounds with another bunch of terrifying bastards like that. "Right then," I calculated, "That makes four when we are two!"

"I'm so glad you're here, college boy, as I had not brought my abacus for my blasted corset would not allow it. Now instead of impressing me with your arithmetic you idiot, why don't you shoot one of them? Now! Yah! C'mon there! Ha!"

I scowled at her, took out the pistol, dug another cartridge from my pocket, quickly reloaded then brought the gun to bear. "Steady, make it count," I murmured, and tried to find the range of the closest horseman. He bounced into my sights and I let him have it, 'Boom!' Holy Christ! I got him and he fell off his horse with a wretched scream. Glancing down at his twisted body as we flew past, I tried to look as nonchalant as possible, though I was probably ready for my new pair of breeches right then.

The other rider spotted us and, seeing his friend gone, steadied his horse in the middle of the road while Weishaupt's coach sped on ahead. This rider, confidently swishing his sword and forewarned of our presence, was an entirely different kettle of fish. He looked mean as mustard and as incensed as a Spartan warrior who had just seen his boyfriend killed in front of him. By me! Curses! I pulled out another cartridge and hurriedly reloaded as we clattered up to him. He went to slash me as we passed and I shot him in the chest, 'Boom!' but he was wearing a breastplate under his tunic which I had not seen and, though he was knocked back by the shot and made only a faltering sweep, he quickly recovered then galloped after us at full pelt.

The coach was no match for the rider and he soon caught us up, then, like a whirlwind, unleashed a storm of powerful blows which smashed away several chunks of the coach. I searched for a cartridge and tried to work out if he was an automaton like the General but, after ducking another swipe, I knew that he was not because of his manly curses and the passion in his eyes. Then -Damn it!- I dropped the gun and it bounced off the footplate.

"How's it going there?" yelled Francesca, seeing my mistake.

"It's going well," I seethed, dodging another slash, "I calculate there are now only three of them and two of us. Tell me, fair maiden, am I right? Maybe you could get your blasted abacus out from your underwear and check for me!"

I got ready as he swung again, only missing my cheek by an inch but, this time, his sword lodged in the coach's roof and, as he struggled to free it, I took my chance. "Take that!" I roared and smacked him in the face, knocking him off his horse and sending him tumbling head over heels down the street. 'That was a good punch,' I reckoned, rubbing my fist as his horse faded and Francesca cracked the whip then pushed ours on with another stream of blue curses. I wrestled the sword free and brandished it at her, taking the chance to draw attention to my heroic deeds, "Did you not see that? Absolutely superb!"

I said this with such swagger that something bad was bound to happen, as so often after a little cockiness comes a fall. Sure enough, at that very moment, we shuddered to a halt behind Weishaupt's coach when it stopped abruptly in front of us and I fell headfirst into the arse of our nearest horse. As I freed my face from the backside of the confused animal and hauled myself back to my seat, Francesca noted, with her crooked eyebrow aloft, "I think that may serve you quite right, *my brave knight*."

What did not serve me right was the next frightening indignity, when, from out of nowhere, a twirling stiletto dagger nailed one of my frilly cuffs to the headboard behind our seat with a heart-stopping 'Thwack!'

"Where the devil did that come from?" I cried, pulling it out and seeing that it had indeed come straight from a devil. For Weishaupt's menacing driver was staring right at us from over the roof of his coach, but, with his eyes hidden in shadow under the brim of his black hat, and a black neckerchief hiding his features, it seemed that he had no face at all. He lashed his team of horses and drove them through the crowds of frightened townsfolk and animals blocking his path, scattering them like flies off a cowpat, as we followed on behind warning everyone to clear the way and weaving through the commotion ourselves.

"There is definitely something of the night about that one!" I moaned as we quickly picked up speed, but the deathly driver had no care for anyone else on the road and soon increased the distance between us by several lengths. Time and time again he took hair-raising risks with his horses and after countless swerves and near-misses, we rattled round a corner scarcely in time to see him steer the coach through the gates of a palatial white house. 'What's this?' I thought, 'Somewhere that Weishaupt feels safe? This doesn't feel like a safe place for us to be.'

We came through the gates then to a halt with a sudden, "Whoa you bastards!" from Francesca who smartly looked about. I shared her surprise, there was no sign of the coach anywhere, yet it had clearly come this way and there was nowhere else to hide. The windows of the grand three-storey house were all shuttered up and there were no signs of life at all. We dismounted and ran up the front steps, Francesca admittedly more hastily than me as I honestly had not expected anyone to answer but, when she beat on the door, to my dismay, it swung open with an ominous creak.

'Oh no, not again.' I groaned inside, remembering the torture chamber and my other deadly run-ins with this dastardly crew. I had secretly been relieved not to find Weishaupt and his sinister driver hiding round the corner. Though *he* had run away from *us*. Was he indestructible or not? I squeezed the handle of my sword and peered into the hallway.

Concerned to say the least about what lay in wait, I whispered, "Look, they think that they're married, Oglethorpe is dead, and we have got away with it. We've been lucky to get this far. Perhaps... we should leave?"

She threw me a disdainful look and frowned. "It's all for nothing without the certificate. We must get it for the fight."

"You've changed the tune you play on your harpsichord. What about, *You're just a stupid boy to think of it any other way*?"

I said this in a faux French accent to provoke her and it worked like a charm.

"You are still a stupid boy!" she taunted, "My views have changed wildly since I have been away."

Most women's views, I had noticed, even by that young age, had the tendency to change wildly in the time it took them to go to the privy so, having not seen this one for a period much longer than that, I resolved to put this down to experience. Though it occurred to me, that if her present plans involved breaking into a strange house, through a mysteriously open door, to chase an unkillable madman into God only knows what sinister shenanigans were bound to befall us next, then why not marriage to me, and children too?

"C'mon," she whispered and I trailed after her along the dark corridor holding out my sword. Anxious that this single weapon would not be enough to defeat whatever lay behind the double doors ahead, when she flung them open with a confident, "Ha!" I was relieved to find an empty chamber lined with purple curtains bathed in the dappling light of several tall oil lamps and, at the far end, lying safely on a wooden altar, the wedding certificate.

"What were you worried about, Wunderkind?" she chuckled, picking up her dress and running over to the altar. "Here they are!"

And there they were. Remarkably, right in front of us. How easy was that? Far too easy. Something was wrong.

"Wait!" I yelled and stuck out my hand, but it was too late. When she reached the middle of the room, a coffin-sized slab fell away beneath her and she disappeared in a flash, squealing, Sebastian!"

"No!" I ran over to the hole and threw myself to the edge, frantically reaching inside, but she was a couple of feet below my grasping hand.

My heart froze when I heard Weishaupt sneer, "Oh, it's a cruel, cruel world that keeps the things we desire out of our reach."

He appeared from behind the curtains next to the altar and flashed me a sadistic smirk then picked up the certificate.

"Damn you!" I roared, trying in vain to grab Francesca's outstretched fingers and having to endure the pitiful look of despair on her face, but -Damn it!- the distance was too great. How could he move stone with such speed?

He read my mind, "Yes, boy. Ingenious is it not? These are the secrets of the ancients used to protect their treasures long ago. A simple trick when you have mastered it, but you have not seen the half of it yet." I daredn't think what was coming next so my hair stood on end when he exclaimed, "Ah ha! Here we go," and a thunderous crunch rumbled beneath us as the walls of the underground chamber began to grind together like a vice.

"Holy Mother of God!"

Francesca desperately tried to climb out, but there was no foothold on the smooth walls and she slid helplessly back down. "Sebastian! Do something! Please! I beg you!"

"Extraordinary is it not?" chatted Weishaupt over her pleas with callous indifference, "The blocks weigh many tons yet, as you can see, the mechanism moves them as though they were pebbles. There is however, one drawback. The process is irreversible." He leaned over the altar and jeered, "So, this time, Herr Drechsler, I promise you, you will *definitely* see her die."

"Pig dog!" I raged and threw my sword at him but it missed clattered across the floor.

"Temper, temper," he scoffed then slid a large knife out from inside his coat.

"Hurry!" cried Francesca, but I could only stretch out my arm and watch her anguished expression as she jumped up and down. Weishaupt circled round us, coming between the door and the pit.

He clutched the certificate with one hand and wagged his knife at me with the other, scolding, "You never were the brightest of students, Herr Drechsler. Have you still learnt nothing yet?"

"I... I..." was all I could incoherantly stammer, unable to accept what was happening.

"Look at you, dressed up like a peacock in your fancy clothes. Is that all it took to entice you here. A bit of dainty lace and linen? Vanity is a powerful vice, is it not? Or was it your lust for this woman that made you come? She *is* very pretty, I'll grant you. But look at her now, crying like a baby, when it's her pride that's got her into this mess. Don't you see? You. Your greedy friend. Her. Everyone. You're all so weak. It is your undoing in the end. *That* is why man will always fail. You see? You are the very living proof of it, but still you don't understand."

I glimpsed my stained cuff dangling in the dark in front of me. Damn it! He was right. I was just a pathetic chump tempted by my weaknesses and lured into this awful trap by my foolishness. The prophecy *was* true. Like Adam, I had fallen.

Weishaupt crowed with triumph, "Imagine the prostitutes, the pimps, the thugs, the lawyers, the priests, the merchants, the bankers, the generals, the politicians, and even the Kings and Queens that we have at our beck and call. The money, the bribes, the traps, and, like you, the credulous simpletons that we have in our clutches. No one can escape us. Everyone falls in the end!"

Francesca screamed as the walls rolled closer and I tried to reassure her, "Fear not, my lady."

But Weishaupt threw back his head and roared with laugher, "Ha ha! Yes fear, you pathetic fool, because fear is all you have!"

"Don't fill the lad's head with that filth you pervert!" rang out a defiant cry. Saints alive! I had wished so deeply for Van Halestrom to appear at that moment that, when the silver-tipped bolt shot from the open doorway, I thought that I was in a dream.

But when it tore the wedding certificate from Weishaupt's hand and propelled it to my side, even I could not have dreamt that. Astonishing! I grabbed the papers and stuffed them in my jacket as Weishaupt shrieked with rage, "Curse you, Van Halestrom! I shall hunt you down one day."

"It is I who shall do the hunting," called the Professor, striding through the doors with his quadre bow at the ready and still dressed in his cassock and shining crucifix. Miracle of miracles! I thanked my lucky stars as trusty Klaus ran in after him and gave me a spirited nod. I was to be saved by my loyal friends in the nick of time. But before I could blink, Weishaupt's ghoulish driver sprang from the doorway behind them and fell on Klaus like an evil shadow.

"Look out!" cried Van Halestrom, but too late. The devil ran Klaus through with a dagger and the friendly man crumpled to his knees with blood bubbling from his mouth and a haunted look in his eyes.

Van Halestrom unleashed a hail of bolts into the fiend and he toppled backwards, pulling down a lamp and spilling a pool of flame across the floor which quickly ignited the bottom of the curtains. Van Halestrom went to find Weishaupt in his sights, but the coward had already vanished in the shadows behind the altar.

"Leave him, Professor! Come and help me! Now!"

"Get a move on you idiots!" bellowed Francesca as the walls ground together and the fire blazed in the corner. Van Halestrom dropped his bow and was next to me in a flash, but I had the plan. "Hold my arm, Professor, and lower me down."

I clasped his hand before edging off the lip and he grimaced with my weight as he lowered me into the hole.

"Come on, Francesca!" I implored, feeling her fingertips touching mine. I strained with every ounce of strength I had to span the vital extra inches and, at last, grabbed her hand.

Clutching it with all my might, I turned to tell the Professor to pull me up but gasped when Weishaupt's maniacal face appeared behind him.

"No!"

The Doctor smirked a sickly grin and kicked the Professor off the lip, sending me crashing down on top of Francesca and Van Halestrom landing heavily on top of us both.

He taunted us from above, "Ah ha ha ha! You clumsy fools! You might have the certificate, but it won't matter if you're all dead." His eyes darted to the fire taking hold around the room. "Though I am sorely tempted to stay and watch you die, I fear that I must leave. But what sweet joy to know you will all be perishing together." He gloated, "You know, it is only Adonai, your God of darkness, who arrogantly reserves the right to vengeance? But we, the Illuminati, are above God, so we claim that privilege for ourselves. For would you not agree, my friends? Vengeance is mine! Wah-ah ha ha ha!"

My rage boiled over as his fiendish mechanism thundered away and he poured scorn down on us. "Damn it! We cannot win against this phantom!"

'Bang!' A deafening explosion rang out next to my ear and Weishaupt fell away from the lip with dread pain etched across his face.

Incredibly, Van Halestrom had shot him with a small pistol hidden up his sleeve and muttered, "He is no phantom, Sebastian. He bleeds like all men."

We struggled to our feet without celebration nor cheer then stood shoulder to shoulder with me in the middle as the dusty walls rumbled only inches from our faces. For surely he had won and we were all going to die anyway, as there was not even room to get on top of each other. What a wretched way to go, the three of us squashed to death in this despicable sarcophagus.

I reached out for Francesca's hand in the dark and, feeling it trembling next to mine, squeezed it tight. Certain that the huge slabs were moving even faster, I closed my eyes and, with all hope gone, instinctively began to pray like my parents, "God of mercy, you have made death a gateway for our eternal life..."

Through the din and the dust Van Halestrom yelled, "Why do you continue with that nonsense, lad?"

"Because *He* is our saviour, sir!"

Even during our last moments on earth, with the jaws of death bearing down on us, he continued to educate me. "What are the chances of one group of believers being right over another? Eh? If you had been born in India you would be a Hindu, or in Persia a Muslim, or, further away than that, maybe even a Buddhist. You have the propensity for faith, that's all. It is much more likely that you are all partly correct and that God, whatever that really means, is a unifying energy that binds us all together..."

"Mon Dieu! Isn't there a better time for this conversation than now?" howled Francesca as the walls crushed in on us. I glanced at her longingly for the last time, knowing that I would never get to do the things with her that would have probably enraged all the Gods because they would have been so jealous. Damnation! With the wall pressing on my chest, I craned my head around and noticed the Professor's silver crucifix glinting in the dark. With an inkling of hope, I grabbed it and tore it from his neck.

"What are you doing?" he hollered, but there was no time to explain. I thrust up the cross as high as I could and instantly felt the walls crushing down on its ends with immense pressure. 'Please God let this work,' I prayed and amazingly, with a monumental crunch, the walls came to a juddering halt.

"Now move!" I called and, using both walls to lean on, hauled myself up on the crucifix and clambered onto the lip then rolled out on the floor gasping, "Quick! We don't have much time!"

Weishaupt was nowhere to be seen, and the room was ablaze with huge flames roaring up to the ceiling. I cowered from the heat but threw my arm into the pit and dragged Francesca out as a heavy burning joist crashed to the floor only a few paces away.

"Hurry!" She called, flinging her arm back for Van Halestrom, who we grabbed by the shoulders and yanked out with one tremendous jerk. There was an ear-splitting creak and we all watched in silent awe as the crucifix bent, then snapped in half, and the walls smashed together with one almighty,'Thump!'

"Everything has its breaking point," assessed Van Halestrom then sprang to his feet and cried out, "Come on!"

The three of us fled the inferno and had to agonisingly jump over Klaus's crumpled body, as we would have burnt to death for certain if we had stayed a second longer. Running for our very lives, we burst from the chamber and raced up the smoke-filled corridor before crashing out of the front door coughing and spluttering for air. Without pause, Francesca and I jumped back onboard our coach and Van Halestrom mounted his then, with much cracking of whips and encouragement of the horses, we all launched into the street together and charged off up the road.

Holy Mother of God! Somehow we had escaped the evil pit and the house of death, though my heart still galloped like our horses and my sweating palms shook like the carriage wheels rattling over the cobbles. I glanced over my shoulder back in the direction of the house, from where I could now see huge leaping flames and a billowing acrid plume of smoke belching up into the sky.

We didn't spare the horses and hurtled out of Vienna which soon disappeared over the horizon. After several miles of brisk trotting, our ragtag convoy pulled up at a deserted crossroads where we dismounted. I took out the all-important marriage certificate from my jacket and handed it to Van Halestrom.

"Well done, lad." He sighed and looked between us, "Sadly, I do not have time to either celebrate our victory or to share the sorrowful words for poor Klaus that we will doubtless exchange in the future. That is for another day. But mark my words, he died fighting for what he thought was right." He smiled stoically. "Now there is much urgent work to which I must attend."

He hugged Francesca warmly.

"Thank you, my dear. You are as courageous as you are beautiful." He kissed her hand then added, with much tenderness, "And you are very courageous."

Francesca appreciated these sentiments greatly, and showed it by performing a theatrical curtsy with a poignant tear in her eye while beaming from ear to ear.

Next Van Halestrom turned to me and offered out his hand. "And thank you, Sebastian."

"For what, Professor?" I asked him, accepting the gesture, "You must have saved my life ten times or more."

"On the contrary, Sebastian, I think it was you who saved us all back there. Remember, my lad, education is a two way thing. Much like life. I believe I've learnt a great deal from you along the way. One day we might even make a teacher of *you,* eh?"

His eyes filled with earnest sincerity and I knew that he meant the inheritance of his work. Overwhelmed by the enormity of this suggestion, I begged him, "But, sir, what should I do now? If Weishaupt is defeated, then surely it is over?"

"Alas, my friend, I fear that it may never be over. But think of it this way. He is certainly injured, and maybe even dead. He has also lost his job, and been banished from Bavaria forever. As for the Illuminati, it has been completely routed, scores of its members have been incarcerated, several despicable ceremonies, not least this illicit wedding, have been ruined, and a barrel full of its fiendish disciples have been dispatched back to the void.

Suffice to say, we have lived to tell the tale, and fight another day. So, for now anyway, I believe we can all breathe a well-earned sigh of relief." He looked between us both with much hope in his eyes then spread his arms out wide and clasped our shoulders. "Well done both of you. It is always an honour to fight with such brave and decent people by your side. You should be very proud. Very proud indeed." *[33.]

He bowed, much deeper than usual then, very deliberately, tapped his heels and winked at me, before turning to walk away. Funny old bird.

As he left, I hesitantly went to ask, "One thing, Herr Professor. Please tell me… What level am I at now?"

He stopped in his tracks and shook his head before turning around. "Though I suspected that you might ask me that, I still had hoped that you would not. I believe that we have been through this before, Sebastian. When you have reached the necessary level, then you will no longer need to ask." He smiled. "But that day is not today, my friend. You've come a long way. Let's see how much further you can go."

---

33. Bavarian Banishment of Adam Weishaupt & The Illuminati 1785. S. Drechsler's recollections are accurate here as most historians are in general agreement with Professor Van Halestrom's appraisal of events. Though Adam Weishaupt survived, his society had been publicly routed and the disgraced scholar spent the rest of his days in exile writing a series of apologist essays in defence of the Order. He was eventually given refuge by Duke Ernest II of Saxe-Gotha-Altenburg who, by strange coincidence, is related to the British Royal Family through Queen Elizabeth II. Make of that what you will. As for the Illuminati, this is a quote from H. W. Coil '***Coil's Masonic Encyclopedia***' (1961). Speaking of this period (mid 1785) he writes, '*Not only Illuminism, but Freemasonry was exterminated in Bavaria and neither ever recovered their former position. The Illuminati seem to have completely disappeared from everywhere by the end of the 18th century.*' Though this last point would seem a more contentious topic about which, if a reliable answer is sought, a great deal of enjoyable research will be required. Good luck!

He climbed aboard his coach, remarking in a more scholarly tone, "I'll be back soon, Herr Drechsler, then we can carry on that conversation about theology. I must say, I found it most *illuminating*."

He waved farewell and cheered to us, "Until then, my friends, good luck, and always remember - Stay in the shadows!"

With a crack and a cry he stirred his horses and rumbled away but without his trusty driver. We waved goodbye to him until he had disappeared down the road then glanced at each other, before leaving very quickly ourselves.

Chapter 33

Homeward Bound

The Professor had told us to go straight to Frau Hoffmeister's for, although it was over two hundred miles away, it was the closest place where we would definitely be safe. So we set course and travelled day and night, receiving many strange looks on the way in our grubby but elegant clothes and our battered but extravagant bridal coach, and it must have been eight o'clock at night, two days later, when we finally arrived at the farmhouse.

I distinctly remember a sensational sunset that evening which painted the entire sky with endless and fittingly romantic pink fluffy clouds. The stable lad was in his usual place in the low branch of a tree sucking a piece of straw and jumped down to run in front of our horses excitedly shouting up ahead so that, when we came round the corner, the homely old woman was already waiting outside her door to greet us.

We dismounted, sore and travel weary from our long journey with the help of the hard-working lad who, afterwards, dutifully led the whole team of horses away to tend to them. I watched him go about his business for a moment and, feeling a mite impetuous in the happy circumstances, I called out after him, "The boy can have one of the horses if he likes."

He turned around, his face a picture of happy astonishment, and the Frau asked me if I was sure. I told her that I was certain as we did not need a whole team of horses to complete the rest of our journey home and surely, it would be selfish to have so many, when others only wanted one.

Sweet Lady Francesca was delighted with my gift and hugged me round the neck, grinning, "I hope you will soon be as generous with me, dear sir."

And so, at last, a few hours later in the humble farmhouse bedroom, I was, and we were, over and over again, and all the riches in the world were finally mine and I cared for nothing more. The delectable Francesca was everything that I had hoped for and so, so much more. I found out how truly ignorant I had been on a great many subjects that night, and the morning too, for our exertions were seemingly without end, such was the desire that we felt for each other. A desire which had been growing for such a long time. Indeed, a whole year had passed since we had first met which, I felt, made it all quite respectable, although I had wished, every time I had seen her during that time, that it had been sooner. Suffice to say, a whole other manuscript could have been penned describing our exploits on that one night alone, but my honour, and all known licensing laws, prevent such carnal publications.

We woke the next morning and sat on the garden bench to see the sunrise together, and the day seemed so perfect that it was as though we were in a dream. I held Francesca close and watched her eyes catch the first light of a new day, thinking that we could have been in Heaven, or even The Garden of Eden, like Adam and Eve so very long ago. Maybe, if I tried hard enough to be a good man, then perhaps God would not forsake us after all. I watched Frau Hoffmeister pick a rotten apple from the tree and throw it to her chickens while she chatted away to them.

Was it really all over, or would I wake up to find myself back in the torture chamber with Weishaupt leaning over me? I reflected that I did not know for certain if anything was real or if it was a dream anymore but, happily that, if it was a dream, then I wished never to wake up again but to carry on sleeping forever, because now my dream was real. I sighed deeply and gathered my thoughts. So much had happened over the past year which I could never have thought possible, but what had I learnt from it all - never mind university?

The escapades, the battles, the fear, the love, the losses and the sweet taste of victory. As the Professor had said, it seemed as though we had suceeded in defeating the Illuminati and, of course, along with all these other incredible experiences, this remarkable triumph had a profound effect on my thoughts.

Even if Van Halestrom was right, as usual, and the evilness that we had fought was not supernatural, but man's own wickedness, I had still witnessed so many truly unbelievable events, that I found it impossible to think that a higher power had not, somehow, been helping me throughout my adventure. For what reason, I do not know. Maybe to use me as a weapon against those who opposed it, but I could not explain the extraordinary feeling of merciful fate in any other way, to say nothing of lightning strikes, crazed dogs, and sheer incredible luck coming to my rescue time and time again.

Paradoxically, it was the sceptical Van Halestrom who was the most miraculous of all. A saving angel, capable of such unfathomable feats of wonder, so improbable in themselves, that any priest would think twice before attempting to explain them to his own doting congregation, let alone any learned men of science. As a student of reason myself, I knew that without the aid of empirical proof, one has to simply make up their own mind and, in the end, I was ready to do just that. For, thankfully, I had seen good prevail over evil, so this is what I believed.

At that moment, I knew that God, *'whatever that meant'* - as Professor Van Halestrom used to say - was good, and that this same goodness existed in man. But, to realise this, man must first overcome his weaknesses. For, if he did not, he might find a darker lord presiding over him. The Professor used to tell me that all energy, from the smallest point of light, to the vast universe, was benign in itself and therefore, as we are made of the same stuff, life's duty was to be benign as well.

To illustrate this point he would recite a little poem:

> Because the sun is warm not cold,
> And summer's fruits not old and dead,
> The World's a ball of wonderment and light my friend,
> So wouldn't it be a shame,
> If we did not try, with all our energy and might, to be the very same.

Touching words I felt, and fine sentiment to boot.

Well, I had done my best to be and, in the end, that is all anyone can do. So I chose to rejoice, content that I had fulfilled my promise to God to stay alive and serve faithfully in His fold. Now I knew that whatever darkness, or light, lay ahead of me on life's long and winding road, I could meet its challenges with a clean conscience and an open heart. For I was certain, beyond my deepest depths, that I had done what I believed was right, and, happily, in doing so, had discovered my 'new self' along the way, which I had first set out to, way back in the begining, all that time ago.

I had also overcome tremendous odds, to triumph against great adversities and lived to tell the tale. And oh, what an incredible tale I had to tell. What an incredible tale indeed.

Sebastian Drechsler, 1852.

Special Thanks

I would like to take this opportunity to thank my tireless editorial team, Robin and Carol, for their dedication, long nights, and general perseverance. I am sure they realise that I could not have done it without them but, on this particular occasion, I feel it is better for them to see it written down in black and white than to hear it. So, once again, thanks. Also, thank you to everyone who was patient with me while I got Sebastian's memoirs ready for release and all those who had to listen to me endlessly talk about this incredible book which I found, not so long ago, in a second hand shop in London. Thanks again.

Whilst republishing the book, it struck me that it contained thirty three chapters, a number which I know, after researching the background of this story, has great symbolism. Though, I also know that one can find these coincidences anywhere, especially if one looks hard enough, so I will leave it up to you - the reader - to decide whether it is or not.

Visit Illuminati Hunter.com **&** Facebook Illuminati Hunter Book for more Information about this fascinating series of paperbacks and 'Live' E books.

Footnote Appendix & Hypertext Addresses.

1. Professor Van Halestrom & Ingolstadt University. Unfortunately, there is no record of a Professor Van Halestrom working at Ingolstadt's university at this time, but staff records are sketchy, at best, so this is no surprise. By 1784 Ingolstadt University was regarded as one of the most influential and esteemed institutes of higher learning in Europe and the free-thinking spirit that flourished throughout the Enlightenment, widely regarded responsible for the French and American revolutions, was reflected in the culture of the campus. The university was finally closed down in 1800 by, the then, Elector of Bavaria, Maximilian IV and, though it is claimed this was due to a lack of funds, it is believed the institution was considered so revolutionarily secular by the broadly Christian authorities, that it posed a threat to the government.

https://en.wikipedia.org/wiki/University_of_Ingolstadt
https://commons.wikimedia.org/wiki/Category:Jesuitenkolleg_Ingolstadt

2. Johann Adam Weishaupt. This immensely intriguing historical figure was certainly lecturing at the University of Ingolstadt in 1784. Although S. Drechsler refers to him as 'The Doctor,' Adam Weishaupt was Professor of Canon Law at the faculty and the first non-Jesuit to hold this position in over ninety years. It is one view that the young academic's education by the Jesuit priesthood, which would have been extremely harsh, was the reason that he adopted his anti-Christian philosophies. By this time he is known to have denounced his Catholicism and adopted the doctrines of the Hermetics, Manicheans and those that revolved around astrology, alchemy, magic, and the mysteries of ancient Egypt, taking special interest in the pyramids at Giza.

https://en.wikipedia.org/wiki/Adam_Weishaupt

3. Katzenstein Castle. This impressive fort, originally built in the Middle Ages, is situated thirty miles west of Ingolstadt on the road to Stuttgart and is featured on the map at the beginning of the book. It will look exactly the same as when S. Drechsler saw it and can be viewed on the internet for those wishing to verify the authenticity of the author's account. Bavaria is home to hundreds of similar castles. The Serpen's Caput constellation, also reffered to as 'The Serpent's Head,' points down to the western horizon in the summer months and can be viewed by E book readers on the Star Gazer app.

https://en.wikipedia.org/wiki/Katzenstein_Castle

4. The Bavarian Illuminati. This most infamous of all secret societies was founded in Bavaria on May 1st 1776. From a very modest beginning of five members, after much administrative, financial and organisational help from other 'free-thinking' collaborators, by 1784 its ranks had swollen to as many as three thousand. Membership included many well-connected and influential figures, such as; Johann Wolfgang von Goethe, Johann Gottfried Herdér and the Dukes of Gotha and Weimar. So much has been written about the order by hundreds of notable historians, and their less reliable counterparts, that it is hard to deny any other quasi-political organisation, apart from perhaps the Freemasons, has been responsible for such speculative hysteria, intriguing legend and conspiratorial myths which still continue to this day.

https://en.wikipedia.org/wiki/Illuminati

5. The Owl of Minerva (Athena). These meetings facilitated an academy in which young initiates of the Illuminati could be selected and groomed for higher positions within the organisation. The class of Minerva was a relatively low rank in the scheme of things. However, it was the soul of the Order and functioned as a sort of assembly line for recruits. Candidates advanced from *Novice* to the *Minerval degree* where they were properly vetted, scrutinised and indoctrinated. Another revealing aspect of owl symbolism was to remind its initiates that the Illuminati does its bidding at night.

https://en.wikipedia.org/wiki/Owl_of_Athena

6. The Cremation of Care Ceremony. S. Drechsler's recollections strangely bear much in common with ceremonies known to take place at a yearly party held for the world's elite at Bohemian Grove in California. Though, judging by the available video footage it appears that no one is actually hurt during the ritual. the owl, in this case, is sometimes referred to as Molech. In antiquity Moloch, the Canaanite deity, is represented as a legless bull with arms. This pagan god would be worshipped by the Israelites during times of apostasy (without religion) and is associated with the sacrifice of children. Lev.18:21, *'Neither shall you give any of your offspring to offer them to Molech.'*

https://odysee.com/@EricDubay:c/The-Bohemian-Grove-Society:3
https://www.youtube.com/watch?v=aQ4YGYSsVfE&t=2s

7. The Illuminati & The Founding Fathers of America. The extent to which the Illuminati had penetrated revolutionary American politics via the Freemasons, of which all the founding fathers were members, is unknowable. However, Thomas Jefferson, Ambassador to France from 1785-1789, knew Weishaupt and wrote sympathetically of his professed basic aim of '*making men wise and virtuous*' and contended that, unlike the new American republic, '*secretive methods were a necessity under the religious and aristocratic tyranny of Europe.*' Hundreds of conspiracy theories persist to this day concerning the Order's involvement with revolutionary America as many have noted the Masonic symbolism designed into The Great Seal of The United States and even upon the street layout of Washington DC.

https://www.youtube.com/watch?v=KEE5woXr_Is
https://historycollection.com/conspiracy-theories-about-our-founding-fathers/
https://odysee.com/@Commentator:e4/masonic_washington:e

8. The Origins of The Illuminati. As S. Drechsler states occult Kabballah, the basis of The Ancient Mystery School Religion, has been the faith practiced by many secret societies throughout history, including the Bavarian Illuminati. I can find no mention of Ordo ab Chao (order from chaos) earlier than 1395, when it was part of masonic philosophy, though it is claimed to have existed long before then. Coincidentally, '***Fire in the Minds of Men***' (1980) J. H. Billington, traces 'the origins of the revolutionary faith' the dream of a global secular order - The world ruled by Man as God - and explores the anti-Christian character of revolutionary ideology from the French Revolution to the present era. Jacques de Molay, known for his Kabbalist faith, was burned to death in 1314 on an island in the river Seine in Paris, not by the Pope as stated, but by order of King Phillip IV of France, for heresy and devil worship in the form of the Baphomet. His Templar Knights, the original Freemasons, are thought to have established the first international system of credit.

https://www.youtube.com/watch?v=ZaNvoO7TTqU
https://www.youtube.com/watch?v=gAs2jPpiN9Y
https://www.youtube.com/watch?v=pivMEyM1u-g
https://en.wikipedia.org/wiki/Jacques_de_Molay
https://bigthink.com/the-past/knights-templar-crusades-finance/

9. Weishaupt's Illuminati Codename: Spartacus. S. Drechsler's recollections are accurate here. The Bavarian Illuminati allocated codenames to important members and these were often taken from Greek or Roman antiquity. Adam Weishaupt's was Spartacus, after the revolutionary Thracian gladiator who led the slave uprising against the Roman Empire in 71 B.C. Other leading lights took secret titles including; Baron Von Knigge; Philo. Johann Christophe Bode; Ameilius, etc. Ancient pseudonyms were also used for cities and states. For instance; Munich was known as Athens, Frankfurt as Thebes and, as the author points out, Bavaria was Achaia.

https://modernhistoryproject.org/mhp?Article=FinalWarning&C=1.2#Growth

10. Weishaupt & The Lodge of The Golden Dawn. It is amazing that S. Drechsler recalls these details. Mainstream historians have always argued that this sect was started by William Wyan Wescott in England circa 1887, but speculation has always existed that Weishaupt was at least partly responsible for its establishment in the 1700's, and even that the order was an ancient satanic cult which provided a meeting place for those with designs of spreading the Luciferian doctrine throughout the world.

https://en.wikipedia.org/wiki/Hermetic_Order_of_the_Golden_Dawn
https://bitterwinter.org/the-illuminati-7-the-golden-dawn/

11. The Spear The Axe and The Arrow. While I can find no record of this particular combination of symbols being used by the Illuminati, the seperate insignias go back to antiquity. The spear mounted with the Phrygian cap has held revolutionary symbolism for centuries. Since ancient Roman times the cap has represented those who seek liberty, as it was worn by slaves who had won their freedom and made infamous during the French Revolution of 1789, with the red of the cap also being linked to Bolshevik and other communist emblems. The axe surrounded with the bundle of birch rods, or fasces, also has its roots in ancient Rome and was the symbol for strength and authority, the birch to whip and the axe to wield the ultimate capital punishment. In the context of the story, it is interesting as these insignias were to be used by opposing political ideologies; Communism; the red cap. Fascism; the fasces and the root of the word 'Fascist.'

http://en.wikipedia.org/wiki/Phrygian_cap

http://en.wikipedia.org/wiki/Fasces

12. The Illuminati & Die Hörig (The Subservient or 'The Slaves'). It is unsurprising that S. Drechsler did not recognise this word as it would have been antiquated, even when he heard it two hundred and fifty years ago, and originates from Middle High German (1050-1350) which might explain why it was not familiar to his ear. *Leibeigen* translates as 'in serfdom' (of a peasant: bound to his lord's land and required to work for him) and as 'unfree' or subject to any form of 'bondage.' Within the context of this story, it would seem quite obvious that what is meant here is 'slave.'

13. Illuminati Agent Jacob Lanz Struck by lightning. Incredibly, though there seems to be some conjecture about the precise timing of this amazing event, according to one of the most notable sources '*Pawns in the Game*' (1958) by William Carr, this top ranking Illuminati agent was struck by lightning and killed on 10th July 1784 near Regensburg Bavaria. When the authorities discovered his body, they mistakenly concluded that he had been carrying the incriminating documents himself. Now it has become widespread belief that Lanz was, in fact, on a mission to deliver the papers to Paris where they would be used to aid the French revolution and that the papers were sewn into his robes. If we are to believe S. Drechsler's version of events, it is fascinating to discover the real truth behind what is already an incredible, but little-known, historical event. Either this is the event chronicled by so many historians and conspiracy theorists alike, or we are party to an absolutely astonishing coincidence.

https://nwodb.com/app/view/2/406#cardId_3_583
https://www.amazon.co.uk/Pawns-Game-William-Guy-Carr/dp/1939438039

14. Franz Lange: Councillor of Eichstatt & The Bavarian Illuminati. S. Drechsler's recollection of this character's gruesome death would seem to explain an anomaly from the official stories. This member of the Bavarian Illuminati is often confused with Jakob Lanz (very similar to 'Lange') who it would appear, after being struck by lightning, also perished on the same night. Interestingly, I can find no official date for the obituary of F. Lange, so it is certainly possible that the author's version of events is true.

https://www.conspiracyarchive.com/2015/07/11/lang-or-lanz-myths-about-the-myths/

15. The Original Writings of The Illuminati. The original documents found with Lanz's body after the lightning strike have not survived, so, unfortunately, there is no record of the text to back up Drechsler's account. Although other papers seized from agents of the Bavarian Illuminati on later dates bear strong similarity to those the author describes and cite the abolition of all; Monarchy, Government, Property, Patriotism, Family and Religion. These documents were reprinted and released by the Bavarian authorities in 1787, to warn foreign countries about the Illuminati and their revolutionary intentions. Interestingly, the text bears a strong resemblance to the mother of all conspiracy documents '***The Protocols of the Elders of Zion***' (1903), a book published in Russia and proved, beyond doubt, to be a hoax and produced for political ends. Though it is an inexplicable coincidence that the document S. Drechsler recalls, bears such a close resemblance to this text released over a hundred years later, forged or not.

https://www.conspiracyarchive.com/2020/03/03/some-original-writings-of-the-order-of-the-illuminati-pp-26-43/
https://modernhistoryproject.org/mhp?Article=FinalWarning&C=1.2#Exposed

16. The First Edict Against The Illuminati. In summer 1784 the first edict banning secret societies was issued by Charles Theodore Elector of Bavaria. Though these measures were seen as 'half-hearted,' tellingly the authorities' suspicion of the Illuminati continued to mount around this time, which may well be explained by the author's exploits. Baron Adolph Knigge, was a prominent aristocrat highly influential within the order, who notably fell out with Weishaupt during this period, and official records agree that the academic had suddenly become unpopular due to growing disquite over his organisation.

https://en.wikipedia.org/wiki/Charles_Theodore,_Elector_of_Bavaria
https://en.wikipedia.org/wiki/Adolph_Freiherr_Knigge
https://www.youtube.com/watch?v=wWDoEt6s1lY

17. Frankenstein & The Illuminati. This must be Drechsler's little joke, though possibly an insightful one. Of course, he would have been familiar with Mary Shelley's novel '***Frankenstein***' (1818), set in Ingolstadt University around the same time. So maybe it was a nickname given retrospectively to one of his more morbid fellow students. He may have also been trying to be cryptic, given the context of the story, as there is much agreed symbolic connection of the Illuminati and '*Frankenstein*.' Mary's husband, Percy Shelly, certainly admired the secert society and there are many fascinating allegorical connections between her romantic Gothic masterpiece and Weishaupt's order.

https://www.youtube.com/watch?v=VtNiV1jDI1k
https://en.wikipedia.org/wiki/Frankenstein

18. The Pyramid & The All Seeing Eye of Providence (The Eye of Horus). This symbol, with its intriguing Latin inscriptions, remains perhaps one of the most famous conspiracies of all time, though the engraving S. Drechsler describes would be slightly different to the one we are familiar with today. Interestingly, an earlier version of the symbol had already been accepted by the founding fathers in 1782 as The Great Seal of America. Perhaps its most celebrated expression is on the reverse of the US one dollar bill, first printed on the notes in 1933 under the auspices of President F.D. Roosevelt. Speculation about this esoteric symbol and its usage, meaning and history would appear to be almost endless and a great deal of time would have to be set aside to research this one topic alone, such is the volume of literature written about it. Good luck!

https://en.wikipedia.org/wiki/Eye_of_Providence
https://www.youtube.com/watch?app=desktop&v=nVBfBVjk4CE

19. Freemasons & The Illuminati. The commonly held belief that the tradition of Freemasonry provides the Illuminati a coven in which to conceal itself, has existed for hundreds of years and been speculated about endlessly. This claim is given weight by the official ratification of the two organisations at the Congress of Wilhelmsbad in 1782. It is said that the leaderships' true goals are only revealed to adepts at the higher degrees while the lower members are unaware of these plans and naturally defend the integrity of the institution. It is interesting that S. Drechsler recalls his mentor describing its influence as a 'hidden hand' a term which has now become commonplace.

http://en.wikipedia.org/wiki/Masonic_conspiracy_theories
https://www.travelingtemplar.com/2013/07/the-1782-congress-of-wilhelmsbad.html

20. Kabbalist Priests' Breastplates. Kabbalah is an arcane form of mysticism of unknown origin which has many different interpretations, some of them quite peculiar, though this ceremony would have been unusual to say the least. According to ancient tradition, these priests would have worn ornate robes and breastplates decorated with twelve precious stones, representing the twelve tribes of the Old Testament. Interestingly, when Satan was banished from Heaven, it is said that he was also given similar jems, but tellingly, only nine. Kabbalah speaks of nine spheres, or dimensions, existing in the universe and some terrifying prophecies eudure as to what is contained within these.

https://en.wikipedia.org/wiki/Priestly_breastplate
https://www.youtube.com/watch?v=KTsCmOM_zqw

21. **Joseph II, Holy Roman Emperor & The Bavarian Illuminati 1784.** S. Drechsler's seemingly outlandish claims to have seen a pyramid at this ritual are intriguingly given credence by the existence of an almost identical structure at the Staatspark Hanau estate in Wilhelmsbad in northern Germany, which E book readers can see here. Coincidentally, this was the location for several meetings of the Bavarian Illuminati and the Freemasons (see footnote 19). While there is no official record of a plot to destroy the Bavarian chancellery, or proof that Emperor Joseph had sought Illuminati membership, there is every chance that they both may have happened. Joseph, very small and frail, historically known as one of the 'Enlightened Despots,' and also the brother of Marie Antoinette, was definitely (though secretly) a Freemason, belonging to a lodge called *Zur neugekronten Hoffnung* (New Crowned Hope), and a member of 'many other' secret societies at that time. Interestingly, before this point, he had dealt favourably with Weishaupt's organisation, but as S. Drechsler's account may explain, at the end of 1784 his relationship with the Illuminati definitely deteriorated. As the memoirs suggest, any other stance may have posed insurmountable political problems. The Old Town Hall in Munich, which I believe is the building S. Drechsler is refering to here, was abandoned by the government exactly one hundred years later. Historical examples of the destruction of buildings for political ends include, as the text mentions, Guy Fawke's failed attempt to destroy the Houses of Parliment in 1605 and also, the more successful, torching of the Reichstag by the Nazis in 1933.

https://en.wikipedia.org/wiki/Joseph_II%2C_Holy_Roman_Emperor
https://commons.wikimedia.org/wiki/File:Pyramide_Staatspark_Hanau-Wilhelmsbad.JPG
https://en.wikipedia.org/wiki/Old_Town_Hall%2C_Munich

22. The Illuminati & Ingolstadt University. Herr Vacchieri is mentioned in a book called '*Little Tools of Knowledge*' (2001) by P. Becker and W. Clark (pages 104-134) and seemed to occupy a role at the university similar to that of a 'school inspector,' though I can find no proof that he was a member of the Illuminati. S. Drechsler also mentions Adam Weishaupt's Godfather, though not by name. Johann Adam von Ickstatt was the Curator of Ingolstadt University up until 1778 and probably instrumental in getting Weishaupt his job. There also seems to be doubt about his membership of the Illuminati though it is hard to believe he did not know, somehow, about the details of his godson's organisation.

https://illuminatisociety.org/university-of-ingolstadt/
http://en.wikipedia.org/wiki/Johann_Adam_von_Ickstatt

23. Adam Weishaupt Sacked from Ingolstadt University Winter of 1785. S. Drechsler's claim to have witnessed the academic's departure are accurate here, as Adam Weishaupt finally lost his position at Ingolstadt University on the 11th February 1785, amidst continuing controversy surrounding his 'not so' secret society. The authorities' first decree in July of the previous year had been quite mild, but both official and public suspicion of the Illuminati was certainly growing around this time, making it impossible for distinguished institutions such as Ingolstadt's university, who enjoyed the patronage of the state, to employ members from its ranks. Never mind the figurehead of its leadership. As S. Drechsler also mentions, as well as other competing rumours of illegitimate relationships, as strange as it may sound, most official histories record that Weishaupt was known to be having an affair with his sister-in-law.

https://www.facebook.com/watch/?v=2082360262140207
https://archive.org/details/proofsofconspira00r/page/n5/mode/2up?q=pregnant

24. Illuminati & 'The End Times' Prophecy. Illuminati speculators have long contested that the Order wish to instigate a social cataclysm mirroring the fateful prophecy predicting the armageddon of civilisation, as described in the Bible's '***Book of Revelation***.' This ominous forecast recalled by S. Drechsler, also sounds strangely similar to extracts from a mysterious letter once rumoured to be kept at the British Museum, which it is claimed, was sent by the then head of world Masonry Albert Pike to Giuseppe Mazzini in 1871. If S. Drechsler's account is to be believed, then it is incredible to think that this frightening prediction for the world was even being talked about as early as 1785.

https://odysee.com/@ApexworldMedia:5/Three-World-Wars:f
http://en.wikipedia.org/wiki/Albert_Pike
http://en.wikipedia.org/wiki/Giuseppe_Mazzini

25. Wolfsegg Castle. Though I cannot find any strong connections linking this ancient castle and the Illuminati, it has had several owners throughout its long and fascinating seven-hundred-year history. Originally built in 1278 by Wolf von Schönleiten, its steeped in legends of supernatural hauntings and, owing to its prominent position, can be seen from several miles away. It is still there to this day, situated 15km north west of Regensburg near the outskirts of Pettendorf, and can be viewed on the internet.

https://en.wikipedia.org/wiki/Wolfsegg,_Bavaria
https://amyscrypt.com/wolfsegg-castle-germany/

26. Charles Theodore & The Banishment of The Illuminati 1785. On March 2nd 1785 the second edict was passed specifically banning membership of the Illuminati and making it an imprisonable offence to be part of the order. Initially, Weishaupt fled to the principality of Regensburg, but finally settled in Gotha under the protection of Duke Ernest II of Saxe-Gotha-Altenburg. He is rumoured to have hidden in many places whilst escaping the authorities including, amongst others, a chimney. Although S. Drechsler does not give a precise date for this evening, we could have expected Weishaupt to have thought the decree inevitable and therefore may well have left his homeland some weeks before, which would tie in exactly with these recollections.

https://nwodb.com/app/view/1/993

27. The Illuminati & The Compte De Viriue. This French aristocrat was made famous by his statements about the Illuminati after attending the order's grand congress in Wilhelmsbad in 1782. He said, *"The conspiracy that is being woven is so well thought out that it will be, so to speak, impossible for the Monarchy and the Church to escape from it."* He could thereafter only speak of Freemasonry with 'horror.' The 'cosmic trigger' has been termed a 'thought tunnel' by Robert A. Wilson, '*Illuminatus*' (1977). Also known in certain traditions as 'The Chapel Perilous,' it broadly refers to an induced public state of mind.

https://en.wikipedia.org/wiki/Fran%C3%A7ois_Henri%2C_comte_de_Virieu

https://en.wikipedia.org/wiki/The_Illuminatus%21_Trilogy

28. General Frederick II, Landgrave of Hesse Kassel. This character, who made his fortune renting Hessian troops to the British Army during the American Revolutionary War, had definite connections with the Illuminati and must be who S. Drechsler is describing. Though his death is recorded as being on 31st October (All Hallow's Eve) 1785, some seven months later meaning that, if the author's account is to be believed, General Frederick would have had to cling on to his life for some time, with an amazing set of injuries, before finally dying. Although, tellingly, S. Drechsler never actually sees him die, so this may explain this intriguing anomaly in his story.

https://en.wikipedia.org/wiki/Frederick_II%2C_Landgrave_of_Hesse-Kassel

29. The Illuminati & The French Revolution. Many historians have long contested that the Bavarian Illuminati were involved in the fermentation of the revolutionary forces that led to the overthrow of decadent King Louis XVI's '*regime ancien*' which ruled in France until 1789. Notable works such as; '*Secret Societies; Illuminati, Freemasons and the French Revolution*' (2007) by Una Birch and John Robison's '*Proof of a Conspiracy*' (1798), document detailed plans of how the Bavarian secret society, along with many influential French Freemasons, conspired to bring about a popular nationwide uprising. A list which included, amongst others; the Duke of Orleans (Freemason), the Marquis de Lafayette (Freemason) and the Jacobin Club, a radical nucleus of the revolt formed by other prominent Freemasons.

https://daily.jstor.org/the-french-revolution-as-illuminati-conspiracy/
https://sacred-texts.com/sro/pc/index.htm

30. The Order of The Rosicrusians. The Rosicrucian order was a secret society founded in late medieval Germany by Christian Rosenkreuz. The sect's manifesto was heavily influenced by Alchemist astrologer and occultist John Dee, Queen Elizabeth I of England's head of security, and Dee's pupil Francis Bacon. As S. Drechsler describes the mandate of the order was one of scientific empiricism over religious dogma especially that of the Roman Catholic Church, which may explain VanHalestrom's philosophical approach, though the Brotherhood certainly did not shy away from mysterious theology themselves. The history of the Rosicrusians and the Illuminati is interestingly intertwined, some historians even comparing the two in purpose and manifesto. Though, if S. Drechsler's comments are to be believed, this seems less likely

https://www.youtube.com/watch?v=qOCdFDXe5jQ
http://en.wikipedia.org/wiki/Rosicrucianism

31. Mozart & The Illuminati. There is no doubt that Mozart was in Vienna at this time. The famous composer was also a friend of Adam Weishaupt and a member of a Masonic Lodge *Zur Wohltatigkeit* (Beneficence). His most famous opera, ***The Magic Flute*** features an array of Masonic rituals and symbolism, and his presence at the wedding shows the influence the Illuminati had on the cultural life of the day, as he would have been at his peak then and very much in demand. Much speculation exits suggesting that he was actually killed by the society for revealing their secrets in his work, and some that his death was brought about by his rival Antonio Salieri. Though, this topic is such a contested one that it would require a book of its own.

https://www.youtube.com/watch?v=1I0eYz8yENs
https://en.wikipedia.org/wiki/Wolfgang_Amadeus_Mozart
https://en.wikipedia.org/wiki/Mozart_and_Freemasonry
https://odysee.com/@GnosticLibrary:3/Mozart--The-magic-Flute:6
https://www.pressreader.com/ireland/the-irish-mail-on-sunday/20210620/282909503482802
https://brutalproof.net/2019/11/mozart-a-freemason-was-poisoned-for-exposing-them/
https://www.readersdigest.co.uk/culture/music/was-mozart-murdered

32. Brigadier James Oglethorpe & The Illuminati. I can find no reliable information suggesting that this venerable English politician and Freemason was an important Illuminati agent, though, interestingly, he was responsible for founding the '13'th state of Georgia in the U.S.A. on the '33'rd parallel. It is also intriguing to note that James Oglethorpe is recorded to have died on 30th June 1785 in London, which would have allowed exactly the right amount of time for his body to be returned to England. Perhaps unsurprisingly, no details of this wedding exist although, if Drechsler's version of events is to be believed, this could have been for any number of extraordinary reasons.

https://en.wikipedia.org/wiki/James_Oglethorpe

33. Bavarian Banishment of Adam Weishaupt & The Illuminati 1785. S. Drechsler's recollections are accurate here as most historians are in general agreement with Professor Van Halestrom's appraisal of events. Though Adam Weishaupt survived, his society had been publicly routed and the disgraced scholar spent the rest of his days in exile writing a series of apologist essays in defence of the Order. He was eventually given refuge by Duke Ernest II of Saxe-Gotha-Altenburg who, by a strange coincidence, is related to the British Royal Family through Queen Elizabeth II. (Make of that what you will.) As for the Illuminati, this is a quote from H. W. Coil '***Coil's Masonic Encyclopedia***' (1961). Speaking of this period (summer 1785) he writes, '*Not only Illuminism, but Freemasonry was exterminated in Bavaria and neither ever recovered their former position. The Illuminati seem to have completely disappeared from everywhere by the end of the 18th century.*' Though this last point would seem a more contentious topic about which, if a reliable answer is sought, a great deal of enjoyable research will be required. Good luck!

https://www.youtube.com/results?search_query=Origins+of+the+Illuminati+-+Where+it+all+beganhttps://encyclopedia2.thefreedictionary.com/Bavarian+Illuminati
https://www.youtube.com/watch?v=z2SYR7ZEMvo
https://www.youtube.com/watch?v=--81aT8XuUQ

Das
verbesserte System
der
Illuminaten
mit allen
seinen Graden und Einrichtungen.

Herausgegeben von
Adam Weishaupt
Herzoglich Sachs. Goth. Hofrath.

Hic situs est Phaeton, currus auriga paterni:
Quem si non tenuit; magnis tamen excidit ausis.
Ovid. Met. B. 2.

Neue und vermehrte Auflage.

Frankfurt und Leipzig,
in der Grattenauerischen Buchhandlung. 1788.